Male, Female, Other?

A Catholic Guide to Understanding Gender

Totus Tuus
—PRESS—

Male, Female, Other?
A Catholic Guide to Understanding Gender

Published by Totus Tuus Press
PO Box 5065
Scottsdale, AZ 85261

Cover design by Devin Schadt
Typesetting by Russell Design
Printed in the United States of America
Hardcover ISBN: 978-1-944578-06-0
Paperback ISBN: 978-1-944578-07-7
E book ISBN: 978-1-944578-08-4

For Mary

For you love all things that exist, and you loathe none of the things which you have made, for you would not have made anything if you had hated it.—Wisdom 11:24

Contents

Introduction

At the age of twelve, Claire began feeling increasingly uncomfortable with her body. She wrestled with anxiety and depression and understood that puberty could be a tumultuous time. But this felt different. She was an outlier at school, didn't fit in with the other girls, and began questioning the source of her distress.

One day, a recommended video appeared online of a charismatic individual who had likewise wrestled with her female identity, but at last found peace by identifying as male. After viewing a slew of similar videos, Claire felt that her discomfort finally had a name. She thought, *"Maybe the reason I'm uncomfortable with my body is I'm supposed to be a guy."* She eventually mustered the courage to inform her parents that she felt she was a boy and wanted to transition by receiving hormones and a double mastectomy.

Her parents—both scientists—took the news well and immediately began researching how to best care for her. Most of what they found online told the same story: "If your kid says she's trans, she's trans. A parent's job is to accept this reality and help her transition so that she can thrive." But something in this treatment pathway felt incomplete to Claire's mother, who had a doctorate in pharmacology. As the family began spending more time together and less time on screens, Claire began questioning whether she had internalized rigid gender stereotypes that might be causing some of her distress.

Looking in the mirror one day, as she was trying to present in a masculine way, she recalled, "My baggy, uncomfortable clothes; my damaged, short hair; and my depressed-looking face . . . it didn't make me feel any better. I was still miserable, and I still hated myself." Her distress slowly began to lift. "It was kind of sudden when I thought: *You know, maybe this isn't the right answer— maybe it's something else . . .* But it took a while to actually set in that yes, I was definitely a girl."[1]

Claire's dysphoria dissipated and she gradually felt at home in her own body. However, many individuals who experience gender dysphoria or who identify as trans haven't experienced the same resolution. The daily stress and discomfort they experience is often difficult for others to comprehend.

Imagine dressing as the other sex for one day. Imagine yourself in the mall, at work, in the gym, in church. What would you feel? Uncomfortable? Disingenuous? Judged? No matter how distressing the experience might be, you could at least look forward to the end of the day, when you could discard the attire that felt so inauthentic. But what if it was your own body that felt out of place?

Euphoria is a feeling of blissful happiness, contentment, and excitement. The opposite is dysphoria: a feeling of sadness, uneasiness, and dissatisfaction. Coming from the Greek *dys* (difficult), and *pherein* (to bear), gender dysphoria is when a person feels distress over the incongruity between his or her sex and their self-perception or deeply felt experience regarding that identity. One individual remarked, "Sometimes dysphoria is described as being in the 'wrong body,' but I think that's just a convenient description of something very difficult to describe." The distress can fluctuate and be relatively easy to manage for some. For others, it could be experienced as a constant and debilitating self-hatred. One man shared with me, "If I am presenting myself as a man in order to please everyone else, then that makes me super lonely because . . . I'm forced to live their vision of who I am instead of allowing myself to outwardly express my own internal life." Similarly, one woman described her experience as spending "decades in a body that feels simultaneously dead and like an eternal wellspring of agony."[2]

Individuals who experience gender dysphoria or who identify as trans—the two are not synonymous—often face many other challenges beyond the incongruence they feel regarding their body. In one survey of more than six thousand individuals who identify as trans, 57 percent of them have family members who refuse to speak to them.[3] They may also struggle to find gainful employment, and sometimes resort to sex work or begging in order to survive, thus exposing themselves to the dangers of both lifestyles.[4] One such individual who lost his job and became homeless recalled the desperation he felt: "I'm screaming at God saying, 'Why are you letting this happen to me, Why? Why me? What did I do wrong to you?'"[5]

If Christians spent as much time talking to individuals who identify as trans as they do talking about transgender headlines in the news, the world would be a better place. Unfortunately, the subject has sometimes been reduced to nothing more than a heretical ideology that needs to be defeated and disproven. With the subject of gender serving as the battlefield, those labeled as "hateful transphobic right-winged fanatics" align their forces on one side of the culture war, while the "confused woke left-wing snowflakes" stand in opposition, poised to counterattack. The scene could also be compared to a husband and wife having a shouting match, while their distressed child sits on the floor between them, feeling invisible.

While it is true that there is a time and place for civil discourse—and that the matters at hand are crucial ones that rightfully stir up passionate debates—argumentation alone is not a sufficient response to the transgender question. Dialogue is needed. Ideologies must be challenged, but first, individuals need to be heard.

To those who identify as trans . . .

If you experience gender dysphoria or identify as trans, the first word you deserve to hear is:

I am sorry if you have ever been made to feel that you don't belong in the Church. You are not the Church's enemy, and there's room for you here as you navigate through your questions about identity. I apologize if this has not been your experience in the past. We see you. We understand that you didn't choose this. The feelings you experience and the questions you ask are not acts of disobedience that incur the constant displeasure of God. You may have experienced rejection from within your family, your faith community, your school, or your workplace. You may struggle to accept yourself. But I'm willing to bet that you're not trying to wage war against Catholicism. You're more interested in living a peaceful life and becoming fully yourself. You're probably open to having God in your life, but you're not always sure what that looks like. All you want is to be authentic, and that desire for authenticity should be deeply affirmed. You're not trying to deceive anyone. You simply want to discover and live out the identity that aligns best with your personal experience. You're not seeking vain attention. If anything, you'd probably prefer to blend in without strangers looking twice at you.

If you're wondering what God thinks about all of this, know that the Church's answer to your questions is not, "Repent and just pick up your cross!" Granted, we all have plenty to repent for, and the cross is an essential element of Christian living. But God loves you right now, even as you read this, no matter how you identify and express yourself. You are not forsaken. As cliché as it might sound, God has a plan for your life. If he could say anything to you, it would probably be, "Come to me, all who labor and are heavy laden, and I will give you rest" (Matt 11:28).

If you're open to this invitation, I ask one thing of you: Please be patient with the Church as we learn to navigate this subject together. Although the Church has an unfathomable treasure of wisdom, Christians are just beginning to understand and engage with individuals who experience transgender inclinations. Therefore, it's probably going to be somewhat messy and clumsy at times. Odds are, I'll probably want to edit portions of this book fifteen minutes after sending it to the printer, wishing I had nuanced portions more carefully.

You might be disappointed in the tools—or lack thereof—that are available to you within the Church. In fact, one individual reached out to me and lamented, "I haven't found any meaningful Catholic resources that offer counseling, support groups, retreats, or even simply a warm welcome to people with gender dysphoria." All I can say to this is: We're working on it. Many compassionate and faithful Catholics are developing these things right now.

Because you deserve love, you also deserve the truth. In this book, my hope is that you will find both. These pages will offer you consolations and challenges. It will invite you to question some of the ideas you may have heard before, while reminding you, as one individual with gender dysphoria reminded me, that "you are not a problem to be solved, but a mystery to be loved."

To those who don't identify as trans . . .

If you are a family member, educator, or friend to someone who identifies as trans, it's likely that the subject of gender often leaves you feeling perplexed. You may have heard that each person has something called a "gender identity" that is in the brain, but not in the body; that it's a social construct, but not defined by stereotypes; that it's innate and unchanging, but is sometimes fluid and "can change every day or even every few hours."[6] Especially for adults who aren't familiar with current terminology, the terrain can feel mystifying.

You're not alone. Young people often experience feelings of bewilderment as well. For example, at the University of Essex, the "Trans Inclusion Guidance" document informs students that those who are pangender identify with a multitude, and perhaps infinite number, of genders.[7] A bemused individual reached out to the university by means of a Freedom of Information Act, inquiring what some of these infinite genders might be. The university replied with a list of about a dozen and added that still others are "unrecognized" or "unknown." Unfazed, he inquired how they would be able to count the genders if they were unrecognized and unknown. Acknowledging that listing all of them might not be possible—since it would take forever—he asked for a sampling of five hundred. The

University of Essex was unable to accommodate his request, noting, "This is due to the self-defining nature and infinite number of genders that an individual could assign themselves to which makes it impossible to formulate a list." He replied, "To be helpful may I suggest that another reason why you cannot provide a list of the infinite number of genders is that the list would be larger than the universe (even if the font size was tiny)."[8]

This exchange encapsulates the problem that often plagues discussions about gender. One group spends ample time with individuals who identify as trans without questioning the logic of the ideology, while the other focuses on the logical inconsistencies of the ideology, without spending much time with the individuals. But what if clarity and charity could meet?

Many who don't identify as trans are led to believe that there are only two possible responses to those who do: Affirm them or reject them. Because most people would rather not be called a transphobic bigot, they keep their doubts to themselves and choose the path of unquestioning affirmation: "You do you."

Rarely is any mention made of accompaniment, walking with individuals in truth and love. No questions are asked about what it means to affirm a person's true identity. Indeed, persons should be affirmed. But to affirm a false idea isn't love. It's false compassion.

Because most people feel unequipped to discuss topics related to transgender identification, they remain silent. Their sense of inadequacy is understandable, though. To engage with another in a meaningful way on these topics seems to require a thorough understanding of endocrinology, pediatric medicine, neurology, biology, psychology, theology, feminism, gender studies, anthropology, and public policy. But no one can be an expert in everything. As Saint Edith Stein remarked, "The individual human being's power is so limited that he or she has to pay for the highest accomplishments in one field by shortcomings or deficiencies in other fields."[9]

Therefore, to create this book, I drew upon the most up-to-date research in each of these areas of study. Should you wish to dive deeper into any of the topics, there are approximately a thousand sources referenced in the endnotes, a vast number of which are peer-reviewed scientific journals. I also sent the manuscript to doctors in each of the fields of study mentioned above, who have offered innumerable helpful corrections and clarifications. I also shared the manuscript with those who do not agree with the Church's teachings, and they have likewise been gracious in helping me to nuance the content more carefully. But perhaps most importantly, I have shared the document you're about to read with individuals who identify as trans or who experience gender dysphoria. Their feedback was the most helpful of all.

The issues in the book are presented in a format similar to what Saint Thomas Aquinas used in his classic work, *Summa Theologiae*. In it, he presents a simple objection in the form of a statement, then offers a series of points to support that claim. In doing so, he does not offer a straw man argument that is easily dismantled, but aims to present the objection with equal or greater clarity and persuasiveness than his opponents might. He then affirms the truth to be found in the objections and builds upon them to arrive at a different conclusion. For Aquinas, the purpose of debate was to journey toward truth together rather than entering into a competition to score cheap polemical points.

What follows are eighteen of the most popular claims in support of gender theory. Some chapters might be most helpful for university students taking a gender studies class, who feel uncertain about how to reply to the claims presented by the professor. Other chapters might offer clarity for parents, educators, and leaders who care for children who experience gender dysphoria. Finally, my hope is that much of the content will be thought-provoking for those who experience a discord between their sex and their identity.

Altogether, the goal of the work is to respond to the challenge issued by Saint John Paul II just before he began delivering a series of addresses known as the Theology of the Body, when he said, "The truth that we owe to man is, first and foremost, a truth about man."[10]

Jason Evert
October 7, 2022, Feast of the Holy Rosary

1.

Each person has their own gender identity.

Gender identity is one's internal sense of self as man, woman, both, or neither.[1] For most people, their gender identity aligns with their sex. For transgender people, however, the two are different. But for everyone, gender identity is how a person feels inside, and how they express those feelings.

The Human Rights Campaign, which is a global leader in promoting LGBTQ+ rights, offers a glossary that defines nearly thirty gender-related words.[2] Among them are terms such as cisgender, gender-fluid, genderqueer, nonbinary, and transgender. However, one word is noticeably absent from the list: Gender.

One reason why conversations over the topic of gender theory are often unproductive is that the word "gender" has evolved through at least four distinct meanings in the past several decades, and people often mean different things when they use it. As a result, they end up speaking past each other.

Originally, the Greek root of the word "gender" meant "the manner in which one generates." The first usage of the English term can be traced to the fourteenth century, in reference to grammar.[3] For example, Latin has three genders for its nouns: masculine, feminine, and neuter, while some languages have as many as five gender categories.

A century later, "gender" was used as synonym for biological sex, but such a usage was rare until the twentieth century.[4] Today, many legal documents and online forms use "gender" and "sex" interchangeably. This usage can also be seen in popular phrases such as a "gender reveal party." Such celebrations aren't revealing anything about an unborn baby's internal sense of "gender identity." It simply means sex. Nonetheless, the word "gender" was predominantly used within the English language in reference to grammar until the 1970s.

The word "gender" was non-existent within medical literature until the psychologist John Money introduced the term "gender role" in an academic paper focused on hermaphroditism in 1955. He defined it as "social norms and characteristics associated with being a man or a woman."[5] For Money, one's identity is "private to an individual," whereas one's "gender role" is a "public expression to others."[6] He later explained, "The majority of people who contributed to this new meaning of gender were hermaphrodites or intersexes."[7] By 1980, the word was used ubiquitously in medical literature, primarily in relation to the gendered social roles that men and women live out. Feminist writers adopted the terminology, viewed John Money's claims as a scientific endorsement for their ideologies, and were quick to point out that socially constructed roles for men and women are malleable and purely culturally conditioned.[8] In turn, the public became habituated to using "gender" to mean "sex" or "sexual difference."

Most recently, the term "gender" is equated with "gender identity." Because gender theorists reject the significance of sexual difference (male/female), they disconnect "gender" from the sex binary. The World Health Organization explains: "Gender identity refers to a person's deeply felt, internal and individual experience of gender, which may or may not correspond to the person's physiology or designated sex at birth."[9] Such definitions partly reveal why the term "gender" is often missing from glossaries of gender theory: How can one define it without reference to the male/female binary?

Even within the field of gender studies and trans activism, many understandings of sexual identity exist. Some trans activists, such as YouTuber Blair White state, "There are only two genders,"[10] adding, "your gender is observed, your gender is not assigned."[11] Another stated, "I don't identify as a female. I don't think that transgender females are women."[12] Fionne Orlander concurred, saying, "I am a trans woman, I am a man, I can't be one without the other."[13]

Many who experience gender dysphoria do not believe they can become the other sex by transition of any kind. Rather, the steps of transition are seen as ways to manage the fact that they will never be the other sex.

Buck Angel adds a different nuance, clarifying, "I don't identify as a trans person[14] . . . I am a transsexual and will never be biologically male. But I do live as a male."[15] Buck added, "When we start wiping out language in order for trans people to feel comfortable in the world, that is insane and I will not be part of that."[16] Meanwhile, others such as Mathilda Hogberg declare, "I don't want to *be* a woman. I *am* a woman."[17]

The reason why the concept of gender seems to be so elusive is that the word itself is prone to shapeshifting, taking on whatever meaning best suits its user. But regardless of how one might define the term "gender," one thing is for certain regarding the recent evolution of its meaning: In the words of Dr. Abigail Favale, "The concept of gender, then, has ultimately served to pry a wedge between *body* and *identity*."[18]

If one's identity is untethered from the body, then it will anchor onto one's personality. However, there are as many personalities as there are persons. Thus, everyone becomes entitled to their own "gender identity." As some activists say, "Your gender is as unique as your fingerprint. No two are the same." When the human person is understood in this way, the effects can be dizzying.

On TikTok, one young woman explained:

I'm a nonbinary transman, which means I'm on the more mas-culine side of nonbinary, so technically I'm a "demiboy" but I don't really like that term so I just refer to myself as transmasc most of the time, and I don't mind being referred to as a boy, but I prefer just being referred to as a person because it makes me more comfortable, but I also plan on medically transition-ing with testosterone, top surgery, and bottom surgery, so that means I like being seen as nonbinary in a social sense, but I also want full male anatomy.

Upon reading this, one might wonder what all these words mean and where she discovered such language to describe herself. While many young people first encounter trans terminology on social media, it's also promoted by some within the medical com-munity. Dr. Diane Ehrensaft is the director of mental health at the Child and Adolescent Gender Center at Benioff Children's Hospi-tal, University of California, San Francisco. Speaking of children who identify as trans, she explains:

They refuse to pin themselves down as either male or female—maybe they are a boy/girl, or a gender hybrid, or gender ambi-dextrous, moving freely between genders, living somewhere in-between, or creating their own mosaic of gender identity and expression. As they grow older, they might identify themselves as agender, or gender neutral, or gender queer. Each one of these children is exercising their gender creativity, and we can think of them as our gender-creative children.[19]

While some dismiss the teens on TikTok and belittle those who promote gender theory, a different approach is needed. Individu-als wrestling with questions about their identity deserve respect and compassion. If the only people who offer them a listening ear are those who will accompany them into a gender clinic to obtain cross-sex hormones, why would they look elsewhere for support?

Imagine if you met someone and fell in love, but their first language was not your own. Odds are, as an expression of love and out of a desire to establish a deeper connection, you would make an effort to learn their language. It shows that they matter to you, and that you wish to connect with them in the way that is most familiar to them. In the same respect, if Christians hope to engage in meaningful dialogue with individuals who identify as trans, it's essential for them to understand the basic concepts of gender theory. Three of the most basic concepts are: gender dysphoria, trans, and nonbinary.

Gender dysphoria

Although the term "gender" is often ambiguous, there's at least some agreement regarding the term "gender dysphoria." According to the Diagnostic and Statistical Manual of Mental Disorders (DSM-5), it is defined as "A marked incongruence between one's experienced/expressed gender and assigned gender, of at least six months' duration," as manifested by various indications, based upon whether the individual is a child or an adolescent/adult.[20] This condition is associated with clinically significant distress or impairment in important areas of functioning. For adolescents and adults, it is diagnosed by at least two or more of the following:

- A marked incongruence between one's experienced/expressed gender and primary and/or secondary sex characteristics (or in young adolescents, the anticipated secondary sex characteristics).
- A strong desire to be rid of one's primary and/or secondary sex characteristics because of a marked incongruence with one's experienced/expressed gender (or in young adolescents, a desire to prevent the development of the anticipated secondary sex characteristics).

- A strong desire for the primary and/or secondary sex characteristics of the other gender.
- A strong desire to be of the other gender (or some alternative gender different from one's assigned gender).
- A strong desire to be treated as the other gender (or some alternative gender different from one's assigned gender).
- A strong conviction that one has the typical feelings and reactions of the other gender (or some alternative gender different from one's assigned gender).[21]

The classification of "Gender Dysphoria" was introduced in 2013. In its previous edition, the DSM referred to the same condition as "Gender Identity Disorder." The monumental effect of this paradigm shift cannot be understated. Initially, the disorder was defined by the disconnect experienced between one's body and one's identity. But with the reclassification, the target of treatment shifted from one's identity to one's dysphoria. This was intended to destigmatize the experience, but now the disconnect isn't viewed as the problem—the distress is the problem. Now, as Drs. Paul McHugh and Lawrence Mayer note, "a biological male who identifies himself as a female is not considered to have a psychiatric disorder unless the individual is experiencing a significant psychosocial distress at the incongruence."[22] Based upon some interpretations of the new definition, it is considered a normal state of mental health for a man to identify as a woman and decide to surgically remove his genitals.

An interesting comparison is sometimes offered with Body Integrity Identity Disorder, which is a condition when individuals feel that a part of their body does not belong to them. They might express jealousy toward amputees or injure themselves to rid themselves of an unwanted limb, even if it is healthy. While some individuals who suffer with this can find a surgeon willing to perform an amputation for them, the consensus among medical professionals is that the therapeutic goal ought to be to conform the mind to the body, rather than vice versa. As Dr. Sabine Müller explains, "Instead of only curing the symptom, a causal therapy should be developed to integrate the alien limb into the body image."[23] Unfortunately, the current approach to treating gender dysphoria is often the opposite.

Some trans activists have lobbied to have gender dysphoria removed from the DSM altogether, arguing that it pathologizes something that wouldn't exist if our society was more accepting toward those who identify as trans. Others, however, insist that it ought to remain so that insurance companies can cover the expense of transitioning. After all, without a diagnosis, there's no diagnostic code to offer an insurance company, and if it's not a mental health condition, why should insurance fund a purely elective cosmetic procedure? As a result, some are proposing a shift away from "gender dysphoria" to "gender incongruence," focusing on sexual health rather than mental health. Still others have argued that removing gender dysphoria from the DSM would lead to less adequate care and support for the real challenges individuals face.

For those who experience gender dysphoria, the distress can feel overwhelming. One individual who wrestled with it for decades wrote, "My gender identity always felt more like a puzzle that I had to put together myself, one in which many of the pieces were missing, where I had no clue as to what the final picture was supposed to be."[24] Others describe feeling "trapped in the wrong body," or as if they were being forced to write with the wrong hand. While some experience distress primarily with their body, others are more triggered by gender roles, expressions, and expectations.

According to the DSM-5, the prevalence of adult males who meet the diagnostic criteria for gender dysphoria ranges from 0.005 to 0.014 percent. For females, the range is somewhere between 0.002 to 0.003 percent. However, the manual adds that these figures are likely to be underestimates.[25] They're also not fair representations of the percentage of individuals who identify as trans, for several reasons. One is that many people who experience distress about their body do not meet the full diagnostic criteria for gender dysphoria. Another is that the percentages are based on those who sought treatment at specialty clinics, which is something most people with gender dysphoria did not do. Also, many people who identify as trans do not experience gender dysphoria at all.

Determining exact figures is a daunting task because some studies measure those who have received hormonal or surgical treatment, while others count only those who have legally changed their sex. Still others measure the number of those who meet the DSM criteria for a diagnosis of gender dysphoria, while others base their assessment on whether the individual identifies as transgender. Using this final measurement, some studies show prevalence rates as high as 0.6 percent of adults who identify as transgender.[26] For young people, studies vary from 0.7 to 3.2 percent.[27]

What's clear, however, is that there has been an exponential increase in the number of young people identifying as trans. Although gender dysphoria has been given different labels, psychologists possess a hundred-year diagnostic history of it, and it had previously affected older males or very young boys by a wide margin. However, across the globe, the demographics have changed, both in terms of the age of onset and the sex of those experiencing gender dysphoria. A meteoric rise of adolescent females who experience gender dysphoria has caused the sex ratio to flip in recent years.

In Sweden, females being diagnosed with gender dysphoria rose 1,500 percent between 2008 and 2018.[28] In 2009, only seventy-seven patients requested the services of the largest children's gender clinic in the UK. By 2022, it soared to 3,895 young—and predominantly female—patients.[29] Similar trends have appeared in many other Western nations, causing global leaders to postulate what might be fueling the shift. If the increase is merely due to wider social acceptance of LGBTQ+ identities, why hasn't there been a surge of middle-aged women coming out as trans? Why has the sex ratio been inverted so that gender dysphoria disproportionately affects adolescent females? These questions will be explored later in the book.

Despite the surge of young people who experience traits of gender dysphoria, the most reliable studies show that more than 80 percent of such children will naturally desist and identify with their biological sex.[30] In the words of Dr. James Cantor, "*every* follow-up study of GD [Gender Dysphoric] children, without exception, found the same thing: By puberty, the majority of GD children ceased to want to transition."[31] The rate of desistance is lower for adolescents and adults. However, it's difficult to predict which individuals will persist, and which will desist.

Trans

As mentioned above, although a small portion of individuals meet the diagnostic criteria for gender dysphoria, a larger segment of the population would identify under the "trans" umbrella. Although many young people are conversant with the concept of transgender identification, a few basic clarifications are helpful for those less familiar with the subject.

The term "trans" is an abbreviation of the word "transgender." It refers to anyone whose self-perception of their identity does not align with their sex. Therefore, the term "trans man" refers to a female who identifies as a man, and the term "trans woman" refers to a male who identifies as a woman.

The word "trans" is not an indication of a person's sexual attractions. Nonetheless, gender dysphoria and transgender identification are not unrelated to sexuality. According to the National Transgender Discrimination Survey, 77 percent of individuals who identify as trans report that they do not identify as heterosexual.[32] (This statistic is complicated, however. For example, some men who identify as female might identify as lesbian.)

"Trans" is not an abbreviated form of the word "transvestite." This term, which was coined in 1910 by the sex researcher Magnus

Hirschfeld to refer to those who cross-dress, is not favored today. It predominantly involves male behavior for entertainment or sexual arousal purposes, and is not necessarily related to one's sense of sexual identity.

"Trans" is also not an abbreviation of the word "transsexual." This term refers more specifically to those who have received surgical or hormonal alterations to their body. It is more commonly used within older medical literature, and often is not used favorably elsewhere.

Individuals who identify as trans do not always receive cross-sex hormones or surgery. Some cannot afford the procedures, and some have no desire to receive them. Overall, about 50 percent report having received cross-sex hormones, and 25 percent, surgery.[33] Women are about twice as likely to receive surgery as men, and "top surgeries" are about twice as common as "bottom surgeries" (8–25 percent versus 4–13 percent).[34]

Terms such as "trans-trender" lead some people to believe that identifying as trans is merely a fad that young people experiment with in an effort to gain popularity and social status. While it's true that social influences often play a role and certain individuals experience immediate affirmation and acceptance upon identifying as trans, many other who experience a discord between their sex and declared gender identity face dire social consequences for expressing these feelings.

What is most important is to realize that each person's story is unique. Although there are certainly patterns of underlying contributing factors that have emerged—which will be explored in depth later in the book—each individual deserves to be heard. Some have felt alienated from their own body since childhood. Others are searching for an answer to the discomfort, dissonance, or dissatisfaction they feel about the expectations placed upon their sex. Meanwhile, some express gender atypical behavior or interests and then discover an identity label that seems to resonate with their experience. In the process, they often discover a community of like-minded individuals with whom they can identify. Because each person's story is different, the only way to fully understand individuals who identify as trans is to become a part of their lives and care enough to learn about them as persons.

Nonbinary

When the word "trans*" appears with an asterisk, it is intended to include those who do not identify strictly as transgender. For example, those who identify as nonbinary might not necessarily consider themselves to fall under the transgender label. More than one third of individuals who identify as trans* consider themselves somewhere under the nonbinary label.[35]

They might not wish to identify with any gender, or they might consider their declared gender identity to be fluid. Michelle Mann adds, "Some non-binary people might identify as more than just non-binary. They can be non-binary and trans, or non-binary and a woman or something else."[36] Within the nonbinary umbrella, various identities and gender expressions might be found, such as agender, bigender, genderqueer, maverique, maxigender, novosexual, pangender, faesari, or centrell. A maverique, for example, is defined as someone whose gender exists on its own plane of gender, independent from all others, while someone who identifies as maxigender wishes to identify with as many genders as are available to them. What all these declared identities have in common is that they imply that a person can "be" something other than his or her sex, despite every cell in one's body being genetically encoded as such.

Nonbinary is a category that many young females are drawn to. Abigail Shrier reported:

> They make little effort to adopt the stereotypical habits of men: They rarely buy a weight set, watch football, or ogle girls. If they cover themselves with tattoos, they prefer feminine ones—flowers or cartoon animals, the kind that mark them as something

besides stereotypically male; they want to be seen as "queer," definitely not as "cis men." They flee womanhood like a house on fire, their minds fixed on escape, not on any particular destination.[37]

Glossary of related terms

The terms above are some of the more common ones you'll come across within the realm of gender theory. But numerous other terms and phrases are helpful to understand when engaging in the topic. For example:

AFAB: assigned female at birth

AMAB: assigned male at birth

Agender: one who feels that they lack a gender

Androgyne: one who identifies as a blend between male and female

Bigender: one who identifies as having two gender identities

Bottom surgery: a surgical procedure to remove one's genitals or create a facsimile of the genitals of the other sex

Cis: a Latin prefix meaning "on this side of"

Cis female: a woman whose sense of identity aligns with her sex

Cis male: a man whose sense of identity aligns with his sex

Demiboy: one who partially identifies with a male identity

Demigirl: one who partially identifies with a female identity

Detransitioner: one who began transitioning, but has halted or reversed the process of change, typically to reclaim one's natal sex as one's primary identity

Gender fluid: one whose sense of gender identity is not stable, but fluctuates

Genderqueer: one who does not identify with or follow the binary norms of male and female

Gender expression: how one shows one's internal sense of gender (this could be to express one's self, to mitigate feelings of dysphoria, for arousal, for performance, etc.)

Gender identity: first used in 1963, this term refers to one's internal sense of being male, female, both, or neither[38]

Gender neutral: one who identifies as belonging to neither gender

Hermaphrodite: generally considered a derogatory term for an individual with an intersex condition

TERF: trans-exclusionary radical feminist, a derogatory acronym for women who disagree with gender theory

Top surgery: a surgical procedure to alter the appearance of one's chest

Trans: A Latin prefix meaning "across" or "on the other side of," used as an abbreviation for transgender

Transgender: A term first used in 1965,[39] it refers to individuals whose sense of gender identity does not align with their sex

Transitioning: a term that may include some or all of the following: a change of attire, names, pronouns, use of puberty blockers, cross-sex hormones, surgery, and updating legal identification documents to identify or express oneself as another gender

Understanding gender

The sheer volume and novelty of many trans-related terms is enough to make any person feel overwhelmed and unprepared to adequately address the subject with any level of confidence. There seems to be a definition for everything that is new, but no definition of what has been since the beginning: male and female.

But this unprecedented exploration of human identity ought to draw all individuals back to the most fundamental set of questions: *What is a man? What is a woman?* Dr. John Finley remarked, "The fact that we are asking this question as a society is an ambiguous sign. It may be reason's equivalent of a slur or a facial droop, indicating a deeper problem. The fact that we can't coherently answer the question is like a brain scan showing a stroke."[40]

In an effort to define "woman," some have offered answers such as, "A woman is anyone who identifies as a woman." But not only does this fail to answer the question, it leaves one to wonder what the bounds are for such logic. Why does the same thought process not work for other realities, such as one's age, race, weight, or height? How is it that a person's beliefs about being male or female suffice to make one so?

Some will propose that a woman is someone who "feels like a woman." But can a male know what it feels like to menstruate or conceive a child? Typically, what is meant by "feeling like a woman" does not mean that the individual has experiential knowledge of living in a female body, but that he feels that he is a woman. But again, the defining factor of womanhood becomes one's self-perception.

In a presentation entitled "Ending Gender," Scott Turner Schofield offers a different answer to the question "What is a woman?" by proposing, "A woman can be anything and anyone can be a woman as long as she is smart and strong."[41] But can a woman be anything? No, she cannot. Even God can't be anything other than who He is. Can anyone be a woman as long as she's smart and strong? No, they cannot. Intelligence and strength are not prerequisites of womanhood. It cannot be earned. Womanhood is a gift from God, and only some individuals receive this gift.

Perhaps instead of asking the question "What is a woman," more progress would be made if the question were reversed: What do you call a person who can conceive and give birth to a child? What name do you give to an adult human female? In an effort to bring clarity to the debate, one feminist took to Twitter and proposed a rather simple answer: "A woman is someone with a female body and any personality, not a 'female personality' and any body."[42]

Beneath the cultural tumult, there lies an unprecedented opportunity for humanity to rediscover itself. One detransitioner recalled, "I was so focused on trying to change my gender, I never stopped to think about what gender meant."[43] While gender can sometimes be used as a synonym for sex, other possible definitions could be "sex lived out," "the social expression of the reality of one's sex," or "the cultural expressions of masculinity and femininity."

Gender can be distinguished from sex, but it cannot be divorced from it.[44] Although expressions of masculinity and femininity shift and evolve, the foundation of sex remains stable. For example, a century ago, pink was a considered a masculine color, while blue was deemed "delicate and dainty," and thus more fitting when worn by girls.[45] But the individuals wearing the pink and blue will remain forever male or female. This is because not one of them was ever born into the wrong body.

One path forward could be to avoid the two extreme positions of denying sexual differences or exaggerating them.[46] Whereas rigid gender stereotypes attempt to force individuals to conform their personality to align with their body, those who promote gender theory aim to conform a person's body to align with their personality. Why not work to create a culture that makes it easier for people to love themselves as they are?

2.

Gender is a social construct.

Men and women are essentially the same. Any distinctions we see between them are only because of cultural conditioning. If children were raised without gender stereotypes, women would be equal to men.

When people claim that "gender" is a social construct, they are typically referring to the social roles lived out by men and women. And while it's true that culture can shape the ways in which men and women express their sexual identity, it's untrue to imply from this that men and women are essentially the same.

In the 1990s the toy company Hasbro decided to test a gender-neutral playhouse that they hoped to market to boys and girls. It didn't go as planned. *The Atlantic* reported, "It soon emerged that girls and boys did not interact with the structure in the same way. The girls dressed the dolls, kissed them, and played house. The boys catapulted the toy baby carriage from the roof. A Hasbro manager came up with a novel explanation: 'Boys and girls are different.'"[1]

While this anecdote is amusing, it's fair to pose the question: But what about the boy who likes to play with dolls or the girl who prefers rough-and-tumble play? Do their preferences indicate that sex isn't as binary as some would like to imagine?

When considering the theory that gender as a social construct, it's helpful to remember that those who initially proposed the idea were often motivated by a desire to establish equality for women.

But equality does not require sameness. In fact, equating women with men dilutes the uniqueness of women.

One such example of the uniqueness of women is their sensitivity. Consider, for example, the experiment that psychologist Dr. Richard Fabes conducted on children between the ages of six and eight, to assess how boys and girls responded to the sound of a crying baby. The children were placed in a room where they could hear the infant crying through an audio system that included a microphone. They had the option of comforting the child through the intercom, or simply turning off the loudspeaker. Most of the boys—in fact, twice as many as the girls—simply shut the volume off to resolve the problem of the crying child![2]

Some might dismiss the results of the study and argue that the girls were simply conditioned by their mothers to be more sensitive to the needs of others. But there's no need to minimize the fact that women are equipped to be more sensitive. In fact, on average, *all* their senses are more sensitive than those of men.

Hearing

Even from within the womb, girls begin to outperform boys in terms of their ability to hear. Females are more sensitive to small changes in volume,[3] and as they mature, will soon be able to detect subtle inflections within the human voice that are imperceptible to the male brain.[4] This is due to the fact that small hair cells in the inner ear of women vibrate more intensely than men's, amplifying their hearing ability.[5] In fact, in order for the average boy to hear as well as the average girl, one's voice needs to be amplified by about eight decibels.[6] Granted, this doesn't guarantee that he's listening, but at least he can hear you!

Although a woman might take it personally that a man seems incapable of hearing her while he's performing another task, there's a good reason for that. Partly because of the greater number of connections between the two hemispheres of a woman's brain, she has an extraordinary ability to multitask. On the other hand, researchers have found that if you scan a man's brain while he's reading, "you'll find that he's virtually deaf."[7]

While these differences might seem lopsided in favor of the women, they also confer certain advantages for males. Men, for example, are comfortable with sounds twice as loud as women. Granted, some males are more sensitive to sound than others. But this is the exception rather than the norm. Although women's hearing is more sensitive, men have a greater ability to locate the source of a sound in three-dimensional space.[8] Meanwhile, because of the testosterone bath that the male brain receives beginning in utero, his auditory system is formed differently, thus giving him a greater ability to tune out ambient noise than the average female brain.[9] This gives men a unique ability to focus intently upon the object of their attention.

Women, on the other hand, tend to absorb the sounds of their environment to the opposite—and sometimes hyperobservant—extreme. While a woman sits at a café across from a friend, she might simultaneously be eavesdropping on multiple conversations at nearby tables while reading the body language of those outside of earshot to assess which couples are getting along, and who is more interested in whom . . . all while fully engaged in a deeply personal conversation at her own table—and without giving her partner any indication that she's mentally performing surveillance of nearby tables.

Seeing

What men lack in terms of their ability to hear, they make up for with their visual capacities. Researchers applied fifteen vision tests to nearly nine hundred men and women, and discovered: "On no test did females significantly outperform males."[10] Although women have a greater ability to discriminate between colors, men have a stronger ability to gauge depth perception and track moving objects in space.[11]

On the surface, it might appear that men have more acute vision than women. But women have a more highly developed capacity to interpret what they see. It's well established that, on average, women are superior at reading facial expressions and understanding body language.[12] They are adept at reading nonverbal messages not only to decipher the validity of the spoken word, but to assess unspoken needs. Although men are better at identifying their emotions, women are better at identifying the emotions of others.[13] This is why, as one researcher noted, "Men generally find statements like 'although I said ABC, the circumstances should have made you understand that I meant XYZ' extremely difficult to comprehend."[14] Women rely more heavily than men upon nonverbal cues in interpersonal relationships, and it's possible that they may rely *more* on this than the spoken word![15] As Pope Saint John Paul II remarked, women "see persons with their hearts."[16]

Smelling

Visit any college dormitory and you'll concur that women smell better than men. Literally. The research is clear: women outperform men at detecting and discriminated scents.[17] In one study, Dr. Pamela Dalton exposed men and women repeatedly to different scents to measure their ability to detect particular odors. With repeated exposure, the men made no improvement in detecting the scent, while the women's ability to detect the odor improved one hundred-thousandfold![18]

Why? On the bottom side of the brain, the olfactory bulb receives signals from the olfactory nerve, which originates from smell receptors in the nose. However, women have on average seven million more cells in the olfactory bulb than men.[19] Evolutionary biologists propose that this superior sense of smell gives mothers an advantage in detecting whether food is safe before feeding it to their children. This also explains why there's such disparity of opinions between mothers and their teenage sons regarding the smell of his room.

Women's sense of smell is stronger than men's especially during ovulation. When a woman at her peak time of fertility each month is exposed to the male pheromone androstadienone, Dr. Louann Brizendine explains that "within six minutes, their mood brightens and their mental focus sharpens. These airborne pheromones keep women from getting into a bad mood for hours afterward. Beginning at puberty, only female brains, not male brains, are able to detect the androstadienone pheromone, and they're sensitive to it only during certain times of the month."[20]

Women are also more impacted by the sweet smell of an infant's head.[21] According to *Smithsonian* magazine, "The smell of newborn babies triggers the same reward centers as drugs."[22] This intoxicating cocktail of about 150 chemicals causes a surge of dopamine in the woman's brain, facilitating a deeper bond between mother and child. Fathers can also detect the scent, but not as intensely as mothers.

Feeling

Women are not only generally more sensitive on an emotional level, research shows that they "showed 'overwhelmingly' greater sensitivity to pressure on the skin on every part of the body . . . women have a tactile sensitivity so superior to men's that in some tests there is no overlap between the scores of the two sexes; in these, the least sensitive woman is more sensitive than the most sensitive man."[23] They also outperform men in temperature detection.[24]

Behavioral differences

Watch any online fail compilation video, and young males excel far beyond their female counterparts at making almost miraculously stupid decisions. Typically, when a female appears in such a video, she's either accompanied by males, or is attempting a gymnastic maneuver during a slumber party.

Sex-specific risk-taking transcends species. In their research of Japanese macaque monkeys, Linda Marie Fedigan and Sandra Zohar noticed that males and females were born at equal rates, but by the time they reached adulthood, the females outnumbered the males five to one. After reviewing more than two decades of data, the researchers concluded that the males were exponentially more likely to make remarkably dumb and risky choices, such as trying to scamper across the road before being crushed by a vehicle, whereas the females simply avoided the road![25]

Human behaviors that many consider to be socially constructed gender stereotypes also appear in primates. Take, for example, young vervet and rhesus monkeys: females prefer to play with dolls, whereas the males opt for toy cars and a ball.[26] Or consider the wild chimpanzee: The females are more likely to cradle a stick in their arms as if it were a baby, whereas the males use the same sticks as weapons.[27] Like humans, if young males apes aren't given the opportunity to play fight with one another, they become *more* violent as adults.[28]

Many of these gender-related behavioral differences are impacted by hormones. Whereas baby girls tend to prefer the sight of human faces and make more eye contact than male babies (who prefer to look at mechanical moving objects), girls who were exposed to higher levels of testosterone in the womb make less eye contact.[29] Females who were exposed to higher levels of testosterone tend to be less interested in children and have a more difficult time interpreting others' emotions, whereas women with lower levels of the hormone are more interested in parenting, wearing makeup, dressing up, cooking, and interior decorating.[30] Those with higher levels of testosterone tend to be more aggressive, to have decreased verbal abilities, and to have better spatial orientation abilities.[31] However, as the DSM-5 points out, "the prenatal androgen milieu is more closely related to gendered behavior than to gender identity."[32]

Although behavioral differences offer evidence that sexual distinctions aren't merely culturally constructed, it should be reiterated that women who engage in gender nonconforming behavior are no less female than the women who exhibit more typically "feminine" behavior patterns.

Biological differences

While some might ascribe the behavioral differences between men and women to cultural conditioning or hormonal variations, the more closely one examines the bodies of men and women, the clearer our differences become.

Researchers have identified 6,500 sex-specific genes.[33] Every cell of the human body that has a nucleus is sexed, and according to Dr. Franck Mauvais-Jarvis, there are "ubiquitous sex differences in the molecular makeup of all male and female cells."[34] This is one reason why a "sex-change operation" is impossible. Every cell of the human body would need to be exchanged. The biological evidence for sex difference is insurmountable.[35]

Dr. Franck Mauvais-Jarvis added, "The combination of all genetic and hormonal causes of sex differences aforementioned culminates in two different biological systems in men and women that translate into differences in disease predisposition, manifestation, and response to treatment."[36]

What this means is that men and women are susceptible to disease in different ways. Women are more prone to autoimmune diseases while men are more susceptible to infectious diseases.[37] Men are more likely to suffer heart disease and are three times more likely to be diagnosed with autism spectrum disorder.[38] Sex differences exist in rates of heart disease, asthma, diabetes, Alzheimer's disease, pneumonia, and autism, to name only a few.[39]

Men and women also exhibit symptoms of disease in unique ways. Whereas men often experience chest pain during a heart attack, women experience pain between their shoulder blades, nausea, vomiting, and shortness of breath.[40] Because women often experience different symptoms when suffering a heart attack, they are more than twice as likely as men to be sent home from the emergency room without being diagnosed and, as a result, are more likely to die after being released.[41]

Males and females also respond to drugs differently, both in terms of efficacy and side effects.[42] Aspirin, for example, is more beneficial to women than men in preventing stroke, but more beneficial to men for preventing heart attacks.[43] In the words of Dr. Maria Ferretti, "When properly documented and studied, sex and gender differences are the gateway to precision medicine."[44]

Often, the solution to a patient's ailment depends upon a doctor's understanding of sex-specific medicine.[45] Dr. Marek Glezerman, author of the book *Gender Medicine*, recalled an instance where another doctor reached out to him for assistance regarding a female patient who suffered repeated epileptic attacks. Her specialists made repetitive changes to her medication to alleviate her ailment, but without success. Dr. Glezerman pointed out to the doctor that the woman's seizures worsened in both frequency and intensity during the second phase of her menstrual cycle, when women experience a surge of progesterone. Progesterone is a natural inhibitor of antiepileptic medication, and therefore the solution was not to change her medication, but to increase the dosage during that window of her cycle. Her doctor implemented this recommendation, and the problem was solved.[46]

These medical considerations are even more important for individuals who identify as trans. If a woman identifies as male, her medical providers still have an ethical obligation to account for her biological sex as a woman when treating her. No amount of self-identification can override the reality of her genetic code. At times, this can make the difference between life and death. Take, for instance, the tragedy that was reported by *The New England Journal of Medicine* when a woman who identified as a man arrived at an emergency room, complaining of abdominal pains.[47] The individual's medical chart listed the patient's gender as male, and so doctors treated the individual accordingly. Unfortunately, the cause of the patient's discomfort was that she was in labor. Because she was not appropriately triaged and evaluated for pregnancy related problems, the child passed away.

Form and function

But why are men and women so unique? Dr. Deborah Blum explains, "Many scientists trace almost every behavioral gender difference—from emotions to competitiveness—back to the different demands of being a sperm-producer or an egg-maker."[48] Put simply, form follows function. In the words of Dr. Andrew Sodergren, "The ultimate purpose of maleness and femaleness—is fatherhood and motherhood, not merely in the act of reproduction but in the full sense of a vocation."[49]

Each person's body is ordered toward his or her reproductive role, and the existence of the human species depends upon one's ability to recognize the "otherness" of the other sex. Granted, a person's ability to procreate does not define his or her identity. Men and women are male and female before they're fertile, after their fertility ends, and even in heaven, when procreation will have ceased.

Nonetheless, the human body's organization for generation is a revelation of one's sexed identity. Just as the electricians who invented the power outlet and the electrical cord designed the two to be united to transmit electricity, human beings are created in a binary and complementary form, for the transmission of human life. Even the smallest details of one's anatomy point toward this reality. For example, during ovulation, a woman not only becomes more sensitive to touch and scents, the chemical composition of her saliva changes, to increase the amount of sugar in it![50]

However, sexual complementarity is not merely about corresponding parts, because sexual differences are shown only in a limited way on the outside.[51] What's visible points to the reality of masculinity and femininity. Even without realizing it, men and women continually manifest their uniqueness. For example, women predominantly carry babies in their left side, regardless of whether they're right or left-handed (closer to the heart, which the baby can feel). Men, however, predominantly carry a baby in the arm that is strongest.[52]

Or consider the wonder of breastfeeding. Many mothers experience an uncontrolled "let-down reflex" of breastmilk upon hearing their baby cry. Sometimes this occurs when the mother simply *thinks* about the baby. What's perhaps even more fascinating, though, are the physiological benefits of breastfeeding, which only a woman can naturally provide.

Some of the greatest threats to the health of infants are bacterial infections within the intestines. Some of these dangerous microorganisms attach to curved cells that line the digestive tract. However, some of the sugars in breast milk mimic these cells, and scientists have postulated that the bacteria mistakenly attach to the sugars and are excreted by the body, thus preventing infection. This may partly explain why formula-fed babies have twice the number of intestinal infections as babies who are breastfed.[53] Breast milk also contains fatty acids that promote brain development in the child. One endocrinologist explained, "Milk is not just a source of nutritional elements, some simple mixture of fats, sugars, and salts. It has a causal effect on the infant. It's really a vehicle by which the mother transfers information to the child."[54]

One of the ways that a woman's breast milk transfers information to her child is through the immune system. When a baby breastfeeds, a small amount of saliva will backwash into the woman's breast. If the child is sick, her breast can detect the infection and it will immediately trigger an immunological response. The chemical composition of her breast milk will change, and she will begin to transmit billions of white blood cells to the baby, specifically designed to boost the child's immune system to fight the specific pathogens. When the illness resolves, the woman's breast milk will resume its normal composition.[55] One woman remarked, "So, the next time someone shames you for breastfeeding in public, just tell them you're performing a diagnostic test!"

Because of the remarkable nature of womanhood, the British novelist William Golding exclaimed, "I think women are foolish to pretend they are equal to men, they are far superior and always have been."[56] Eric S. Gray added, "Whatever you give a woman, she will make greater. If you give her sperm, she'll give you a baby. If you give her a house, she'll give you a home. If you give her groceries, she'll give you a meal. If you give her a smile, she'll give you her heart. She multiplies and enlarges what is given to her."[57]

Upon reading this, some might feel offended that such a quote relegates all women to domestic life. But the unique gifts of womanhood do not determine a woman's destiny or require her to become a biological mother to lead a fulfilling life. Rather, they indicate that she has been entrusted with a unique capacity to nurture others. In the words of Saint Edith Stein, a woman's soul is designed "to be a shelter in which other souls may unfold. Both spiritual companionship and spiritual motherliness are not limited to the physical spouse and mother relationships, but they extend to all people with whom woman comes into contact."[58] Or, as Mother Teresa remarked, God's most precious gift to women is "the ability to love as a woman."[59] Perhaps this is why the devil is so desperate to convince women that they need to become masculinized in order to become powerful.

In light of all of the above scientific evidence of the uniqueness of men and women, imagine if something similar were true for individuals who experienced gender dysphoria. Imagine if every cell was imprinted with genetic evidence of a transgender identity, and the organs and gametes were oriented toward such an identity. Those who disagreed with gender theory would be scorned for the absurdity of their anti-scientific beliefs. And yet the biological evidence reveals unequivocally that humans are sexually dimorphic creatures, and that sex is stable, unchanging, objective, and meaningful.

To each of the above points, some might argue, "Anatomical information is irrelevant because gender identity has nothing to do with biology. In fact, the stubbornness of biology is precisely what lies at the core of gender dysphoria. So it doesn't matter if there are 6,500 sex-specific genes or 6.5 million of them. Those who seek to transition aren't trying to change their sex. They're trying to align their body more closely with their gender identity."

In response, one might ask, "What if young people are being culturally conditioned to believe that their gender can be divorced from their body? What if gender theory is the social construct after all?"

3.

Some people are trans.

It is profoundly disrespectful and dismissive to deny the reality of transgender people. Just as no one questions the existence of cisgender individuals, it's unreasonable and uncharitable to pretend that people who are trans are any less real. When Christians make statement such as "No one 'is' transgender,"[1] it makes trans individuals feel erased and unseen.

There is no question that many individuals exist who experience gender dysphoria or identify in a way that does not align with their sex. But is there such a thing as a trans person? Some individuals understandably feel offended that such a question would even be raised. In the words of trans YouTuber Samantha Lux, "Referring to trans women as masculine for no reason other than the fact that we were born male is just not necessary . . . this language is not appropriate. You cannot call us biological boys or even biological males and expect us to think that you're coming at us in good faith. That is the language of a transphobe and you will be treated as such."[2]

But to question whether humans should be categorized as *cis* versus *trans* is not intended to imply that the lived experiences of any individual who identifies as trans is fabricated or disingenuous. The question is intended to raise a profoundly important matter: What is it that defines a person? Do feelings of self-perception reveal the deepest truth of a person's identity?

When a person claims that he or she *is* trans, it cements a feeling into an identity, and an ontological status. It becomes *who* they are, rather than *what* they feel. But if a person's identity hinges upon their feelings or beliefs—even if those experiences are persistent and deeply felt—the process of self-identification becomes unnecessarily difficult. If the body cannot be trusted to reveal the truth of the person, then why should feelings be trusted? For example, YouTuber Ash Hardell recommends that viewers experiment with different names, pronouns, and outfits to see what feels right. She suggests to her audience that they "try different things, and then you can kind of figure out like what pings your euphoria, and then that is like a good way to figure out your gender and your gender identity."[3] Other online influencers, such as Kaylee Karol, propose that taking hormones is "probably the best way to actually tell if you're trans anyways."[4] But are such drastic measures necessary?

Fifty years ago, a young woman who had predominantly masculine interests would be labeled a tomboy. Now, with the evolution and power of language, she might conclude she is trans and would benefit from a double mastectomy because she was born in the wrong body. But something can be learned from history here: Is the better approach for such a woman to discard womanhood and appropriate manhood, or to broaden her culture's understanding of what it means to be a woman? Gender nonconformity does not require people to identify as something other than their sex. After all, everyone is either a male person or a female person. There is no subset of human beings for whom sex is irrelevant.

By introducing the idea that some people "are trans," gender theorists and other influencers are attempting to use language to shape reality by informing cultures how to think about it. In the words of Professor Judith Butler, "the alteration of gender at the most fundamental epistemic level will be conducted, in part, through contesting the grammar in which gender is given."[5] Or, in the words of one trans activist, "It's time for trans experience to move from being an object of knowledge to being one of its creators."[6] If the trans identity becomes fundamental to one's thought, it becomes the lens through which life is understood. By redefining human identity, some have proposed that it then becomes possible to change language, philosophies, politics, and even science.[7]

However, what these ambitious thinkers fail to realize is that when God speaks, new realities are created. When humans speak, the only thing created is sound. This is a substantial ontological difference. As Dr. Abigail Favale explains, "Divine speech makes reality; Human speech identifies reality. . . . [O]ur language does not project meaning onto things. Rather, meaning intrinsically exists in what God creates. Moreover, this meaning is intelligible to us, and language, a mark of God's image in us, enables human beings to proclaim that inherent meaning."[8]

Therefore, humans cannot add the word "trans" as a prefix to another word and create a new reality. For example, a gentleman named Oli London identifies as transracial and has received eighteen reconstructive surgeries to appear Korean. After a series of procedures, he announced, "I'm so happy finally. I've been trapped in the wrong body for eight years. And that's the worst feeling in the world, when you're trapped, and you don't feel like you can be yourself. But finally, I'm Korean. I can be myself and I'm so, so happy."[9]

Similarly, some individuals experience species dysphoria and identify as transspecies. Take, for example, a man in the United Kingdom named Ted, who identifies as a parrot. To become like them, he not only tattooed feathers onto his skin, but had the whites of his eyes tattooed. He surgically removed his ears, transformed his house into a birdcage, and lives off the same food as the pets. He explained, "You just can't trust people like you can trust parrots."[10]

Some individuals might be offended by such comparisons. Although emotional reactions are sometimes justified, sometimes they are a mechanism to avoid responding to a difficult question. If a transgender activist were asked, "Do you hate Ted and Oli?" the activist would likely deny any feelings of ill will. But the question becomes, "Then why can't these individuals transition to become another race or species, so that they can become their authentic selves?" A libertarian reaction might be to endorse their right to augment their bodies according to their personal wishes. But does anyone believe that the deepest truth about these individuals is that they *are* transracial or transspecies? Such an identification does not bring them closer to the truth of who they are, but further away from it.

In a similar way, when a person identifies as transgender, although this might provide them with a term that they feel helps them to talk about a complicated experience and communicate that to others, an important question must be asked: Does this title enable them to be their authentic self, or to reject the deepest truth of their identity? Put differently, does it affirm the person . . . or the dysphoria?

For these reasons, Dr. Deborah Soh argues, "There is no such thing as a transgender child. The stringing together of 'transgender' and 'child' is part of a lexicon pushed by activists to co-op the young into their political movement. Many people, including parents, unknowingly use the term, not knowing there is a difference between 'being transgender' and being 'gender dysphoric.'"[11] As a result, some parents will make declarative statements such as, "My daughter was born transgender."[12] But as one man who underwent reassignment surgery later observed, "If you believe there are trans kids, you'll seek different solutions than if you believe there are children who suffer from gender dysphoria."

What does it mean to be human?

The philosopher Josef Pieper once said that it is impossible for a man to know the essence of a single gnat.[13] If this is the case, then it is important to approach the subject of the human person with a posture of reverence and humility. Ultimately, man is a mystery. This does not mean, however, than we cannot know *anything* about man. It simply means that we cannot know *everything* about the subject. There is much that can be learned through the physical and psychological sciences, but without the contribution of divine revelation, we will arrive at an impartial picture of what it means to be human. Saint John Paul II pointed out, though, "Modern rationalism *does not tolerate mystery*. It does not accept the mystery of man as male and female."[14]

For ages, philosophers and scientists have grappled with the question of what it means to be human. Thousands of years ago, Gnostics and Manicheans adopted a dualist view of the human person. In short, it is the creed that professes "I'm not my body." A similar philosophy was promoted by the French thinker René Descartes, whose idea of the human mind was summarized by others as the "ghost in the machine." This view of the human person now serves as the foundation of gender theory: that if gender is tied to sex, the person becomes a slave to his or her body. As Robert P. George wrote, "The idea that human beings are non-bodily persons inhabiting non-personal bodies never quite goes away."[15]

The Church's answer to this disintegration of the human person is an integrated vision of man. To the question, "Can we trust the body to reveal the truth of the person?" the Church would utter an emphatic *yes!* The human body reveals the person. This teaching, rather than being an imposition from religious authorities, is something people naturally believe.

For example, if you were to say, "I am going to the store," it's safe to say that your body is going there as well. In other words, you don't *have* a body. You *are* a body. It's not something you merely *have*, like you have a pair of jeans. Your body *is* you. This is not to say that a person is the sum of his or her parts. A woman is not a woman because she has female parts. Rather, she has female parts because she is a woman.

Because the body reveals the person, it is a visible expression of the reality of who you are as a man or woman. So, instead of the materialistic idea that chromosomes plus gonads plus anatomy equals sex, the Church would propose that the human person is not a sexless being that "has" a male or female body. Rather, it is the human person—male or female—who is sexed, and this reality is expressed in and through the body. As Saint John Paul II explained, "It is typical of rationalism to make a radical contrast in man between spirit and body, between body and spirit. But man is a person in the unity of his body and his spirit. The body can never be reduced to mere matter: it is a *spiritualized body*, just as man's spirit is so closely united to the body that he can be described as *an embodied spirit*."[16] In fact, the human body is the only creation of God that makes a person visible. Angels are personal beings, but they do not have a body. Animals have bodies but are not personal beings. Therefore, the human body alone has the power to make visible the invisible reality of personhood.[17] Put simply, your sex is not *what you have*, but *who you are*. Thus, a person's identity is revealed in and through the body, not by one's feelings about the body.

If the body is a reliable revelation, this is good news. It means that the body is not meaningless, but meaningful! The body is the firm foundation of man's sexual identity. One's sex defines our identity, expresses the person, and reveals the soul.[18] As Cardinal Christoph Schönborn declared, "The beauty is real and reliable. Its light can be traced back to God's original guiding intention for man and woman."[19]

Nature's enemy

What many people overlook is that the devil is not only the enemy of the soul. He is the enemy of human nature. What God has joined, he desires to separate. So, if God has joined together a husband and wife, the devil seeks divorce. If God has united the body to the soul, the devil desires their division, which is death. But if the devil can rupture the union that exists between the body and the person, the image of God becomes obscured. After all, if the body is meaningless, then so are the terms: man, wife, father, daughter, and family. Contrary to what many believe, gender theory does not aim to create an endless spectrum of genders, but to abolish sexual differences. The ultimate goal is to erase what Saint John Paul II called "the spousal meaning of the body." After all, for diversity to exist, there must be objective differences. However, the ultimate diversity is male and female.[20]

This might strike some as an apocalyptic exaggeration, but consider the testimony of the family of Robert Arquette. Robert was an American actor who identified as trans and passed away in 2016. After Robert's death, his family released the following statement:

> Our brother Robert, who became our brother Alexis, who became our sister Alexis, who became our brother Alexis, passed this morning. . . . In the days leading to her death, she told us she was already visiting the other side, and that where she was going, there was only one gender. That on the other side, we are free from all of the things that separate us in this life; and that we are all one.[21]

What's perhaps most fascinating about this statement is not the fluidity of Robert's gender identity and expression, but the idea that sexual differences separate men and women, and that the solution to this division is to eliminate such distinctions.

Saint John Paul II proposed a very different perspective of sexual difference. In his Theology of the Body, he proposes that *the spousal meaning of the body* is the fundamental truth about the human person. In order to understand what it means to be human one must understand this. It means that the human body has "the power to express the love by which the human person becomes a gift, thus fulfilling the deep meaning of his or her being and existence."[22] He adds that the spousal meaning of the body is "the spiritual beauty of the sign constituted by the human body in its masculinity and femininity."[23]

What he means by this is that humans are made in the image and likeness of God, who is love. Therefore, the human person images God not merely in a spiritual way or as individuals, but most profoundly in our complementarity as male and female. He writes, "Man becomes an image of God not so much in the moment of solitude as in the moment of communion. . . . [This] constitutes perhaps the deepest theological aspect of everything one can say about man."[24]

In the one-flesh union of a husband and wife, the two make visible the invisible mystery of God: that the Blessed Trinity is a communion of persons, an eternal exchange of life-giving love. Therefore, the sexual difference has a transcendent meaning that points beyond the individual. As Christopher West explained, "our bodies as male and female are not only *biological*, they are *theological*."[25] Our bodies not only reveal something about us (who we are and that we are called to make a gift of ourselves in love); they reveal something about God, in whose image we are made. This, Saint John Paul says, "can be said to sum up *the whole of Christian anthropology*,"[26] that man "becomes fully himself to the extent that he gives himself as a free gift to others."[27]

But if the human body is a sign that makes visible the invisible mystery of God, then what happens if the sign is obscured? If man loses sight of God, he loses sight of himself. In the words of Vatican II, "When God is forgotten, however, the creature itself grows unintelligible."[28] In other words, if man loses sight of supernatural realities, it will come to the point where man can no longer see natural realities. G. K. Chesterton predicted that such times would come. He wrote,

"The great march of mental destruction will go on. Everything will be denied. . . . Fires will be kindled to testify that two and two make four. Swords will be drawn to prove that leaves are green in summer."[29]

If obscuring the sign of masculinity and femininity causes man's vision of God to be eclipsed, consider what happens when masculinity and femininity *are* lived out according to God's plan: Sexual difference would not reveal competition, but complementarity. Sexual difference would not be viewed as the cause of oppression, but the revelation of life-giving love. It would not be an obstacle to unity, but rather the invitation to communion.

Although it's common to speak of "the opposite sex," male and female are not opposites or simply two types of bodies. Male and female are two ways of being made in the image of God.[30] The other is not just *another* sex, but *the* other sex. The sexed body reveals that the human person is from others and for others.[31] Without this complementarity, where does the body point? What is the natural complement to a person who is nonbinary or genderfluid? Without sexual differentiation, we deprive ourselves of our own identity and knowledge of self. In the words of Pope Francis, "Learning to accept our body, to care for it and to respect its fullest meaning, is an essential element of any genuine human ecology. Also, valuing one's own body in its femininity or masculinity is necessary if I am going to be able to recognize myself in an encounter with someone who is different."[32] What he means is that we only understand our own sexed reality when we accept and encounter the reality of the other sex. When that is erased, so are we.

Masculinity and femininity, although expressed in various ways through history and cultures, are ordered toward an end: spousal union and parenthood.[33] However, the truth of sexual difference does not require men and women to fit into narrow cultural expectations of gender. In fact, there are many ways for individuals to express the natural reality of our sexed identities as male and female. Take, for example, Sister Deirdre Byrne, who is a missionary religious sister, a board-certified family practitioner and surgeon, and a colonel in the United States Army. She is well aware that there is more than one way for a woman to express her femininity. She did not do these things instead of motherhood. Rather, she mothered through these things. In the words of Saint Edith Stein, "Thus the participation of women in the most diverse professional disciplines could be a blessing for the entire society, private or public, precisely if the specifically feminine ethos would be preserved."[34]

Dr. Abigail Favale added:

> St. John Paul II's unique understanding of the terms "masculinity" and "femininity" could be helpful here. He uses these terms exclusively in reference to males and females respectively. Masculinity is simply the way of being a man in the world, and is thus uniquely inflected by each individual personality. Thus, when my husband, Michael, is caring for our children and cooking dinner, these are masculine acts, because they are being performed by a male human being. Similarly, my femininity is exhibited as much in my assertiveness during a staff meeting as when I am breast-feeding—because it is the *person* who is gendered, not the act or trait. This embodied, personalist understanding of masculinity and femininity reaffirms the meaning of the sexed body, without collapsing cultural stereotypes into natural categories.[35]

This insight leaves room for the expansion of gender expression without erasing the binary nature of sex. So, rather than saying that a woman is masculine if she engages in things that men typically engage in, is it possible she could change the oil in her car in a feminine way? Does she cease to be a woman if she expresses her femininity in a manner that stretches cultural expectations of womanhood? After all, a woman doesn't become one by having stereotypical female interests or mannerisms.

If a person does not feel at home in his or her body, the Church would not conclude that the person *is trans*. Rather, the Church believes that original sin obscured humanity's ability to see themselves, others, and God. Saint John Paul II explained that in the beginning, because of "original innocence," the man and woman were able to see one another as God sees them. The body was a clear revelation of the person, and thus, of one's call to love. But with original sin came shame, and the desire to conceal the body. The pope noted that this resulted in "the collapse of the original acceptance of the body as a sign of the person in the visible world."[36]

Original sin disrupted not only the unity between men and women, but also the unity within each person. John Paul pointed out that this "brings with it an almost constitutive *difficulty in identifying oneself with one's own body*."[37] Although he was not addressing the question of gender dysphoria in this passage, the fact remains that each person, in his or her own way, experiences a division between the body and soul. Speaking of Adam after the fall, John Paul continued, "It is as if he had experienced a specific *fracture of the personal integrity of his own body, particularly in that which determines its sexuality*."[38] Every person will experience this challenge in a unique way, but each person is given a task to rediscover the meaning of his or her body.

Whereas gender theory considers feelings of gender incongruence to be a guide that should be followed toward fulfillment, claiming to offer people the ability to embrace the full truth about their identity, a bold question that was asked above must be revisited: What if gender theory only gives people permission to reject it? What if the Church's goal isn't to erase anyone's identity, but to help them rediscover it? What if the Church's hope is to help individuals avoid the challenging question that Corinna Cohn once posed: "Why did I need to become a lifelong medical patient and have a dangerous surgery to reveal my 'authentic' self?"

These questions are not easy ones, but they explain why feminist philosopher Luce Irigaray once wrote, "Sexual difference is one of the important questions of our age, if not in fact the burning issue. According to Heidegger, each age is preoccupied with one thing, and one alone. Sexual difference is probably that issue in our own age which could be our salvation on an intellectual level."[39]

Ultimately, sexual identity is not something we define, but something we receive. As Saint John Paul II explained, "The fundamental fact of this existence of man in every stage of his history is that God 'created them male and female'; in fact he always creates them in this way, and they are always such."[40] Therefore, the question is not simply *what* makes you a man or a woman, but *who* makes you a man or a woman. It is not merely *something* that establishes our sexual identity but *someone.*

4.

Sex is assigned at birth.

According to Dr. Deanna Adkins, one's internal sense of gender is "the only medically supported determinant of sex. . . . It is counter to medical science to use chromosomes, hormones, internal reproductive organs, external genitalia, or secondary sex characteristics to override gender identity for purposes of classifying someone as male or female."[1] Therefore, when a child is born and a doctor assigns the child male or female, such a premature judgment can be damaging to the individual. According to The New England Journal of Medicine, "Sex designations on birth certificates offer no clinical utility, and they can be harmful for intersex and transgender people."[2] Because some boys have vaginas and some girls have penises, we can't know someone' sex unless they tell us.

In the words of trans activist Decker Moss, "imagine a world, where gender isn't left up to doctors or judges, one where we are all able to claim our own gender based on what's between our ears, rather than have it assigned to us based on what's between our legs. Here, we're all able to self-identify as male, as female, as both, or as neither."[3]

Although gender theory proposes the idea that every child is "assigned" a sex at birth, this language originated in the medical field for babies who are born with genital ambiguities. In such difficult situations doctors and parents were left with a difficult task of discerning how to proceed. Dr. John Money believed that clinicians had a responsibility to assist parents in assigning such children a sex and then establishing a plan of hormonal and surgical interventions if necessary, followed by social conditioning, to ensure the child will live out his or her gender role.

Thankfully, many medical professionals and clinicians today take a more cautious and less invasive approach. When a child is born with ambiguous genitalia, a team of specialists will assist the parents in navigating this challenging situation. Often, this will involve the consultation of experts in genetics, urology, endocrinology, psychiatry, and pediatric medicine. If the sex of the child is not obvious, sometimes an ultrasound or chromosomal, hormonal, or genetic tests can give the parents greater clarity. However, 99.98 percent of the time, the genitals of a child clearly indicate his or her sex.[4]

To apply the language of "assigning sex" to children when their bodies are clearly male or female is a linguistic maneuver by gender theorists. Despite the binary nature of human sexuality, gender theorists treat every child as sexually ambiguous. Margaret McCarthy summed up their intentions well: "It is as though we are all effectively hermaphrodites regardless of our anatomy or any other physiological make up."[5] Supposedly, all that a parent or obstetrician can do is "assign" a sex based upon their best guess, as an external, arbitrary authority. But if sex can be assigned, it can be reassigned. This is the ultimate motive behind adopting such language.

For a child whose sexual development in utero is typical, doctors and parents are not *assigning* a child's sex. They're recognizing a biological reality that was determined long before the child's birth and identifying it. As Dr. Paul McHugh explained, "The language of 'assigned at birth' is purposefully misleading and would be identical to an assertion that blood type is assigned at birth. Yes, a doctor can check your blood type and list it. But blood type, like sex, is objectively recognizable, not assigned. In fact, the sex of a child can be ascertained well before birth."[6]

According to biologists, sex can be defined by the type of mature reproductive cells, or gametes.

Neuroscientist Dr. Deborah Soh explains:

Contrary to what is commonly believed, sex is defined not by chromosomes or our genitals, or hormonal profiles, but by gametes, which are mature reproductive cells. There are only two types of gametes: small ones called sperm that are produced by males, and large ones called eggs that are produced by females. There are no intermediate types of gametes between egg and sperm cells. It is not a spectrum.[7]

The classification of human as male and female is not arbitrary. As one physician replied to *The New England Journal of Medicine's* article about eliminating "unnecessary legal sex classifications," for children, "I'm a pediatrician. The growth curves for male and female babies are notably different. Am I just to give up on tracking normal growth and development?"[8]

Therefore, the language of "assigning" sex should be rejected. Similar terms could also be questioned. For example, the term "born male" or "born female" can undermine the stability of sex. Was the person any less male before his delivery? Can a man cease to be male at a later point in time? What is so extraordinary about the moment of birth? Sex is such a stable reality that thousands of years after one's death—and for all eternity—the fact of being male and female persists. Even government agencies such as the United States Selective Service acknowledge this when they declared that for the military draft, "US citizens or immigrants who are born male and changed their gender to female are still required to register. Individuals who are born female and changed their gender to male are not required to register."[9]

Not all creatures have a sexual nature as stable as humans. Although most organisms do not change their sex, some kinds of animals do.[10] Take, for example, the goby fish. If the dominant male dies or is removed from a habitat, the largest female becomes male. If the male is reintroduced into the habitat, the female who had replaced him as a male reverts back to a female and is interested once again in mating with him.[11] A small fraction of less than one percent of animals possess this capacity, known as sequential hermaphroditism.[12] For the Bluehead Wrass fish, the metamorphosis, including the outward appearance and ability to produce sperm cells, takes only a few days![13] Similarly, some plants reproduce asexually, while others can even change their sex based upon environmental conditions.[14]

However, even in the case of these fascinating creatures, sex is understood the same way as it is for humans: *Sex is defined by how an organism is organized for reproduction.* Therefore, male and female are not like two colors among many. Rather, the two sexes are intelligible only in relation to one another. They become aware of their own uniqueness only in light of their complementarity. One discovers oneself in the other. A man's body is naturally ordered toward fatherhood, and a woman's toward motherhood. Some might counter, "Then what about people who are infertile?"

Infertility does not negate the fact that humans are a sexually dimorphic species. In fact, it supports the fact. For example, if a man is unable to become pregnant, it's not because he's infertile. It's because he's not a woman. Just as no man can gestate, no woman can fertilize an ovum. Even in the case of men and women who have intersex conditions, they cannot self-fertilize. Like all other people, they can either impregnate, become pregnant, or if their fertility is not functioning properly, they can do neither. But if a person's procreative potential is impaired by age or disease, this does not make the person any less male or female. It simply shows that the potential that they have for reproduction cannot be actualized. If fertility was a prerequisite for determining one's sex, then no one could know their own sex prior to parenthood. Thankfully, long before then, one's sex can be determined by how one's body is organized for reproduction.

5.

Intersex people prove that sex is not binary.

According to Anne Fausto-Sterling, a professor of biology and gender studies, as many as one in fifty people are born intersex.[1] These common variations in sexual development reveal that sex is anything but binary. In fact, at least five different sexes can be identified. Therefore, biological sex is a spectrum, and it is unscientific, simplistic, and outdated to think otherwise.

"Intersex" is an umbrella term sometimes used to include more than forty different kinds of disorders of sexual development (DSDs). Most people who experience one of these conditions do not identify as trans. In fact, some resent being used to promote transgender ideology and being lumped into the LGBTIA category. After all, intersex conditions are not a reflection of a person's sense of identity or sexual orientation. Those are different issues altogether, and it's a leap in logic to believe that variations in biology support the idea that a person can be something other than his or her sex. Moreover, nearly all people who identify as trans were born with a biological sex that is anything but ambiguous, and this is precisely what those with gender dysphoria express dysphoric feelings about.

Nonetheless, disorders of sexual development are often presented as an argument to undermine the binary nature of human sexuality and promote the myth that sex is a social construct.

Before scrutinizing the evidence used to support this claim, it's helpful to establish an accurate estimate of the prevalence of children born with such conditions.

Anne Fausto-Sterling and others have reported that as many as one in fifty people are intersex, making the condition as common as having red hair.[2] However, others report that the frequency is one in five thousand live births.[3] The hundredfold discrepancy between these figures (2 percent and .02 percent) can be explained by how broadly each researcher (or activist) chooses to define the term "intersex." When most people hear the term, they assume it refers to someone who is born with ambiguous genitalia, whose sexual identity is therefore uncertain.

A closer examination of the "2 percent" statistic proposed by Anne Fausto-Sterling reveals how she was able to arrive at such an astounding number: The top five most common conditions she lists are not intersex conditions![4] According to Dr. Leonard Sax, "[T]hese five conditions constitute roughly 99% of the population she defines as intersex."[5]

For example, 88 percent of the people she included are individuals who have an enzyme deficiency known as late onset congenital adrenal hyperplasia (LOCAH).[6] However, this is not an intersex condition because the genitalia of these babies are normal and in alignment with their chromosomes. In fact, most are unaware of their condition until their midtwenties.[7] Many of the women born with LOCAH can conceive and bear children, and yet activists claim that they're neither male nor female. When these individuals are removed from the popular 2 percent statistic, it plummets to less than .2 percent.

The next most common "intersex" conditions listed within the remaining .2 percent affect individuals who have chromosomal deviations from the typical XX, XY configuration, but who do not have any genital ambiguity, such as men who have Klinefelter syndrome or women who have Turner syndrome. Klinefelter syndrome is when a male inherits an extra X chromosome from his mother or father. He is XXY, or sometimes XXXY or XXXXY. Typically, such individuals are unambiguously male, despite often being infertile and having smaller testicles and sometimes enlarged breast tissue. In fact, many men with Klinefelter syndrome are unaware of having the syndrome until it is detected while seeking treatment for their infertility. Fertile men who have Klinefelter syndrome often live their whole lives unaware of their condition. Nonetheless, Fausto-Sterling wishes to define such individuals as intersex.

Women who have Turner Syndrome have only one X chromosome in most or all of their cells. They are often shorter than typical females and lack sufficient hormones to induce typical physical development at puberty. Such women are infertile because two X chromosomes are needed for a woman's ovaries to properly develop. Men with Klinefelter syndrome and women with Turner syndrome do not constitute a third or fourth sex. Although they do have a disorder of sexual development, according to *The Journal of Sex Research*, "There is therefore no clinical sense in which these individuals are intersex."[8] Therefore, such exceptions do not disprove the rule of a sexual binary. In fact, the exceptions prove the rule because they rely upon it to be deemed exceptional.

When non-intersex conditions are removed from Fausto-Sterling's claim of 2 percent of all people being intersex, the odds of being born with such a condition decreases to two out of every ten thousand live births.[9] This is the more accurate figure of intersex individuals and provides a clearer definition of them: They are men and women who are not easily classifiable as male or female, or whose chromosomal makeup is inconsistent with their genital appearance.

Fausto-Sterling's broad definition of intersex is based on her presumption that the true sexual dimorphism is a "Platonic ideal," and that people ought to relinquish the "proposition that for each sex there is a single, correct developmental pathway."[10] One is left to wonder if she's equally open to relinquishing the "Platonic ideal" for how many chambers the human heart should have or how many fingers a normal hand ought to possess. Instead, she proposes the notion that if something occurs within nature, it must be normal, which is a naturalistic fallacy.

To buttress her claim that sex is a spectrum, she compiled a list of more than twenty chromosomal, genital, gonadal, or hormonal attributes that males and females must possess to meet the platonic ideal of their sex. Any deviation from these norms results in an individual being labeled "intersex." And in her mind, the more intersex individuals there are, the more easily society will disengage from the idea of sex as binary. In her words, "The implications of my argument for a sexual continuum are profound. If nature really offers us more than two sexes, then it follows that our current notions of masculinity and femininity are cultural conceits."[11]

Disorders of sexual development (DSD)

Because activists often utilize the work of Fausto-Sterling to promote the idea that sex is a spectrum, it's helpful to become familiar with the conditions that are most often cited as evidence for such a claim. Early in embryonic development, unborn babies share structures that usually proceed down a clearly male or female pathway. For example, the same structure that develops into fallopian tubes for a female will become the sperm transport system for males. On rare occasion, the typical developmental pathway does not unfold in the usual manner and the sexual differentiation of the child may be ambiguous at birth. While it's true that there are only two sexes, it is untrue that every person's sex is unambiguous.

Individuals who have disorders of sexual development are often classified into three groups: People with XY chromosomes who develop female characteristics, those with XX chromosomes who develop male characteristics, and those with more than one set of chromosomes, who may develop certain male and female characteristics.

Consider first the XY group. Whereas many people believe that human sexuality is reducible to whether a person has XX or XY chromosomes, this is untrue. Having a Y chromosome doesn't always determine male identity. The gene typically responsible for determining the male sex is the SRY gene (sex determining region on the Y chromosome). Therefore, XY individuals who lack an SRY gene will develop into females.

Some individuals who have XY chromosomes and an SRY gene can still develop as females, though. For example, a woman who has complete androgen insensitivity syndrome (CAIS) has XY chromosomes. However, because she has a variation in the receptor for androgen, her body does not respond to testosterone in the typical manner. Thus, she may have XY chromosomes and internal testes (which are unable to produce viable sperm), but will develop the secondary sex characteristics of a woman, with external genitalia but no uterus or ovaries. This condition is rarely identified at birth because such babies appear fully female. However, because they lack a uterus and ovaries, such women do not menstruate. In fact, the absence of menstruation is often what leads to the detection of CAIS. Interestingly, her internal testes will continue to produce hormone levels typical of a man, but her body converts the hormones into estrogen so that she develops typical female secondary sex characteristics. However, because undescended testes can lead to cancer, they are often removed after puberty.

One remarkable disorder of sexual development for XY individuals occurs in children who have been called the *Guevedoces*, which literally means "testes at twelve." The genetic defect primarily impacts boys from a small group of villages in the Dominican Republic. When they are born, they have a female appearance, with undescended testes and a penis that is underdeveloped to the extent that it looks like an enlarged clitoris. As a result, they are raised as girls—but develop into boys at puberty. Because their bodies have failed to develop the enzyme 5-alpha reductase, this deficiency causes a delay in the masculinization of the body, which typically occurs in the womb. When the male body at last produces sufficient quantities of testosterone during puberty, full masculinization occurs (genital growth, descended testes, narrowed hips, increased muscle mass, facial hair, deepened voice, etc.). Nearly all such individuals identify as males in adulthood, even if registered female at birth.[12]

Consider next the XX group. Some individuals have XX chromosomes and an active SRY gene. As a result, they will develop into infertile males. But their lack of a Y chromosome does not cause them to be women.

Also included in the XX group are those who have the most common disorder of sexual development: congenital adrenal hyperplasia (CAH). This disorder of the adrenal glands causes higher levels of testosterone to circulate within the body and can have many outcomes. Boys can also have CAH, but because it does not cause them to have ambiguous genitalia, it is not considered to be an intersex condition in those cases. However, it can virilize the appearance of female genitalia. Thus, the prevalence of individuals who have intersex-related CAH is approximately one out of every thirty thousand people.[13] Due to their higher levels of testosterone, girls with CAH often prefer playing with boys and stereotypical male toys and are often considered tomboys.[14] Many also identify as lesbian.[15] But none of these characteristics cause them to be anything but female.

Ryan Anderson summarizes:

An XY without SRY will develop as a female, while an XX with SRY will develop as a male. An XY with SRY but without the ability to respond to androgen (CAIS) will develop as a female, while an XX without SRY but with too much androgen (CAH) will develop as a female with virilized external genitalia. These are just a couple of the ways in which minor genetic or hormonal abnormalities can lead to disorders of sexual development.[16]

The third group of individuals who have disorders of sexual development are those who may have more than one set of chromosomes. For example, they might have both an XX and XY or X and XY chromosomes. Sometimes two different sperm, one with an X chromosome and another with a Y, fertilize the ovum simultaneously. As a result, the individual will have XX and XY cells. This is called an XX/XY mosaic. At other times, two eggs can be fertilized by two separate sperm. If one of the twins dies, it can be absorbed into the other embryo, thus giving it two different sets of DNA. However, individuals who experience this condition (chimerism) are often unaware, and typically do not have ambiguous genitalia. They could be categorized as having DSDs, but not true intersex conditions.

The rarest of all disorders of sexual development is ovotesticular DSD, formerly known as "true hermaphroditism." Only about five hundred cases have been reported, and it can affect individuals with various chromosomal patterns, such as 46XX, combined 46XX/46XY and 46 XY. Although it is rare, it is worth noting that it still exists in a binary reality. Ovotesticular DSD is characterized by the presence of both ovarian and testicular tissues in the same person, who often has ambiguous genitalia as an infant, but can also have typical genitals.[17] However, typically only one type of gonad will be functional, and if testes are present, they are usually undescended. Sex is typically determined in these cases on "the appearance of the external genitalia, the formation of the glands, and the potential for fertility."[18]

All intersex conditions and DSDs are variations of the two sexes, not a new kind of sex. In order for more than two sexes to exist, there would need to be a third kind of gamete, which does not exist. Because nothing exists other than the sperm and egg, it's unscientific to propose the idea of sex as a spectrum. In fact, the only way to identify a DSD is in contrast to the binary reality of human sexuality. Therefore, the binary reality of sex is not disproven by the fact that sex is sometimes ambiguous. As Pope

Saint John Paul II wrote, "Every human being is by nature a sexual being, and belongs from birth to one of the two sexes. This fact is not contradicted by hermaphroditism—any more than any other sickness or deformity militates against the fact that there is such a thing as human nature."[19]

6.

Some people have the brain of one sex but the body of the other.

In a Harvard online journal, Katherine Wu reported, "Transgender people appear to be born with brains more similar to the gender with which they identify, rather than the one to which they were assigned."[1] For example, studies of trans women show that regions of their brain are more similar to biological women than to men. These studies and many others explain why scientists have postulated the idea of an intersex brain.[2] What we can learn from these findings is that one's gender is innate and that some people are born trans.

In the popular children's book *I am Jazz*, the main character, Jazz, declares, "I have a girl brain but a boy body. This is called transgender. I was born this way."[3] While it cannot be questioned that Jazz sincerely feels this way (and those thoughts are located within Jazz's mind), the idea that a female brain can reside within a male body is pseudoscience.

Some studies have proposed the idea that people who identify as trans have brains that more closely resemble the brains of the sex with which they identify, rather than their biological sex. For example, in 1995, Jiang-Ning Zhou published an article entitled, "A Sex Difference in the Human Brain and its Relation to Transsexuality."[4] In it, he compared a region of the brain known as the bed nucleus of the stria terminalis (BSTc) and found that for men who identified as trans, this area of the brain was more similar in size to females than to males.

News headlines followed, announcing, "Possible Transsexual Brain Trait Found."[5] However, those who read the headlines most likely didn't realize that the study sample included only six deceased men, all of whom had received feminizing hormones. Five of the six men had also received an orchiectomy (an operation to remove the testes). The author of the study admitted, "As all the transsexuals had been treated with estrogens, the reduced size of the BSTc could possibly have been due to the presence of high levels of estrogen in the blood."[6]

Research shows that cross-sex hormones change the structure of the brain, bending regions of the male brain to more closely resemble those of women, and vice versa. In an article entitled, "Changing Your Sex Changes Your Brain," *The European Journal of Endocrinology* explained, "anti-androgen + estrogen treatment decreased brain volumes of male-to-female subjects towards female proportions, while androgen treatment in female-to-male subjects increased total brain and hypothalamus volumes towards male proportions."[7] Dr. Mark Yarhouse pointed out yet another problem with Zhou's conclusions, noting, "Also, when we consider research on identity, it is hard to imagine it being located in the hypothalamus. Self-concept is not rooted there but rather in the cortex."[8]

Five years after Zhou's initial study, he published a second, entitled, "Male to Female Transsexuals Have Female Neuron Numbers in a Limbic Nucleus," that measured the number of a specific type of neuron in the BSTc.[9] It showed similar results in the BSTc region of the brain: that the neuron count of men who identified as transsexual was within the range of the thirteen women in the study. However, this study was subject to many of the same limitations as the first.

Then, in 2011, researchers published new findings that studied individuals who identified as trans, but who had not yet taken cross-sex hormones.[10] In it, they found that the white matter microstructure of women who identified as trans was more similar to males than females. Three years later, other neurologists discovered that the white matter microstructure of some who identify as trans was somewhere in between that of men and woman.[11] Still other studies have shown that the brains of people who identify as trans are aligned with their biological sex rather than their gender identity.[12]

Drs. Lawrence Mayer and Paul McHugh summed up the current state of research on the subject, writing, "[T]he current studies on associations between brain structure and transgender identity are small, methodologically limited, inconclusive, and sometimes contradictory."[13] They added that the studies to date "demonstrated weak correlations between brain structure and cross-gender identification. These correlations do not provide any evidence for a neurobiological basis for cross-gender identification."[14] Numerous limitations within the current body research led the American College of Pediatricians to conclude:

A properly designed brain difference study needs to be prospective and longitudinal; it would require a large randomly selected population-based sample of a fixed set of individuals, would follow them with serial brain imaging from infancy through adulthood, and would have to be replicated. Not one brain study to date meets a single one of these requirements to be considered rigorous research design.[15]

However, even if such a study existed, at least five other challenges would remain. The first is the question of neuroplasticity. Dr. Paul McHugh remarked, "Even if evidence existed that brain studies showed differences, which they do not, it would not tell us whether the brain differences are the cause of transgender identity or a result of identifying and acting upon their own stereotypes about the opposite sex, through what is known as neuroplasticity."[16] This term refers to the fact that repeated behaviors alter the structure of the brain.[17] Put simply, it's possible for one's actions to cause brain differences rather than for brain differences to determine one's actions.[18]

A second limitation of the "trans brain" theory is that differences in brain functioning and structure can also be a sign of related conditions such as autism, rather than gender dysphoria. Such conditions, in turn, are correlated with a person's likelihood of embracing a trans identity.[19]

A third limitation is the question of individuals who have brains that do not fully masculinize or feminize, but do not identify as trans. For example, males who have a polymorphic AR gene have regions of their brains that are not responsive to testosterone, while females who have a polymorphic ERβ gene are not receptive to estrogen. As a result, the brain structures do not masculinize or feminize normally.[20] Certain regions of their brains might resemble features of the other sex, but it does not follow from this that such individuals will identify as trans.

A fourth limitation would be individuals who identify as trans, but who have brain structures in alignment with their biological sex.[21] For example, critics of the "trans brain" theory point out that the region of the brain in question does not become sexually dimorphic until adulthood and therefore it cannot explain gender dysphoria in youth.[22]

Even if all these difficulties could be overcome, one final challenge would remain: If scientists could isolate a region of the brain that determined one's internal sense of gender without any ambiguity, it would still would not change a person's sex. It would simply reveal how they experience being that sex.

In the absence of conclusive evidence in favor of the "trans brain" theory, some have proposed that transgender inclinations might be genetically determined. However, if this were the case, identical twins—who share 100 percent of their DNA—should have the same perceived gender identity. However, the largest study on transgenderism and twins shows that this is only true 28 percent of the time. By comparison, when one identical twin struggles with anorexia, 44 percent of the time, the other will as well.[23] Therefore, current evidence for a genetic cause of transgender identification is weak.

Although current research does not demonstrate that one's internal sense of gender is predetermined and biologically innate, it's reasonable to acknowledge that there are biological factors that could contribute to gender dysphoria.

For example, girls who were exposed to higher amounts of testosterone in the womb tend to exhibit more masculinized, or "tomboyish" behavior. Similar results have been observed in animal studies, where rats injected with testosterone not only become more aggressive but improve their navigational abilities when challenged to solve a maze. If such a girl is raised in a culture that promotes the message that gender nonconforming behavior could be an indication that she's really "trans," she may be more likely to embrace such an identity.

But if researchers can look to the brain to provide scientific evidence of one's true "gender identity," why can't they look elsewhere on the body? Why strain to find evidence under a microscope that is visible to the naked eye? This reveals the most fundamental contradiction with such an approach: If one's gender exists independently from the body, why look to the body to reveal evidence of one's identity?

Is Your Brain Male or Female?

Whereas the evidence in favor of a transgender brain has proven to be underwhelming, *The Journal of Neuroscience Research* published a 791-page issue explaining the differences between men's and women's brains and "documenting sex differences at *all* levels of brain function."[24] One of the authors, a professor of neuroscience from the University of California Irvine remarked, "So overpowering is the wave of research that the standard ways of dismissing sex influences (e.g., 'They are all small and unreliable,' 'They are all due to circulating hormones,' 'They are all due to human culture,' and 'They don't exist on the molecular level') have all been swept away, at least for those cognizant of the research."[25]

Unfortunately, proponents of gender theory often don't seem cognizant of the research. Take, for example, Dr. Kristie Overstreet, who explained transgender identification by saying, "Gender identity is sense of self, so think of it as what's between your ears: sense of self, who you are. This is very different than biological sex, right? Hormones, genitalia, chromosomes: That's what's between our legs."[26]

Her level of imprecision is both astounding and irresponsible. As a clinical sexologist, she should be aware of the fact that one's chromosomes and hormones aren't isolated to the genital area. Furthermore, what's between one's ears reveals one's biological sex. If a gender theorist wanted to retreat to any place in the human body to escape from the reality of the binary nature of human sexuality, the brain would be the last place to hide.

In her book, *Sex and the Developing Brain*, Dr. Margaret M. McCarthy explains, "[E]very cell in a male brain is to some degree fundamentally different than every cell in a female brain."[27] Dr. Larry Cahill added, "[S]ex influences on brain function are ubiquitous, found at every level of neuroscience."[28] Not only are brain cells and functions unique for men and women, entire regions of the brain grow in different proportions. For example, the medial preoptic area, which is associated with sexual pursuit, is 2.5 times larger in men. The dorsal premammillary nucleus, which is in charge of signaling the need for territorial defense, is also larger in males. However, the mirror-neuron system, which is in charge of reading others' emotions, is larger in women. The same is true of the prefrontal cortex, which is in charge of inhibiting impulses.[29]

Some have argued that the very idea of a male or female brain is outdated science caused by "neurosexism."[30] However, as Dr. Maria Ferretti pointed out, "Although the field is indeed rife with misinterpretation and methodological flaws, that is no justification for dismissing sex differences in neuroscience."[31]

To be fair, critics are correct that it is an oversimplification to speak of a "male brain" versus a "female brain." A close examination reveals extensive overlap in the structures and functions of the brains of men and women. Like their bodies, the brains of males and females have much in common, and much that is distinct.[32] Therefore, rather than speaking of a male or female brain, it is more precise to speak of the brain of a male or female. It is the person who is sexually dimorphic, not one's brain itself.

However, there are also profound sexual differences in the brain.[33] Whereas males have a greater number of white matter connections running from the front to the rear of their brain, women have more connections between the two hemispheres.[34] High levels of fetal testosterone results in a smaller corpus collosum in brains of men, which serves to transmit information from one side of the brain to the other.[35]

When performing identical activities, different regions of the brain are activated, based upon one's sex. For example, a specific region of the left brain is activated during speech for males, whereas women experience activation in different regions on both sides of the brain.[36] This explains why men take longer to recover speech following a stroke.[37] It also explains why a man might become mute after being injured on the left side of his head, whereas a woman struck in the same location is likely to keep on talking![38]

7.

The idea of a rigid gender binary is the result of Western colonialism.

Before Europeans imposed their values on Indigenous people, cultures around the world celebrated third gender individuals and even revered diverse gender identities and expressions. The Native American two-spirit people, the Indian hijra and sādhin, the fa'afafine of Samoa, and the kathoey of Indonesia are just a few examples that dispel the myth that only two genders exist.

There's no question that cultures around the world and throughout history display a broad range of gender expressions and social roles for men and women. Such societies also use a wide range of titles to describe individuals who don't fit into stereotypically masculine or feminine categories. However, these historical facts do not prove that a "third gender" exists. Such an argument falls short on three accounts: It is guilty of primordialism, it is historically inaccurate and oversimplified, and it is anachronistic.

Guilty of primordialism

When university professors of gender theory attempt to promote the idea of "third gender" individuals living in an idyllic past, they want students to believe that before white Europeans descended upon civilizations untouched by Western dogmas, Indigenous people across the globe were blissfully unaware of the modern colonialist idea that men aren't women. Instead, they enjoyed liberation and were free to be their authentic selves.

In their article "Romancing the Transgender Native," Evan Towle and Lynn Morgan—who identify as transgender themselves—present a blistering critique of this narrative. They argue that it "falsely places other cultures in an idealized 'primordial location,' a Garden of Eden where gender diversity flourished before the Fall into Western modernity . . . in an age before oppressive gender ideologies were invented."[1] They continue, "[Such] accounts of historical and non-Western gender variability are used to suggest that our contemporary (trans)gender variability is both ancient and natural . . . 'Third gender' societies are accorded a primordial, foundational location in our thinking, as though they underlay or predated Western gender formulations."[2]

According to this narrative, the transgender native becomes an icon of Indigenous innocence repressed by patriarchal structures. But, in the words of Towle and Morgan, the transgender native is actually "a literary trope often used in transgender testimonial writing. . . . It serves in several texts as a generic, seductive figure who lives an idealized existence in a utopian place and time."[3] In the words of one trans-activist, "In some cultures, including Native American cultures, transgendered people were not only accepted but revered."[4]

A sober look at the historical evidence reveals that while individuals who lived outside of the typical framework of masculinity and femininity were sometimes revered, they often faced overwhelming ridicule, harassment, and violent persecution within their own cultures, long before being influenced by European social norms.[5] Minimizing their struggles might help promote the myth of an ideal past, but it's not historically accurate.

Historically inaccurate and oversimplified

Most people have never heard of the hijra, sādhin, or fa'afafine. As a result, when such names are used in gender theory classes to promote the idea of a "third gender," most students have no option but to listen and "learn." A closer examination of these titles reveals that they don't fit neatly into the Western concept of gender. One reason for this, according to Towle and Morgan, is that "The 'third gender' concept lumps all nonnormative gender variations into one category, limiting our understandings of the range and diversity of gender ideologies and practices."[6]

Perhaps the most glaring example of this is the fact that segregating sexuality from gender is a distinctively Western concept. This can be seen in popular catchphrases such as, "Sexuality is who you go to bed *with*, but gender is who you go to bed *as*." In many cultures, the two are intertwined: Your masculinity or femininity are revealed by how you express your sexuality.

Take, for example, the *hijras* (also known as *kinner*). Within parts of Indian culture, these are sexually impotent males who have their genitals removed in a ritual, while facing an image of a goddess, to achieve ritual powers. They often wear women's clothing, assume their mannerisms, take on feminine names, have male sexual partners, and are often used as prostitutes. However, according to anthropologist Adnan Hossain's research of *hijras* in Bangladesh, their identity is rooted more in their sexuality than in their religious roles.[7] They are not understood to be women. Rather, they are castrated males considered within Hinduism to have received a calling from their goddess. If they refuse to assume this role, their punishment is that they will be reborn impotent seven times.[8]

Another gender variant within Indian culture is the *sādhin*. These are young women who refuse to marry and sometimes take on certain traditionally male roles. Within traditional Hindu culture, the only accepted roles for a female are those of wife and mother. Since the *sādhin* do not embrace these roles, they form their own social niche. However, they are not considered to have changed their sexual identity.

Rather than labeling such a person a "third gender," a more accurate understanding could be gained by understanding the social pressures that might influence a young Hindu woman to choose celibacy. The Hindu moral legal text *Manu Smriti*—which has been quoted in supreme court judgments in India—contains regulations regarding a woman's role within marriage.[9] It states, "Though destitute of virtue, or seeking pleasure (elsewhere), or devoid of good qualities, (yet) a husband must be constantly worshipped as a god by a faithful wife."[10] If a woman opts out of marriage because she finds this lifelong misogynistic arrangement to be less than ideal, she does not cease to be a woman. To use her experience to prove gender theory is reductive and unconvincing.

Samoan culture provides another example where a foreign concept of gender doesn't fit the into Western framework. The word *fa'afafine* means "like a woman" or "in the manner of a woman." These are effeminate males who often take on the social roles of women and dress accordingly. However, they don't typically experience distress over their bodies or seek surgical changes. Paul Vasey, a Canadian psychology professor, explains:

If a fa'afafine went to New Zealand or Australia and had a sex-change operation and returned to Samoa, no one in Samoa would say that individual is now a woman. . . . But traditional, non-Western frameworks for understanding masculine women or feminine men as "third genders" are often warped when viewed through a Western lens, which reinterprets them as transwomen or transmen. It's a type of colonialism.[11]

Take, for example, Lauran Hubbard, a forty-two-year-old from New Zealand who competed in men's weight lifting when younger with moderate success. In 2019, he won the gold medal at the Pacific Games competing in the women's division. The Samoan prime minister—who is the patron of the Samoan Fa'afafine

Association—remarked, "This fa'afafine, or male, should never have been allowed by the Pacific Games Council President to lift with the women. . . . It's not easy for the female athletes to train all year long to compete, and yet we allow these stupid things to happen. The reality is that gold medal belongs to Samoa."[12] As someone who is obviously not prejudiced against gender nonconforming individuals, he did not mince words for those who inject Western ideas of gender into traditional Samoan culture.

Another popular example of a "third gender" is the Native American *two spirit*. These men were originally labeled by the Europeans *berdache*, which is a pejorative term to describe a male prostitute. Because of its negative connotation, a new name needed to be created. According to anthropologist Serena Nanda, "Two spirit" is not an ancient Native American gender. Rather, it's a title "coined in 1990 by urban Native American gays and lesbians."[13]

Regardless of when the title was created and by whom, Native American gender variants were not considered to be individuals who changed their sex. Rather, they were individuals who often expressed an interest with the occupational activities of the other sex.[14] For example, the Navajo *nádleeh* were effeminate males who often dressed and took on gender roles of women. The Mojave *alyha* were males who donned female attire, imitated feminine roles, and often took on a homosexual role within the culture, while the Mojave *hwame* were females who associated with more masculine norms. Nanda explains, "Among the Kaska, a family who had only daughters might select one to 'be like a man,' as her hunting role could help provide the family with food."[15] However, they were not considered to *be* the other sex. Such ideas, according to Nanda, "were not culturally acknowledged and to some extent, were ridiculed."[16] Scholars concur that these layers of diversity within Native American cultures reveal how the idea of "third gender" oversimplifies a complex subject.[17]

Moving from North to South America, one discovers a similar pattern in Brazilian culture. In this society, gender diversity is also understood to be rooted in one's sexual roles and behaviors. For example, the *bicha*, *viado*, and *transvestí* are effeminate males whose male sexual partners are interestingly *not* considered homosexual because their role within the relationship is that of the masculine counterpart. Some who identify in this way make hormonal or minor surgical alterations to their bodies, but they believe it is impossible for a man to become a woman.[18] Serena Nanda notes that "they believe that sex-change operations do not produce women, but only castrated homosexuals . . . transvestís modify their bodies not because they feel themselves to be women, but because they feel themselves to be 'like women' in their behavior, appearance, and particularly in their relationships with men."[19]

A similar pattern is seen in Indonesia among the *waria* and *calabai*, who are also homosexual males who cross-dress and are often involved in prostitution. However, they do not identify as "gay," because they seek only heterosexual male partners who relate to them in a feminine manner. Surgical change is typically not sought by *waria*, since changing one's sex is not seen as a possibility. Similarly in Thailand, the term *kathoey* was originally reserved for individuals who had disorders of sexual development, but it now primarily refers to homosexual males who appropriate feminine attributes and are often involved in prostitution.

In other cultures, gender is intermingled with religious practices. In Indonesia, the *bissu* are androgenous shamans, most often homosexual males who enter into possession trances in order to commune with spirits. Gender-variant individuals also play an important role within Afro-Brazilian religions such as *Candomble*, where individuals enter a possession trance whereby a spirit enters one's body. The priests of this religion are either females or effeminate males who must take the passive role in relation to the gods in order for the spirit to enter them.[20]

Many more examples of gender-variant roles could be offered, such as the *mashoga* of Kenya, the Maori *whakawāhine*, and the

Hawaiian *māhū*. However, a close examination of each shows what many of the above cultures reveal: If a person does not fit into binary gender roles within a society, it does not mean that he or she was born into the wrong body or needs to surgically modify it. In fact, when people surgically modify their bodies to "become" the other sex, they perpetuate a binary understanding of sex. In the words of one anthropologist, "Transsexuals, then, far from being an example of gender diversity, both reflected and reinforced the dominant Euro-American sex/gender ideology in which one had to choose to be either a man or a (stereotypical) woman."[21]

Although cultures will vary in terms of how they express the concepts of masculinity and femininity, Fr. Malichi Napier offers an important reminder when we're considering a universal definition of gender. He explains:

> [G]ender refers to the cultural expressions of normative behaviors and characteristics of men and women, which reflect the natural differences that exist between them. The nuance needed is to have in mind the fact that every culture is marked by the disorder of sin, and so gender is neither an absolute manifestation of the essence of man and woman, nor is it some free-floating artifice without relationship to our ontological reality.[22]

Anachronistic

Anachronism is the act of attributing something to a period of time to which it does not belong. It's when historians stare down the well of history and see their own reflection at the bottom. For example, one of the immediate challenges that arises when claiming that other cultures have a "third gender" is the fact that this term is a Western concept that wasn't introduced until 1975.[23] While it's true that many cultures have individuals who do not conform to rigid gender stereotypes, Towle and Morgan point out the problem in imposing Western concepts onto these cultures to understand them:

[M]embers of North American transgender communities . . . treat "third gender" natives of other cultures as part of their own imagined communities. . . . Invoking "third gender" examples in an oversimplified way or citing them out of context to underwrite Western social agendas is an unwitting kind of neocolonial (or at least ethnocentric) appropriation that distorts the complexity and reality of other peoples' lives. We join an increasing number of anthropologists who caution against using caricatures of other cultures to advance locally situated arguments. . . . [B]eware of re-creating the worlds of other cultures "to suit our own intentions." . . . The danger inherent in this strategy is that the other becomes merely a rhetorical device for forwarding the identity of the self.[24]

While gender theory professors accuse Europeans of eradicating gender diversity through colonizing Indigenous people, developing nations today argue that the opposite is true. Western nations are now exporting the concept of gender theory into developing nations by tying foreign aid to the adoption of their ideologies. Pope Francis explains:

[A] minister of education asked for a large loan to build schools for the poor. They gave it to her on the condition that in the schools there would be a book for the children of a certain grade level . . . in which gender theory was taught. This woman needed the money but that was the condition. . . . This is ideological colonization. . . . Every people has its own culture. But when conditions are imposed by colonizing empires, they seek to make these peoples lose their own identity and create uniformity.[25]

8.

More people are coming out as trans only because society has become more accepting.

Many people assume that those who experience gender dysphoria, possess intersex conditions, or are gender nonconforming didn't exist before the internet. While there has been surge of interest in these topics in recent decades, history provides ample evidence that such individuals have been part of humanity for thousands of years. It's only because of greater visibility and tolerance that they're now finally free to be themselves.

Varied expressions and understandings of sexual identity are indeed as old as humanity itself. More than two thousand years ago, the Roman emperor Elagabalus claimed he was a woman and preferred to be called a lady rather than a lord. Blurring gender distinctions was also a common practice woven into many ancient religious rites. In ancient Mesopotamia, gender-bending priests offered worship to various goddesses, including Ishtar. One of the poems written about her, dating back to the 23rd century B.C. states, "To destroy, to create, to tear out, to establish are yours . . . To turn a man into a woman and a woman into a man are yours."[1]

Similarly, Roman priests known as the Galli castrated themselves and dressed as women and serve the goddess Cybele, an intersex deity, said to have been born with male and female features. In his classic work written in the fifth century, *The City of God*, Saint Augustine said of them, "As recently as yesterday, they plied the streets of Carthage, with their oiled hair, their powdered faces, their languid limbs, and their feminine gait."[2] Saint Augustine also mentioned individuals who had intersex conditions. He wrote, "As for the Androgyni, or Hermaphrodites, as they are called, though they are rare, yet from time to time there appears persons of sex so doubtful, that it remains uncertain from which sex they take their name."[3]

Therefore, cultures throughout history offer clear evidence that expressions of sexual identity have been understood and lived out in a variety of ways. However, what accounts for the unprecedented rise in the number of young people who identify as trans? The answer is complex, and cannot be reduced to increased visibility and tolerance, though this does play a role.

Imagine the flood of a river, swollen beyond its banks. If you were to trace the origin of each drop, you might find that a certain portion originated in heavy rainfall. Perhaps a dam had broken, or recent weather changes rapidly melted snowcaps. Springs may have opened from underground sources. As a result of each of these factors, smaller streams and rivers became engorged and the flow of their tributaries poured into the larger waterway that is now uprooting villages in the current downstream.

A similar cascade of historical factors has contributed to the current deluge of interest in the topic of gender theory. To understand the various forces at work, a thorough examination of the intellectual foundation and architects of gender theory is essential. By examining the evolution of gender theory over the past century, it becomes clear that the exponential rise in individuals identifying as trans cannot be attributed to social acceptance alone.

Marxism

Karl Marx and Friedrich Engels were socialist philosophers and political theorists who believed that class struggle defines history.

Together, they authored *The Communist Manifesto*, which is a brief political document that called for communist revolution and a "forcible overthrow of all existing social conditions," and predicted that socialism would replace capitalism.

Economic philosophies might seem unrelated to the modern concept of gender theory, but the bridge to understanding the connection is the Marxist framework itself. Marx believed that the upper class (the Bourgeoisie) possessed the unfair advantage of wealth that the working class (Proletariat) did not. Therefore, the problem of class struggle could only be resolved by erasing class distinctions. Through this, a dictatorship of the proletariat could be created.

Gender theory is built upon the same framework: Those who are cisgender possess an unfair culture of acceptance that transgender individuals lack. By eliminating the concept of a sexual "binary," a dictatorship of gender theory can arise: Then, the freedom to manifest sexual identity apart from the "oppressive" force of the binary can be realized. One definition of binary is "a division into two groups or classes that are considered diametrically opposite." Viewing masculinity and femininity as diametrical opposites rather than complementary creations is a distinctly Marxist concept.

Much of Marx's thought was influenced by the dialectic idea of the German philosopher Georg Wilhelm Friedrich Hegel, who proposed that history progresses toward utopia, via revolution. However, if the most basic class of society is marriage and family, and history is essentially the story of class struggle, then to create justice, a revolution is needed to overthrow the family structure itself. Then, utopia will follow. Thus, the manifesto declares: "Abolition of the family!"[4]

In his work, *The Origin of the Family, Private Property and the State*, Engel spoke of what he considered the antagonism between men and women in monogamous marriage. He noted, "the first class oppression coincides with that of the female sex by the male."[5] Through marriage, "the woman was degraded and reduced to servitude; she became the slave of his lust and a mere instrument for the production of children."[6] In Engel's worldview, the family is the foundation of the "domestic slavery of the wife."[7]

Engel proposed that the solution to this injustice is to insert women into the workforce, and "this in turn demands the abolition of the monogamous family as the economic unit of society."[8] While it may seem that Engel is gallantly hoping to protect women from lust, he explains that these societal changes will hopefully "bring about the gradual growth of unconstrained sexual intercourse."[9]

Nonetheless, many radical feminists saw in this system an opportunity for liberation. If the relationship between men and women is dialectical, then equality can only be established by erasing sexual difference. As one trans advocate later argued, "Women couldn't be oppressed if there was no such thing as 'women.' Doing away with gender is the key to doing away with patriarchy."[10]

Simone de Beauvoir

Born into a Catholic family in Paris, Simone de Beauvoir desired at one point in her childhood to become a nun. However, she lost her faith as a teenager after her cousin "took her slumming and gave her a taste for alcohol and for louche nightlife that she never outgrew."[11] Her philandering father told her that she'd never marry, and his premonition was correct. Instead of marrying, she settled for a man who—like her own father—considered fidelity to be restrictive.

During college, Beauvoir met Jean-Paul Sartre, who would become one of the century's most well-known atheist philosophers. The two began a lifelong open sexual relationship that included some of his female companions, and Beauvoir became a staunch atheist herself. The couple indulged in an endless string of affairs, some with Beauvoir's teenage students, with whom they engaged in a quasi-incestuous relationship.[12]

In 1949, Simone de Beauvoir published her landmark work *The Second Sex*, which ushered in a new era of feminism, laced with Sartre's thought. According to Sartre, "[T]here is no human nature since there is no God to conceive of it. Man is not only that which he conceives himself to be, but that which he wills himself to be."[13] Beauvoir echoes his sentiments: "In truth, nature is no more an immutable given than is historical reality."[14] She argued that "nothing is natural," because from her viewpoint, liberation for women could only be achieved by escaping biological determinism—especially the procreative potential. By dismantling pre-existing categories and creating new meanings, women could at last be free from the notion that biology is destiny.

Such an objective was essential for Beauvoir because of the disdain she felt toward motherhood. During an interview later in life, she said, "I hadn't wanted to get married or have children, so I didn't have to lead a domestic life, which is the most suffocating part of the female condition. So, I escaped the servitude of the female condition."[15] She considered fertility to be a curse, encouraged women to rise above the "animal" act of giving life, and insisted that "the family must be abolished."[16] In her words, "The revolution is impotent as long as the notion of family and family relations subsists."[17] No sentence in *The Second Sex* is more often quoted—and misinterpreted—than her declaration, "One is not born, but rather becomes, a woman."[18] Feminist author Céline Leboeuf remarked, "[T]o intone this sentence at the beginning of a work of feminist theory is tantamount to genuflecting at the family pew."[19] Some gender theorists misrepresent Beauvoir to support the idea that one's sex is not biologically determined. But this is an anachronistic reading of Beauvoir. She is clear that "Males and females are two types of individuals who are differentiated within one species for the purposes of reproduction."[20] Her intention behind the famous statement about one not being born a woman is that women needed to be liberated from the idea that one's gender roles in society are determined by one's sex. This is the biological determinism that she sought to deconstruct.

Judith Butler explains:

Beauvoir, of course, meant merely to suggest that the category of women is a variable cultural accomplishment, a set of meanings that are taken on or taken up within a cultural field, and that no one is born with a gender—gender is always acquired. On the other hand, Beauvoir was willing to affirm that one is born with a sex. . . . Beauvoir's theory implied seemingly radical consequences, ones that she herself did not entertain. For instance, if sex and gender are radically distinct, then it does not follow that to be a given sex is to become a given gender; in other words, "woman" need not be the cultural construction of the female body, and "man" need not interpret male bodies. . . . If gender is not tied to sex . . . then gender is a kind of action that can potentially proliferate beyond the binary limits imposed by the apparent binary of sex.[21]

Although these consequences were not intended—or perhaps even conceived—by Beauvoir, her successors in feminist thought and gender theory built upon her destabilized foundation. Some, such as Michel Foucault, reaffirmed the idea that sexuality is not essential or natural, but is mobile, fluid, and ever changing. He declared, "[N]othing in man—not even his body—is sufficiently stable to serve as the basis for self recognition or for understanding other men."[22] Because the human body lacks the power to reveal one's identity, one's feelings or desires become the defining factor.

Judith Butler

Although Simone de Beauvoir did not use the term "gender" in *The Second Sex* because she predated its use within the field of feminist studies, this word is central to the thought of Judith Butler. Her book, *Gender Trouble*, is praised as "the most authoritative attack to date on the 'naturalness' of gender."[23]

For Butler, gender is something that is "performative." By this, she doesn't mean that individuals are acting. Rather, she clarifies, "to say gender is performative is to say that nobody really is a gender from the start."[24] Gender identity is an "illusion" because one's identity is an effect that is produced by one's acts.[25] Therefore, "There is no gender identity behind the expressions of gender."[26] Interestingly, she added, "I don't believe one is radically free to choose one's gender. I don't think that we exercise personal liberty in ways that defy all cultural norms. That's actually not my position, although it is sometimes attributed to me."[27]

In *Gender Trouble*, she explains:

[W]hat we take to be an internal essence of gender is manufactured through a sustained set of acts. . . . Because there is neither an "essence" that gender expresses or externalizes nor an objective ideal to which gender aspires, and because gender is not a fact, the various acts of gender create the idea of gender, and without those acts, there would be no gender at all.[28]

By untethering gender from biology and deriving its meaning from one's actions, Butler opens a pathway for gender to be destabilized and reconstructed. She noted, "The distinction between sex and gender has been crucial to the long-standing feminist effort to debunk the claim that anatomy is destiny. . . . With the distinction intact, it is no longer possible to attribute the values or social functions of women to biological necessity."[29]

Not only does Butler argue that gender is not a fact, she considers the binary nature of sex to be fundamentally unnatural.[30] The very idea of "natural," in her view, is just a hegemonic idea constructed by prevailing systems of power to oppress. Detached from the apparent binary of sex, she declared, "That the gendered body is performative suggests that is has no ontological status apart from the various acts which constitute its reality."[31]

Her proposition—that the body has no objective meaning or truth—establishes the foundation of modern gender theory. She explains:

> When the constructed status of gender is theorized as radically independent of sex, gender itself becomes a free-floating artifice, with the consequence that man and masculine might just as easily signify a female body as a male one, and woman and feminine a male body as easily as a female one. . . . If the immutable character of sex is contested, perhaps this construct called "sex" is as culturally constructed as gender; indeed, perhaps it was always already gender, with the consequence that the distinction between sex and gender turns out to be no distinction at all.[32]

She adds, "Genders can be neither true nor false, neither real nor apparent, neither original nor derived. As credible bearers of those attributes, however, genders can also be rendered thoroughly and radically *incredible*."[33]

Shulamith Firestone

If Simone de Beauvoir sought to divorce gender roles from sex and Judith Butler aimed to divorce gender from sex, Shulamith Firestone took their premises to their "radically incredible" conclusion.

Raised in a strictly observant Orthodox Jewish home, Shulamith recalled asking her father why she had to make her brother's bed. His reply? "Because you're a girl." As Susan Faludi reported, "In the Firestone home, a girl who did not follow the rules was destined to be cast out." This did not bode well for Shulamith, who had a fiery temperament and mind of her own. Her younger sister recalled, "My father threw his rage at Shulie." At the age of sixteen, her father shouted at her during a physical altercation, "I'll kill you!," while Shulamith yelled back, "I'll kill you first!" Firestone was beaten in high school by her brother for breaking a Jewish law, and her sister was banished from the house at seventeen for violating the Sabbath by reading a book in bed with a flashlight. Shulamith left the home soon after and found herself in a physically abusive relationship with a boyfriend. Her friend recalled his repeated beatings: "[O]ne time, he hit her so hard that he knocked a tooth out of place. I think she was afraid he was going to kill her."[34]

These tragic details of the young woman's life are essential for understanding the crucible of suffering from which Shulamith Firestone created her revolutionary book *The Dialectic of Sex*. Dedicated to Simone de Beauvoir and written in 1970, when she was only twenty-five years old, it was hailed as a landmark of feminist thought.

The Dialectic of Sex is based upon Marx and Engels's principle in *The Communist Manifesto* that all of history is the history of class struggles: "struggles between exploited and exploiting, between dominated and dominating classes."[35] Her book argues that the core of women's oppression is the traditional family structure: If the source of oppression is the unjust organization of classes of society, and the family is the most fundamental unit of culture, it must be abolished. She explains, "Marx was on to something more profound than he knew when he observed that the family contained within itself in embryo all the antagonisms that later develop on a wide scale within the society and state. For unless revolution uproots the basic social organization, the biological family, . . . the tapeworm of exploitation will never be annihilated."[36]

In perhaps the most well-known summary of her own manifesto, she elucidates her Marxist plan for the extermination of the family through the elimination of sexual differences:

So that just as to assure elimination of economic classes requires the revolt of the underclass (the proletariat) and, in a temporary dictatorship, their seizure of the means of *production*, so to assure the elimination of sexual classes requires the revolt of the underclass (women) and the seizure of control of *reproduction*: not only the full restoration to women of ownership of their own bodies, but also their (temporary) seizure of control of human fertility. . . . And just as the end goal of socialist revolution was not only the elimination of the economic class *privilege* but of the economic class *distinction* itself, so the end goal of feminist revolution must be, unlike that of the first feminist movement, not just the elimination of male privilege but of the sex *distinction* itself: genital differences between human beings would no longer matter culturally. (A reversion to an unobstructed *pansexuality*—Freud's "polymorphous perversity"—would probably supersede hetero/homo/bi-sexuality.) . . . The tyranny of the biological family would be broken.[37]

According to Firestone, if women are to be liberated, it will require "freedom from sexual classification altogether rather than merely an equalization of sex roles."[38] For liberation to become possible, feminists must question not simply the organization of culture, but further, "even the very organization of nature."[39] In her words:

Humanity has begun to outgrow nature; we can no longer justify the maintenance of a discriminatory sex class system on the grounds of its origins in Nature. Indeed, for pragmatic reasons alone it is beginning to look as if we must get rid of it. . . . The whole sphere of the conditions of life which environ man and have hitherto ruled him now comes under the dominion and control of man who for the first time becomes the real conscious Lord of Nature, master of his own social organization.[40]

Firestone, understandably, deplored the idea of family. She described childhood as "hell"[41] and "a supervised nightmare," and, in her case, it absolutely was.[42] In terms of motherhood, she writes,

Male, Female, Other?

"Let me then say it bluntly: *Pregnancy is barbaric.* . . . Pregnancy is the temporary deformation of the body of the individual for the sake of the species."[43] Therefore, "it has become necessary to free humanity from the tyranny of its biology."[44] For her, one solution to this was contraception, which liberates women "from the tyranny of their sexual-reproductive roles."[45]

But since women are likely to become pregnant nonetheless, she proposed that child-rearing roles be diffused to society as a whole, including "twenty-four-hour child-care centers."[46] Mothers, in her opinion, should not be overly attached to their children. She writes, "A mother who undergoes a nine-month pregnancy is likely to feel that the product of all that pain and discomfort 'belongs' to her. ("To think of what I went through to have you!"). But we want to destroy this possessiveness."[47] Firestone then envisions a future of artificial reproduction through "cybernetics," whereby the very act of childbearing can be taken over by technology, and even men could bear children.

She adds that "in our new society, humanity could finally revert to its natural polymorphous sexuality—all forms of sexuality would be allowed and indulged."[48] By "all forms," she includes incest. She explains that if a young boy "should choose to relate sexually to adults, even if he should happen to pick his own genetic mother, there would be no a priori reasons for her to reject his sexual advances, because the incest taboo would have lost its function."[49]

She continues:

Age-ist and homosexual sex taboos would disappear, as well as non-sexual friendship (Freud's aim-inhibited love). All close relationships would include the physical, our concept of exclusive physical partnerships (monogamy) disappearing from our psychic structure. . . . *With the disappearance of motherhood, and the obstructing incest taboo, sexuality would be re-integrated, allowing love to flow unimpeded.*[50]

91

One might presume that Firestone's extreme views are not representative of other feminist thinkers, but Judith Butler likewise taught that incest isn't necessarily traumatic. Rather, She stated that social stigmas make it so.[51] Similarly, Michel Foucault sought to decriminalize sex with minors, while Simone de Beauvoir concurred that thirteen-year-old girls ought to be able to have sexual relations with men.[52] But as Dr. Abigail Favale remarked, "If your philosophy leads you there, there is something rotten at the root."[53]

Despite—and to some extent, because of—the radical nature of some of her ideas, Shulamith Firestone was catapulted into the national spotlight and earned a place among the most prominent thinkers of feminist theory. However, her meteoric rise was followed by an equally precipitous descent. Kate Millett once wrote about a sizable list of her fellow feminist authors who had "disappeared to struggle alone in makeshift oblivion or vanished into asylums and have yet to return to tell the tale," or who fell into "despairs that could only end in death."[54] The same sad fate met Shulamith Firestone, who never lived to see her utopian Marxist dream arise from the ash heap of the traditional family.

Instead, she became delusional, disowned her parents, and battled paranoid schizophrenia for decades. After her brother committed suicide, she admitted that this "contributed to my own growing madness."[55] Living alone in a small apartment in New York, her neighbors complained that Firestone "was screaming in the night and that she had left the taps running until the floorboards gave way."[56] One of her few remaining friends flew to New York and "found Shulamith emaciated and panhandling, carrying a bag holding a hammer and an unopened can of food."[57] Fearing that her food was poisoned by conspirators, she gradually starved and was found dead on the floor of her apartment, alone.

Firestone's difficult upbringing and unfortunate passing ought to lead those who admire her work to examine more carefully her theories. One cannot fail to wonder what was missing from her worldview, based upon where it came from and where it led her.

Julia Serano

While Beauvoir, Butler, and Firestone envisioned a world in which one "becomes . . . a woman," where "gender is not a fact," and where "genital differences between human beings would no longer matter," Julia Serano embodies these hopes. Julia's book *Whipping Girl*—which has been lauded as "a 21st century feminist" classic—has one quality that cannot be said of the three previous feminist works: It was written by a man. However, Julia clarifies, "I do not identify as a 'male-to-female'—I identify as a woman."[58]

Serano popularized the term "cisgender" and proposed that "trans" should be used an as adjective to describe one's identity. Julia argues that just as there are *Catholic* women and *Asian* women, there are *trans* women.[59] Therefore, trans women are women.

Some questioned that such an individual should be writing a book about feminism, but Julia railed against those who believe that transitioned men lack the authority to speak on behalf of women:

> Their claims that they somehow understand "womanhood" better than trans women do by virtue of having been born and socialized female is just as naive and arrogant as my claiming to understand "womanhood" better because, unlike most women, I have had a male experience to compare it to. Any claim that one has superior knowledge about womanhood is fraught with gender entitlement and erases the infinite different ways for people to experience their own femaleness. . . . And the very idea that the femaleness of my mind, personality, lived experiences, and the rest of my body can somehow be trumped by the mere presence of a penis can only be described as phallocentric.[60]

Many feminists today are at a loss for how to argue against such claims, after having spent decades establishing the foundation of Julia's conclusions. The analogy could be offered of a snake that begins to swallow its own tail and then isn't certain what to do when it reaches its own head.

Feminism's original desire was a good one: to eliminate injustice and oppression against women. As Pope Francis remarked, "[H]istory is burdened by the excesses of patriarchal cultures that considered women inferior."[61] A fundamental error, however, came in thinking that the removal of sexual difference is the solution to the oppression of women. As Judith Butler summarized, "[A] feminist view argues that gender should be overthrown, eliminated, or rendered fatally ambiguous precisely because it is always a sign of subordination for women."[62] But what if the opposite is true? As Beatriz Vollmer Coles wrote, "I believe the key to a new and more enriching feminism for this new millennium lies in the reunion of sex and gender."[63] Without this, feminism cannibalizes itself. An initial desire to be liberated from stereotypes has resulted in more women than ever questioning their own womanhood if they don't fit cultural stereotypes, while men appropriate womanhood by living out the same stereotypes.

The sexual revolution

Perhaps the most overlooked precursor to gender theory is the widespread modern acceptance of contraception. While some people have never considered the connection between the two, many second-wave feminists blamed fertility for their inability to "overthrow their oppressive roles."[64] But if women could employ technology to acquire the same reproductive roles as men, then at last they could achieve equality.

However, if human beings are sexed according to their reproductive roles, and reproduction is divorced from the sexual act, the significance of sexually distinct bodies is obscured. Dr. Abigail Favale points out, "A surgeon can make a vagina out of a wound, because the vagina is no longer seen as the door to a womb."[65]

Before becoming Pope Benedict XVI, Cardinal Joseph Ratzinger explained:

Detached from the bond with fecundity, sex no longer appears to be a determined characteristic, as a radical and pristine orientation of the person. Male? Female? They are questions that for some are now viewed as obsolete, senseless, if not racist. . . . It is not by chance that among the battles of "liberation" of our time there has also been that of escaping from the "slavery of nature" . . . But one cannot struggle against nature without undergoing the most devastating consequences. The sacrosanct equality between man and woman does not exclude, indeed it requires, diversity.[66]

He continues:

The words of the creation account: "male and female he created them" (Gen 1:27) no longer apply. No, what applies now is this: it was not God who created them male and female—hitherto society did this, now we decide for ourselves. Man and woman as created realities, as the nature of the human being, no longer exist. Man calls his nature into question. From now on he is merely spirit and will. The manipulation of nature, which we deplore today where our environment is concerned, now becomes man's fundamental choice where he himself is concerned. From now on there is only the abstract human being, who chooses for himself what his nature is to be. Man and woman in their created state as complementary versions of what it means to be human are disputed. But if there is no pre-ordained duality of man and woman in creation, then neither is the family any longer a reality established by creation.[67]

Christians who accept contraception but decry gender theory are now presented with a dilemma. Marc Barnes points out, "Between arguing that the body tells us who we are, while tacitly accepting that we can and should spend good money to shut the body up—it seems that conservative America has a choice to make."[68] In other words, if the created order of the body should be respected and not altered for the sake of transitioning, why is it permissible to alter the body's natural capacity to procreate through devices, hormonal contraception, and sterilization surgeries?

Because the widespread use of contraception blurred the reality of sexual difference, Angela Franks remarked, "sex [becomes] about bodies and pleasures. Because fertility doesn't matter any more, it does not matter whether the bodies are male or female; they are all just raw material for anonymous couplings."[69] As a result, contraception paved the way for the acceptance of homosexual acts. After all, if a man and a woman can engage in a sexual act that is not ordered toward reproduction, then why can't members of the same sex do the same? Sexual difference becomes irrelevant.

For this reason, Judith Butler rightly observed that "sexual practice has the power to destabilize gender."[70] She explained that if one is a woman to the extent that one functions as one within the dominant heterosexual frame, then to call the frame into question "is perhaps to lose something of one's sense of place in gender."[71]

The convergence

If gender theory could be compared to a flooded river, the above philosophies and cultural shifts act as the precipitation and melting snowcaps that flow from the distance into various streams of influence. Four streams that converge directly into the ideology of gender theory are those of education, the media, politics, and medicine.

Educational programs that promote gender theory are often inserted into school curricula nationwide under the guise of anti-bullying programs. While programs to prevent harassment and discrimination against children who experience gender dysphoria are necessary, the programs typically serve as a Trojan horse for the deconstruction of any norms around sexual identity. For example, the Massachusetts Department of Elementary and Secondary Education required all teachers in the school system to read an assortment of books to children, starting at the age of four, that teach things such as:

> When a baby is born, a grown-up says, "It's a boy!" or "It's a girl!" If a brand-new baby could talk, sometimes that baby might say, "No I'm not!" When a baby grows up to be transgender, it means that the grown-up who said they were a boy or a girl made a mistake.[72]

These lessons were presented to more than 450,000 children and were authored by individuals who believe that some boys have vaginas and biological sex is not a fact.[73] Meanwhile, in New York, groups such as Drag Story Hour NYC have received more than $200,000 in taxpayer funding to enter grade schools and instruct children about gender fluidity.[74]

Upon hearing these lessons, a boy who wrestles with the idea of fitting into rigid gender stereotypes of masculinity might begin to conclude that his body is the source of his problem. If he approaches a teacher who promotes gender theory, the adult is likely to inform him that if an adult loves him, they'll never question his desire to transition. They will only affirm his gender journey of becoming his (or her) authentic self.

Indoctrinating classrooms of children into gender theory violates the privacy and natural development of the students. For students who aren't questioning their sexual identity, such programs introduce unnecessary confusion. But for those who do experience gender dysphoria, it is a deeply personal and often painful reality for children and their families. To propose that the solution is as simple as professing an alternative gender identity and pursuing social and medical transition undermines and fails to appreciate the complexity of individual people struggling. In fact, many young children with gender dysphoria are not interested in transitioning, and to tell them that most people inevitably will misrepresents the research in this area.

Imagine if a young girl who had been instructed in the above ideologies were to be given a smartphone at the age of eleven. Upon discovering social media, she would inevitably discover the videos with the hashtag #Trans that have been viewed more than 26 billion times.[75] In some clips, adolescents share their thoughts on being nonbinary or reveal the results of their latest surgery. Meanwhile, surgeons routinely create videos to market their reassignment surgeries to adolescents.

If a parent begins searching the internet for ideas on how to best support a child who experiences gender dysphoria, they're likely to be told that the only loving choice is to affirm the child's self-perception. They might even stumble across online stores that now offer "kid's concealing briefs transgender underwear," available in extra small size 2, for toddlers just getting out of diapers, adorned with rainbows and cartoon characters.

Within the halls of academia, dissention from the creed of gender theory has become an unforgivable offense. At the University of Southern Maine, students walked out of class and demanded that professor Christy Hammer be removed because she taught that there are two sexes.[76] In Ireland, Enoch Burke was suspended from teaching because of his refusal to refer to a student as "they" and then arrested when he continued to show up to work.[77] Numerous students have also been either suspended or expelled for similar reasons.

Meanwhile, government leaders and activist groups have worked behind the scenes for decades to ensure that one's internal sense of gender identity becomes a protected category against discrimination.[78] Laws have been passed in dozens of states that could lead to lawsuits against therapists who seek to assist clients in resolving gender-related distress while aligning with their biological sex.

Corporations are expected to conform to gender theory and are weighed on the scales of the Human Right's Campaign's Healthcare Equality Index to determine whether their business policies are sufficiently trans-friendly. So as not to offend, some have removed any reference to women, and have adopted terms such as "cervix havers," "menstruators," "chest feeders," "pregnant people," "uterus bearers." (Curiously, similar creative titles aren't often given to men.) In 2019, a disgruntled individual tweeted, "Just wondering why there's a female symbol on sanitary products when men get periods too. just a bit shocked when I saw it that's all." Within two weeks, Procter & Gamble issued a press release and removed the female Venus symbol from all their sanitary pads.[79]

It is hard to imagine that every executive enacting these policies is deeply convicted about the principles of gender theory. Rather, they hold to the tenets of the ideology only insofar as it is socially and financially expedient to do so. As Upton Sinclair remarked, "[I]t is difficult to get a man to understand something when his salary depends upon his not understanding it."[80]

The medical revolution

Not many factors behind gender theory were as influential as the seismic shift that occurred within the field of medicine during the past century. Many people attribute the rise of trans medicine to Dr. John Money, who opened the first gender clinic in the United States in 1966. While he played a pivotal role, it's enlightening to examine the origins of his beliefs.

In 1919, a German physician and sexologist named Dr. Magnus Hirschfeld founded the Institute of Sexual Science in Berlin. Hirschfeld was known to sleep with his male students and cross-dress, and created a bizarre museum of items that included among other things, sexual torture devices.[81] Dr. Magnus's sexual partner and "woman of the house" was a man thirty years younger than him, who eventually committed suicide. Hirschfeld disbelieved in the idea of sex as simply male/female and proposed that homosexuality was a third sex. He even experimented with transplanting testes into men in an effort to "cure" them of homosexuality.[82] He was the first to use the term "transsexual" and began experimenting with sex-change operations, performing a castration in 1922 and a mastectomy 1926, followed by the first penectomy in 1930, and soon after, a vaginoplasty (to a patient who died fourteen months later due to the complications caused by the operation, after an "abyss of suffering").[83]

Just before his patient died, Dr. Hirschfeld was invited by an American endocrinologist named Harry Benjamin to give a speaking tour in the United States to promote his research, and was hailed as the "Einstein of Sex."[84] Dr. Benjamin became focused on promoting medical transitioning in 1948 after being introduced to a transsexual individual by the sexologist Alfred Kinsey. Benjamin had been involved in selling a fake tuberculosis vaccine, and after his fraud was exposed, turned to promoting testosterone and vasectomies as anti-aging remedies.[85] Next, he began offering patients sex-change surgeries, and soon became the world's leading expert on the subject.

At the time, most people who wished to receive such procedures traveled to Casablanca, where thousands of surgeries were conducted by Dr. George Burou.[86] He said, "I don't change men into women. I transform male genitals into genitals that have a female aspect. All the rest is in the patient's mind."[87]

Harry Benjamin wished to make such procedures more available within the United States, and founded the Harry Benjamin Foundation, which in 2006 was renamed the World Professional Association for Transgender Health. Today, WPATH claims to establish "medical standards of care" for individuals who identify as trans. To provide surgical solutions for them,

Benjamin led a research group whose purpose was to establish an American sex-change program. One of the members of this team was Dr. John Money.

John Money was raised in a strictly religious home by an abusive father who whipped him at the age of four because of a broken window. Although the father passed away when John was eight years old, Money explained that the experience of being lashed by his father helped to seal his lifelong rejection of "the brutality of manhood."[88] After his father's death, John was raised by his mother and spinster aunts, whose incessant derogation of males made him feel guilty for being one. Remarking of his own genitals, he later wrote, "I wore the mark of man's vile sexuality."[89] He also pondered whether the world "might really be a better place for women if not only farm animals but humans were gelded [castrated] at birth."[90]

John eventually married, but the relationship soon ended in divorce and John remained childless throughout life. He went on to practice an openly bisexual lifestyle and praised the ideas of open marriage and nudism. He also defended pornography as a "cleansing" activity that could strengthen marriages.[91]

In 1986, he published an exhaustive study that sought to destigmatize unspeakable sexual perversions and became an advocate for pedophilia, explaining that "[a] childhood sexual experience, such as being the partner of a relative or of an older person, need not necessarily affect the child adversely."[92] He argued that as long as a ten-year-old's sexual relationship with a man decades older than him is "positive," and "totally mutual," it "should not be broken up precipitously."[93] In order to desensitize medical students at Baltimore's Johns Hopkins Medical School to sexual perversion, he showed films of people engaging in bestiality and consuming human waste, and taught that incest sometimes pleases wives because it removes from them the burden of being the man's only sexual outlet.

Money never obtained a medical degree, but rather specialized in psychology. After completing his doctoral dissertation in 1952 on the topic of hermaphrodism, he was invited to join the staff of Johns Hopkins, the location of the world's first and largest clinic for treating and researching intersex conditions. There, he studied more than one hundred patients who were born with disorders of sexual development. Based upon his premise that gender is socially constructed, he explored how children with ambiguous genitalia could be steered into whichever sex the medical team decided was best for them. However, due to the level of available surgical technology, it was easier to castrate males and "assign" them a female gender than to reconstruct male genitalia.

Money believed that *all* children are psychosexually neutral, not only those born with intersex conditions. In his mind, nurture, not nature, determines one's sense of self sexually. When asked how he arrived at some of his revolutionary ideas about sexuality, he remarked, "I frequently find myself toying with concepts and working out potential hypothesis. . . . It is like playing a game of science fiction."[94] Nonetheless, his theories offered psychological credence to surgically modify the children whom he considered to be "experiments of nature."[95]

At this time, because adults who wished to obtain sex change surgeries needed to travel overseas for such procedures, advocates began lobbying for such operations to become available in the United States. As a result, the Gender Identity Clinic was founded at Johns Hopkins, and performed its first such operation in 1965. Soon, John Money happened upon an "opportunity" that would forever change the course of his career.

In 1965, Ron and Janet Reimer welcomed twin boys, Bruce and Brian, into their marriage. Unfortunately, the children suffered from a condition known as phimosis, which made it difficult for them to urinate. Their pediatrician informed the young parents (aged twenty and twenty-one) that the issue could be resolved by means of circumcision, and so the routine procedure was scheduled at a local hospital for the boys, who were now eight months old. The doctor opted to use a Bovie cautery machine, which allowed wounds to be cauterized by means of an electric current to prevent bleeding. Bruce was scheduled first for the procedure, but due to a mishap during the circumcision, his penis was destroyed. Brian's procedure was immediately cancelled, and the parents returned home traumatized by the experience and unsure of what to do next.

Nearly a year after the tragic accident, Ron and Janet saw Dr. John Money being interviewed on television, promoting the groundbreaking work of gender transformation that was under way at Johns Hopkins Hospital. The couple wrote to Money and traveled to meet him in 1967. The doctor immediately realized that the twins offered him the perfect matched control to demonstrate his theory. Therefore, he advised the parents to castrate the child and promised them that his team could fashion a perfectly functional vagina for their baby, and although "she" would be unable to bear children, Bruce could be psychologically female, attracted to men, and could one day marry and adopt children (with the help of his psychological, social, and hormonal conditioning).

Ron and Janet weren't ready to operate immediately on their child and returned home to consider what had been promised to them. Wanting to avoid a lifetime of humiliation and confusion for the boy, they heeded the counsel of Dr. Money, and began socially transitioning Bruce to appear female, giving him the name Brenda. Money wrote to them about his concern that they were procrastinating about the operation, and so two months before his second birthday, Bruce underwent surgical castration. The parents also continued to follow the guidance of Dr. Money so that Bruce could seamlessly transition to Brenda.

At the Reimer house, however, the change was anything but smooth. When his mother first attempted to put him in a dress,

Brenda tore at it to remove the costume. He refused to wear makeup and cried at the age of four when he was told that he could not shave like his father. Rather than taking an interest in dolls, Brenda was solely interested in building forts and playing with guns. After being given a jump rope as a gift, he remarked that the only thing he'd use it for is to tie people up and whip them with it. Upon receiving the gift of a toy sewing machine, he promptly disassembled it to see how it worked.

Meanwhile, Dr. Money unveiled his "twins case" to more than a thousand scientists, academics, and reporters at the American Association for the Advancement of Science in Washington D.C., proclaiming that Brenda was a well-adjusted "mother hen" who was keenly interested in dolls and kitchen work, not at all like her brother. He published papers and graciously delivered speeches and interviews globally, hailing the success of his theories and claiming that Brenda's behavior and interests are so typically female that no one would ever question the matter.[96]

Texts of psychology, sociology, and women's studies programs were updated to reflect these cutting-edge findings. In the words of *Time* in 1973, "This dramatic case . . . provides strong support . . . that conventional patterns of masculine and feminine behavior can be altered. It also casts doubt on the theory that major sex differences, psychological as well as anatomical, are immutably set by the genes at conception."[97]

As the twins aged, Money insisted that they visit him in Baltimore to continue Brenda's gender development. During the visits with the young boys, Money began exposing them to adult and child pornography, which he saw as an essential element of childhood sex education. He assured them, "I want to show you pictures of things that moms and dads do."[98] This grooming led to Money forcefully instructing the boys to disrobe in his office and mimic sexual acts with one another while he photographed them. Money considered childhood sexual rehearsal play to be an essential element of cementing their gender roles and healthy gender identity. It allows "children to grow up to be sexually normal."[99]

By the age of seven, Brenda became increasingly resistant to traveling to Baltimore for the routine meetings with Money and rejected his idea of a second genital surgery to further construct a pseudo-vagina. But because the sexual abuse was happening without Brenda's parents' knowledge—and Brenda sadly assumed that they consented to Money's actions because they were responsible for his upbringing—the family continued making visits at the request of Money, for the psychological well-being of their child.

At the age of nine, Brenda had a nervous breakdown, shaking and crying in a corner at home. He recalls his mother crying, screaming, committing adultery, and attempting suicide while the father drank to drown the pain of their dashed hopes of a happy marriage and family. Brenda fell into a deeper depression, blaming himself for their marital problems. When grade school classmates teased him for being a "cavewoman" and "gorilla," Brenda beat up the boys who teased him, which only served to further alienate him from his male peers. Meanwhile, based upon the reports of Money, the media announced that Brenda was "sailing contentedly along through childhood as a genuine girl."[100] He added, "The girl's subsequent history proves how well all three of them [parents and child] succeeded in adjusting to that decision."[101]

In their final trip to see Dr. Money in 1978, he introduced Brenda to a transsexual man who was wearing makeup and explained to him the benefits of sex-change surgery. After the conversation, Dr. Money reached out for Brenda's shoulder, and because the boy feared that the men were going to force him to the operating room, Brenda fled out of the office, chased by people in lab coats. He escaped down four flights of stairs and out of the hospital's rear exit, into the parking lot, and eight blocks away from the facility. When reunited with his family, Brenda informed them that he would kill himself if he was ever forced to see Money again.

In 1980, during a visit to the endocrinologist, Brenda reached a tipping point. After refusing to remove his hospital gown for a breast exam (due to the hormones he was being given), the doctor exclaimed, "Do you want to be a girl or not?" He looked up and shouted in the face of the physician, "No!"[102] The endocrinologist shared with Brenda's psychiatrist that he believed it was time for Brenda to know the truth, and after being picked up from his weekly session with the psychiatrist, on March 14, 1980, Brenda witnessed his father cry for the first time as he explained the full truth. When the story was complete, Brenda asked one question: "What was my name?"

Bruce was overwhelmed with a range of emotions and a deep sense of relief in knowing that he hadn't been crazy for knowing all along that he wasn't female. He immediately transitioned to his true sex and took the name David, in recognition of the Goliath that he had slayed in enduring such trauma. In defense of his parents, David remarked, "My parents feel very guilty, as if the whole thing was their fault. But it wasn't like that. They did what they did out of *kindness* and love and desperation. When you're desperate, you don't necessarily do the right things."[103] Dr. Money, astoundingly, continued to hail his experiment as a success and lamented that the Reimer twins had been lost to follow-up.

After learning that thousands of other infant sex reassignment surgeries were performed based upon the "success" of Money's experiment on him, David went public and shared the details of his experience with researchers and journalists. Although it took years for a scholarly publication to be willing to expose Money's fraud and overturn decades of disinformation, other victims soon emerged, sharing their own harrowing experiences with Dr. Money.[104] David eventually married and adopted three children, but wrestled with mental health issues and divorce, and committed suicide in 2004. His brother, Brian, died in 2002 due to a combination of antidepressants and alcohol.

Not all the experts at Johns Hopkins agreed with Dr. Money's theories and methodologies. One of his greatest critics was Dr. Paul McHugh, who insisted that transsexual surgery is a modern-day equivalent of the once common practice of frontal lobotomy. Since his arrival at Johns Hopkins in 1975, he sought to end the practice because it seemed to do more harm than good.[105] He noted, "Policy makers and the media are doing no favors to the public or the transgendered by treating their confusions as a right in need of defending rather than as a mental disorder that deserves understanding, treatment and prevention."[106]

Based upon research of the long-term follow-up of patients who had been treated since the clinic was founded in 1966, McHugh discovered that none showed measurable improvement. Dr. Jon Meyer, who was the director of the sexual behaviors consultation unit, reported that there were "no differences in long-term adjustment between transsexuals who go under the scalpel and those who do not. . . . My personal feeling is that surgery is not a proper treatment for a psychiatric disorder, and it's clear to me that these patients have severe psychological problems that don't go away following surgery."[107] As a result of these findings, the Gender Identity Clinic was closed in October 1979. Thirty-eight years later, in 2017, it was reopened.

9.

Puberty blockers are a safe, effective, and reversible way to pause puberty.

Sometimes when children are exploring their gender, they need more time to decide what's right for them. In fact, going through puberty can cause tremendous and unnecessary distress to some young people. But, as Dr. Johanna Olson noted, "If we get kids early enough in the process, we put them on puberty blockers or medications that actually keep their body from progressing through that wrong puberty . . . and then put them through the right puberty that corresponds to their brain." Then, if they decide to go on cross-sex hormones or receive surgery later, it "gives them a body that is much closer to their internal gender identity."[1] This will not only relieve their dysphoria, it makes them less suicidal.[2] Then, if a young person decides puberty blockers are not right for them, they can just resume puberty. Dr. Polly Carmichael explained, "[T]he good thing about it is, if you stop the injections, it's like pressing a start button and the body just carries on developing as it would if you hadn't taken the injection."[3] To be fair, there are risks to any medical treatment. But as one medical ethicist at the University of Manchester noted, "anything is better than life in an alien body."[4]

In the early 1990s an "adventurous pediatric endocrinologist" in Amsterdam halted the puberty of a thirteen-year-old girl known as "B" by administering to her an off-label drug known as a gonad-otrophin-releasing hormone agonist, or GnRHa.[5] When adminis-tered to a child, it pauses the development of his or her secondary sex characteristics. For a girl, this means she will not experience normal breast development, menstruation, or typical fat distribu-tion. A boy, meanwhile, will have lower muscle mass, less facial hair, decreased height, and his voice will not deepen.

At the time B received GnRHa, it was only used to chemically castrate male sex offenders and to treat prostate cancer. It has also been used to treat uterine fibroids and endometriosis in women—but for no longer than six months. Doctors also sometimes pre-scribed it to treat the rare condition of precocious puberty in children (when puberty begins before age eight in girls and before age nine in boys). However, such drugs were never approved for treating gender dysphoric children who were otherwise progress-ing naturally through puberty. After all, puberty is not a disease. In fact, the absence of puberty is a disease, known as Kallmann syndrome. When puberty blockers are given to healthy children, physicians are using drugs to induce a diseased state in the patient.

When B turned sixteen, researchers followed up with her and her treatment became the foundation of what is now known as the Dutch Protocol. This means that in the Netherlands, "gender dys-phoric adolescents may be eligible for puberty suppression at age 12, subsequent cross-sex hormone treatment at age 16, and gender reassignment surgery at age 18."[6]

To administer the puberty-blocking drug, patients might receive injections of leuprolide or triptorelin either once per month or every three months. Or they might receive an implant that is inserted under the skin of the upper arm that will continuously release histrelin into the bloodstream for twelve months, at which point a new implant can be inserted. The chemicals halt the pro-duction of gonadal sex steroids (testosterone and estrogen). With-out insurance, the annual cost ranges from $4,000 to $25,000.[7]

In order to know if the time is right to give a child such potent chemicals, gender clinics often recommend following the lead of the child. As Dr. Courtney Finlayson explains, "We just really need good research that we don't have yet. . . . This generation of kids are really . . . the pioneers. They are going to be the ones to teach us."[8] Or, in the words of Dr. Diane Ehrensaft, "[I]t's the children who are now leading us."[9] Experts such as Ehrensaft believe that these medicines are helpful for children as young as eight years old, and that "[w]hen children are supported—and that means accepted— they will do beautifully."[10]

Such early interventions often create misgivings for even the most progressive of parents. As one mother said, after injecting her eleven-year-old son, "It's always scary . . . I often ask myself, 'Are we doing the right thing?' But I don't feel like it's been my decision. I really just got out of her way. I just am letting her be who she is."[11] However, in what other area of medicine do doctors follow the diagnosis and treatment protocol of the patient, especially when the patient hasn't finished grade school?

No long-term studies have been done to confirm the safety or efficacy of using puberty blockers to treat gender dysphoria in children. However, the studies that have been conducted offer troubling results that aren't often shared with parents when visiting their local gender clinic.

Emotional impact

The makers of puberty blocking drugs such as Lupron and Supprelin warn that possible side effects include emotional instability, mood changes, aggression, nervousness, anxiety, agitation, confusion, delusions, insomnia, and depression, adding that you should "monitor for development or worsening of psychiatric symptoms during treatment."[12] Depression is considered a common side effect of puberty blockers, and according to drug manufacturers, "may be severe."[13]

Girls who take GnRHa experience a significant increase in behavioral and emotional problems and are more likely to self-harm.[14] According to the largest gender clinic in the UK, after a year of being on puberty blockers, there was a significant increase in young women who agreed with the statement "I deliberately try to hurt or kill myself."[15] It should be noted, however, that there was no control group in this study, and so one cannot infer causation. What's clear, though, is that the drug was hardly curing the psychological distress of the children who took it. Rather, they expressed *greater* dissatisfaction with their bodies after being on the drug.[16] In the words of a team of researchers who promote the treatment, "It is therefore unlikely that GnRHa treatment will result in significant reduction in body dissatisfaction."[17]

Understanding the role of hormones in brain functioning helps to explain why the drugs could have a negative emotional impact. Puberty blocking drugs shut down the production of estrogen and progesterone. However, researchers believe that estrogen can have a protective effect against mental illnesses such as depression, acting as "nature's psychoprotectant."[18] Dr. Karen Berman, a senior investigator for the National Institutes of Mental Health, studied the effect of Lupron on the female brain. After injecting women with the drug, she scanned their brains with a PET scan and found that the activity in the frontal lobes of their brains had slowed to a near stop.[19] This leads to dulled or inappropriate emotions, lack of motivation, impulsiveness, and altered mental states such as delirium, disorientation, and confusion.[20] Studies also showed that puberty blockers cause memory problems and stunt brain development, which is the last thing a young person needs when making life-changing decisions about his or her future.[21] Therefore, those who argue that the outcomes of puberty blockers are uncertain are guilty of what some psychologists call "HARKing:" hypothesizing after the results are known.

Physical side effects

Hormones play a significant role in bone development for young people, and when natural hormones are suppressed, unnatural consequences follow. Within three years of being on puberty blockers, the average girl will have bone density lower than 98 percent of children her age.[22] While proponents of puberty blockers claim that a child's bone density won't decrease while using the drugs, this is beside the point. Bone density needs to *increase* during adolescence. Children on puberty blockers also have lower spine bone mass density and can develop osteoporosis in their teens.[23] Dr. Michael Biggs reported, "After two years on GnRHa, perhaps 30% of those with puberty suppression could meet [the] threshold for spine bone density."[24]

Although using puberty blockers to treat gender dysphoria is a relatively new practice, many people who took the drug to treat precocious puberty have reported experiencing adverse effects. For example, Sharissa Derricott took Lupron for several years. At twenty-one, a surgeon replaced her deteriorated jaw joint. Then she was diagnosed with degenerative disc disease and fibromyalgia. Her teeth began to shed enamel and crack. Nothing made sense until she discovered thousands of women like herself on forums and online groups who had taken Lupron. She was one of the first patients to take the drug, thirty years ago, and now she says she's had more surgeries than her seventy-nine-year-old father and suffers from a blood disorder and bone and joint problems. "Excuse my language, but it's hell," she said.[25] A mother whose child suffered many of the same effects from the drug lamented, "As a parent, I kick myself . . . What was I thinking?"[26]

Sexual development is also a serious concern when putting a child on puberty blockers. One significant consequence is that some individuals never develop the capacity to orgasm if the puberty blockade is followed by cross-sex hormones.[27] Others, such as the first girl who took puberty blockers in Amsterdam, reported twenty-two years later that she still struggled with depression and due to dissatisfaction and shame about her genital appearance and "feelings of inadequacy in sexual matters," she found it difficult to sustain a romantic relationship as an adult.[28]

Although some assert that the effects of puberty blockers are reversible, these claims are based upon children who took the drugs to treat early puberty, and then experienced puberty at the age-appropriate time. Research is lacking to measure the effects of medically delaying puberty at the natural time and then withdrawing the medication so that puberty occurs after the appropriate window of development has passed. After all, a medically delayed puberty is not the same as a natural puberty. These are biologically, psychologically, and socially different experiences.

One of the "benefits" of puberty blockers, according to its proponents, is that it makes it easier for individuals to pass as the other sex, due to the lack of development of secondary sex characteristics. For example, males will appear more feminized because they never experience the effects of male puberty. However, since puberty blockers halt the natural development of one's reproductive organs, this could create difficulties when males pursue gender "affirming" surgery later. One reason for this is because the individual will lack the necessary amount of tissue to construct a pseudo vagina.[29] In the case of Jazz Jennings's vaginoplasty, the surgeon needed to harvest his intestinal tissue for the procedure. Despite all of these drawbacks, the makers of Lupron proudly announced to their shareholders that the drug generates more than $700 million annually in revenue.[30]

Makers of Lupron know that many doctors might be hesitant to prescribe such a drug to their patients. To help ease their discomfort, the drug manufacturer offers doctors bonuses upwards of $100,000 annually to overcome their hesitancy. In 2001, the manufacturer of Lupron was fined $875 million for using illegal practices to entice physicians to prescribe the drug. The FBI discovered that the sales reps were offering doctors trips to expensive golf and ski resorts, free products, and money disguised as "educational grants."[31]

Puberty blockers: a gateway drug

Gender clinicians claim that puberty blockers serve as a "pause button" so that children can have time to "explore their gender identity." However, Dr. Biggs rightly remarked, "Using GnRHa to block puberty does not mean pressing a pause button . . . it is more like pressing fast forward into cross-sex hormones and ultimately surgery."[32]

Studies of children who go on puberty blockers show that more than 95 percent of them go on to receive cross-sex hormones afterward.[33] These drugs don't give a child time to decide; they initiate a cascade of clinical interventions. In fact, researchers have found that "there are virtually no published reports, even case studies, of adolescents withdrawing from puberty-suppressing drugs and then resuming the normal pubertal development typical for their sex."[34]

In one study of young people that was conducted before the widespread adoption of social affirmation, every child who received puberty blockers continued to experience gender dysphoria, whereas more than 90 percent of those who did not receive the puberty blockade found that their dysphoria resolved naturally![35] By stopping a child's natural development, endocrinologist William Malone remarked that doctors are halting the process that could lead to resolution of the dysphoria.[36]

For this reason, many gender clinics in Europe are changing their mindset, hoping that a more conservative approach will yield a natural resolution to the child's difficulties. Many gender clinics in Sweden and Finland have either tightened their restrictions for prescribing puberty blockers and cross sex hormones or have altogether stopped routinely using them to treat gender dysphoria.[37] Nowadays, if a young person approaches a Dutch gender clinic in search of puberty blockers, they're likely to be put on an eighteen-month waiting list, followed by a nine-month evaluation before the clinic will make their recommendation.[38] An adolescent who demands puberty blockers might object, saying, "I need to wait two years? By then, puberty will be over!" But from the Dutch perspective, the answer is, "Exactly."

It is understandable that children would want to receive cross-sex hormones after being given a puberty blockade. Imagine an eleven-year-old boy who takes puberty blockers for five years. At the age of sixteen, when all his male peers have deeper voices, facial hair, and broader shoulders, but he looks like a prepubescent eleven-year-old, is he going to feel more connected to his masculine identity or less?

One of the most regrettable consequences of these interventions is that when a child goes straight from puberty blockers to cross-sex hormones, he or she becomes permanently sterile.[39] Explaining the significance of this to adolescents is a difficult task, because they have a difficult time forecasting the consequences of their decisions. As Abigail Shrier wrote:

> But try convincing a teenager that something she wants to do carries risks. Imagine telling her that she might not want to damage her breast tissue; that she might one day want to have children and, having birthed those children, to nurse them. It's a little like informing her the sun will burn out five billion years in the future.[40]

Nonetheless, because of the high rate of continuation from puberty blockers to cross-sex hormones, children and parents have a right to know of the impending risks. Not all trans-activists agree, though. YouTuber Samantha Lux argues, "That doesn't make any sense to me. These are totally different procedures . . . this is so ridiculous." Samantha scoffs at the idea that some people think that before going on puberty blockers, "you need to be aware of all of the risks that are associated with gender transition and down along the line. No they don't!"[41]

10.

Cross-sex hormones are beneficial for people who experience gender dysphoria.

The World Professional Association for Transgender Health (WPATH) is the global leader in establishing the standards of care for transgender individuals and they contend that hormonal therapy can be "medically necessary."[1] For many, it is a lifesaving remedy that allows them to feel more at home in their bodies. In fact, a year after going on hormonal therapy, studies show that patients experience a reduction in anxiety, depression, and symptoms of dysphoria.[2] To withhold such treatment from individuals who need it— or simply want it—is cruel and bigoted.

The most common medical intervention to treat gender dysphoria is the administration of cross-sex hormones. For men, this includes estrogen and other medications that suppress testosterone. These drugs do not cause individuals to develop the primary sex characteristics of the other sex (reproductive organs). Rather, they stimulate changes to promote secondary sex characteristics. For example, a male's chest and hips will begin to develop in a more feminine manner. He will gradually have less facial hair, decreased muscle tone, softer skin, testicular atrophy, and some breast development. Conversely, when a woman receives injections of testosterone, changes include a cessation of her periods, vaginal atrophy, increased muscle tone and facial hair, a deepened voice, and a redistribution of fat. If male pattern baldness runs in her family, she may begin to lose her hair.

The current Endocrine Society guidelines recommend that cross-sex hormone treatment is suitable for some individuals prior to the age of sixteen.[3] However, some doctors begin administering the drugs to children as early as eight years old.[4] Meanwhile, injections of testosterone are available for only ten dollars per month under student health plans at numerous colleges.[5] Planned Parenthood will even provide cross-sex hormonal therapy after an initial thirty-minute consultation without lab work follow-ups, which is essential to ensure the safe prescription of hormones.

WPATH recommends that such medication be given only after individuals receive a psychosocial assessment and informed consent has been obtained by a qualified health professional.[6] However, countless young people attest that obtaining the medication is sometimes as easy as a brief conversation over the phone with a gender clinician who isn't a doctor or psychologist. One young woman received hormones at the age of seventeen and recalled, "When you go to a therapist and tell them you have those kinds of feelings, they don't tell you that it's okay to be butch, to be gender nonconforming, to not like men, to not like the way men treat you. They don't tell you there are other women who feel like they don't belong, that they don't feel like they know how to be women. They don't tell you any of that. They tell you about testosterone."[7] However, what they don't often tell young people about such hormones are the potentially life-altering side effects.

Side effects

When a female takes cross-sex hormones, her testosterone level soars ten to forty times beyond what is normally present in the female body, into ranges that are normally present in a woman who has an androgen-secreting tumor. Besides the masculinizing effect it has upon her external appearance, it also causes a host of changes internally.

Tissues within her reproductive system will begin to atrophy, including her uterus and ovaries. Uterine atrophy is often excruciating, and doctors recommend that after five years of being on testosterone, a woman should receive a hysterectomy because of the increased risk of endometrial cancer. The vaginal atrophy often results in painful intercourse, and the thinning of the vaginal wall increases her risk of contracting sexually transmitted diseases. Depending upon the woman, and how long she receives testosterone, it can also cause infertility.

Giving testosterone to a woman quadruples her chance of heart disease because it increases her red blood cell count.[8] When a woman's testosterone levels are raised to the level of a man's, her body does not react to the hormone in the same manner as a male, because her cells are female. Her risk of suffering a stroke is also significantly increased.[9] This is why ongoing lab work is critical, albeit not standard practice at some places where people acquire hormones.

Testosterone also wreaks havoc on a woman's emotions. One YouTuber named Gibby remarked, "Being on testosterone has made me cry less . . . I wish I could cry right now, but it's not going to happen."[10] Some infer from this that testosterone helps to ease depression, but a woman's inability to process emotions is not a sign of improved mental health. Because testosterone boosts confidence, some who receive the drug might feel that their challenges in life have lessened. One woman noted, "It puts a Band-Aid on all of your problems for a while until you realize that it hasn't fixed anything."[11] Keira Bell recalled that while she was taking testosterone, "I couldn't release my emotions." But when she halted the hormonal treatments, she noted, "One of the first signs that I was becoming Keira again was that—thankfully, at last—I was able to cry. And I had a lot to cry about."[12]

While some women who take testosterone don't experience these side effects, many do. Helena Kerschner believed that testosterone would be the right choice for her, but discontinued the injections and recalled:

> I would have like such overwhelming rage attacks that I actually would end up hurting myself instead of hurting others because I was just so out of control. I couldn't control myself. I felt like a monster . . . before I was on testosterone when I would have a really strong emotion, it might move me to tears and I would just cry and sob. But while I was on testosterone, I lost the ability to cry very easily. So I would get that intense emotion but there would be no outlet and then for one reason or another that would trigger anger. I would get so angry and frustrated and that anger was just so overwhelming. And I got the urge to really externalize it. I got the urge to hit things or throw things. I just didn't want to do that. I felt so out of control that I would just kind of take it out on myself to calm myself down and to be an outlet for that rage.[13]

Because these side effects were so troubling, she scaled back on her use of testosterone. Reflecting on how the promises she heard about transitioning weren't materializing, she said, "This is not matching up to that fantasy I had as a teenager. As a teenager I was kind of promised, you know, like this is going to save your life. This is going to make you feel authentic. This is going to make you your true self. This is going make you so happy. . . . It's trans joy."[14]

In males, cross-sex hormones likewise carry unique risks. Because estrogen enhances blood clotting, a man's risk of blood clots will rise. However, because estrogen treatments alone are often insufficient to produce the desired amount of feminizing effects, other anti-androgen drugs are used off-label and can lead to conditions such as jaundice or hepatitis.

When given to a man, cross-sex hormones will cause his genitals to atrophy. One man noted, "The very first change that I noticed—which came during my first few weeks on estrogen/anti-androgens—was a sharp decrease in my sex drive."[15] As mentioned above, if a boy transitions straight to cross-sex hormones from puberty blockers, he will be sterilized for life. When considering this, one thirteen-year-old boy admitted, "I think about it constantly. Cry about it sometimes. Really sad. But my excitement to start the cross-sex hormones completely overrules my, like, despair to just not have a child of my own."[16]

Many who have used cross-sex hormones testify that while taking the drugs, their obsession regarding their body's appearance intensified. One detransitioner, Erin, shared, "Even though it's making me sick, a couple of months after taking it, I would be thinking about it all day and be like, 'I can't wait to put on the gel when I come home.' I just got obsessed with it. And I noticed in the support groups, people were talking about it. And it just made me think, 'Is this dysphoria or is this addiction?'"[17]

When the body becomes the sole target for treating one's distress, a person's mental and emotional energies can sometimes be consumed by the fantasy of transformation. As a result, interests outside of one's goals of transition often become stagnant. One young woman recalled that the time she spent attempting to transition was the most stagnant period in her life in terms of personal growth: "What I saw as positive change was actually the thing that was dragging me the down most in my life at that time."[18]

One of the challenges of relying upon hormones to transform one's body is that it will always want to bend back toward its original state. Three weeks after receiving a shot of testosterone, a woman's hormone levels will return to baseline and some of the visible effects may begin to revert. Should a person wish to keep up the appearance of being the other sex, he or she will need to accept the reality of a lifelong medication regimen. This is because he or she does not possess the gonads to naturally produce sufficient levels of the hormones of the other sex.

Some effects, such as facial hair, bodily changes, and a masculinized voice may endure, however. This creates a difficult situation for those who decide to stop taking hormones, leaving them with a look that is in between sexes, thus causing further distress.

Cross-sex hormone "therapy" does not always produce the effects that a patient expects. According to Dr. Carl Heneghan, a clinical epidemiologist who is also the editor in chief of the *British Medical Journal*, cross-sex hormones cause significant irreversible side effects, are unproven to work, and are unsafe to be applied to children and adolescents.[19] Some advocates cite isolated studies that seem to support cross-sex hormone therapy, but Dr. Heneghan points out that "the evidence is limited by small sample sizes; retrospective methods, and loss of considerable numbers of patients in the follow-up period. The majority of studies also lack a control group."[20] The Endocrine Society guidelines also reported that the strength of evidence for treating adolescents with hormones such as puberty blockers or cross-sex hormones falls into the category of "low or very low."[21]

Informed consent

One has to wonder how many young people who are prescribed cross-sex hormones are aware of the above information. Even if they knew all the facts, how does an adolescent experiencing co-occurring mental health concerns consent to lifelong sterility and an increased risk of heart disease? Dr. Robert Garofalo, who prescribes such drugs to children, acknowledged, "I mean, I know we do informed consent, but really, how realistic is it to believe that a fourteen- or fifteen-year-old or a sixteen-year-old has really the capacity to make that kind of decision for him or herself?"[22]

Adolescents may not have this capacity, and the High Court of England agreed, in a monumental ruling in favor of twenty-three-year-old Keira Bell in 2020. At the age of sixteen, she visited a gender clinic and was soon prescribed puberty blockers. A year later, she was given testosterone and then referred by an adult gender clinic to receive a double mastectomy after two appointments, at the age of twenty. None of the clinicians addressed Kierra's underlying issues, such as her anxiety and depression stemming from her childhood rape, her mother's alcoholism, and the toxic environment of domestic violence in her home. She recalled:

> But the further my transition went, the more I realized that I wasn't a man, and never would be. We are told these days that when someone presents with gender dysphoria, this reflects a person's "real" or "true" self, that the desire to change genders is set. But this was not the case for me. As I matured, I recognized that gender dysphoria was a symptom of my overall misery, not its cause.[23]

Five years after beginning her transition, Keira halted the process, and she reidentified with her sex. Her legal team argued convincingly to the court that puberty blockers are part of a single pathway treatment and that children under the age of sixteen are unlikely to understand the ramifications of sterility and sexual dysfunction. She lamented, "There was never anyone telling me to love myself and that I was fine the way I was. It was just, "Change yourself and you'll be better."[24]

The judges ruled in her favor and declared that for a young person to consent, he or she should be able to understand the following eight factors:

1. The immediate consequences of the treatment in physical and psychological terms
2. The fact that the vast majority of patients taking PBs [puberty blockers] go on to CSH [cross-sex hormones] and therefore that s/he is on a pathway to much greater medical interventions

3. The relationship between taking CSH and subsequent surgery, with the implications of such surgery
4. The fact that CSH may well lead to a loss of fertility
5. The impact of CSH on sexual function
6. The impact that taking this step may have on future and lifelong relationships
7. The unknown physical consequences of taking PBs
8. The fact that the evidence base for this treatment is as yet highly uncertain[25]

Because of how unrealistic it is to expect teens to recognize the weight of these ramifications, the court ruled that such children can't give informed consent to puberty blockers. They also declared that studies demonstrated that those who received hormone blockers showed "no overall improvement in mood or psychological wellbeing."[26] Therefore, clinics and physicians were required to obtain a court order for each patient under the age of eighteen for whom they wish to give puberty blockers to treat gender dysphoria. Unfortunately, in 2021, a UK appeals court overturned the ruling of the High Court, arguing that it should be left for clinicians to exercise their judgment on the matter. However, in 2022, the gender clinic involved in the lawsuit was ordered to be closed down.[27]

Unfortunately, gender clinics in the United States don't always seem concerned with adequate informed consent for minors.[28] For example, Dr. Johanna Olson-Kennedy is the medical director for the Center for Trans Youth Health and Development at Children's Hospital in Los Angeles. She surveyed 101 people in her practice with gender dysphoria who wanted to go on cross-sex hormones and discovered that 30 percent had moderate to severe depressive symptoms, 49 percent thought about suicide, over 30 percent had attempted suicide, and among them was "a lot" of drug use, sexual activity, and some engaged in prostitution for food or a place to

Jason Evert

live.[29] What did she do to improve their lives? She helped all of them receive cross-sex hormones.

Lawsuits may soon surge as more young adults begin to wonder where all the adults were when they were making these life-altering choices. As Dr. Lappert remarked, "We are headed for a medical scandal never before seen in human history. Whole medical institutions will be bankrupted by the legal consequences of this disaster."[30]

11.

Gender-affirming surgery is a life-saving intervention.

A meta-analysis of twenty-eight studies showed that gender-affir-mative surgery lessens dysphoria and improves the quality of life for individuals who are trans.[1] Furthermore, it has been proven that the rates of regret are as low as 2 percent.[2] Therefore, it is cruel to with-hold such treatment from people—especially adults—who sincerely want to feel at home in their own bodies. Besides, if women can receive cosmetic breast surgery for no other reason than to appear more stereotypically feminine, why can't individuals receive top sur-gery to find relief from gender dysphoria?

Those who do not experience gender dysphoria often dismiss indi-viduals who seek surgical treatments as being delusional masoch-ists. A more compassionate approach would be to exercise reverent curiosity about what it would feel like to experience such profound distress about one's body that a person would go to such great lengths to find relief.

Gabriel Mac wrote about this experience in an essay published in *New York* magazine: "I spent weeks before my 2019 hysterectomy up late in bed, hot and sleepless, fantasizing about the moment the medical-waste-disposal team at UC San Francisco would batch-in-cinerate my uterus, which swirled with dysphoria like nausea from the depths of my soul."[3]

While individuals such as Gabriel crave surgery and often describe an overwhelming sense of urgency for such procedures, many who identify as trans have no interest whatsoever in modifying their bodies. Some even argue that the expectation of such modifications perpetuate gender stereotypes. For example, Julia Serano noted, "No qualifications should be placed on the term 'trans woman' based on a person's ability to 'pass' as female, her hormone levels, or the state of her genitals—after all, it is downright sexist to reduce any woman (trans or otherwise) down to her mere body parts or to require her to live up to certain societally dictated ideals regarding appearance."[4]

Nonetheless, individuals often experience an internal conflict between the persistent desire to have surgery and the apprehension regarding the outcome. One wrote, "One of the ways I had tried to suppress it was to convince myself that I would be such an ugly freak of a pseudo-woman that there's no way that transitioning would help my dysphoria, but I realized that the dysphoria is such a big part of my life that maybe being a freakish pseudo-woman wouldn't be so bad." This person's vulnerable admission should help individuals who don't experience gender dysphoria to understand the angst that drives many people to seek surgery.

Procedures

The term "sex-change operation" has evolved into a host of other more commonly used titles, including "sex-reassignment surgery," "gender-reassignment surgery," "gender-affirmation surgery," "gender-confirmation surgery," and "genital-affirmation surgery." Although these titles speak of "surgery" in the singular, a wide variety of procedures are available, depending upon what level of bodily augmentation the individual requests.

Some procedures known as facial masculinization or feminization surgery involve recontouring of the jaw or reduction of the forehead, while another procedure known as tracheal shaving can reduce the size of one's Adam's apple. Other operations focus on reconstruction of the breast tissue by means of a radical double mastectomy or breast implants. Some of the procedures that involve genital reconstruction or removal are known as "bottom surgery" and include phalloplasty, penectomy, vaginoplasty, vaginectomy, metoidioplasty, salpingo-oophorectomy, and orchiectomy, among others. Meanwhile, some individuals who identify as neutrios, nullo, or eunuch may seek gender nullification surgeries to erase any marker of sexual distinction.[5]

When Johns Hopkins University's Gender Identity Clinic first began offering some of these procedures, they only approved twenty-four of the first two thousand requests they received.[6] Nowadays, discretion is largely left up to the individual rather than the institution, and about 25 percent of people who identify as trans have had some form of transition-related surgery.[7]

The most common operation among females is a double mastectomy, commonly referred to as "top surgery." In fact, more than twice as many women receive top surgery as men (21 percent versus 8 percent).[8] However, because the procedure costs upwards of $10,000 and is often not covered by insurance, more than forty thousand young women can be found on the popular crowdfunding website Gofundme.com, soliciting donations to cover the cost of the operation.

Many individuals express relief and satisfaction immediately following their procedures. But even when surgeries go as planned, the results can sometimes spawn new forms of dysphoria rather than relieving it. One YouTuber admitted after having her breasts removed, "I know for me, it started making me way more dysphoric about my hips."[9]

Bottom surgery isn't nearly as popular as top surgery but is five times more common among males than females (10 percent versus 2 percent).[10] Dr. Mark Litwin, a urologist at UCLA, explained on YouTube that the "risks are pretty minor" to have one's testicles removed, and then casually describes the possibilities of infection, scarring, decreased libido, infertility, and nerve damage.[11]

Most women have no interest in bottom surgery, even if they identify as male. Also, procedures such as a phalloplasty, which involves the construction of a pseudo-penis, often involve a high failure rate and can leave the patient with a catheter and sexually dysfunctional genitals that resemble neither sex.

Gabriel Mac was well informed of such risks and purchased a burial plot in advance of the operation, just in case. In preparation for the procedure, Gabriel recalled listening to an individual in an online transmasculine support group meeting whose surgery had failed. After the surgeon harvested skin from the woman's arm to begin the procedure, "all the fat and skin had been stripped from their left forearm from wrist to nearly elbow, along with major nerves, an artery, and veins, and then shaped into a tube and connected, in careful layers, to skin and blood vessels and nerves in their pelvis."[12] Despite the doctor's best efforts, the surgery was a failure and the appendage died three days later, after a second, eight-hour surgery that could not save it. Gabriel recalls the individual's resolve, "But here they were, already getting ready for their surgeons to harvest a whole other part of their body within the month with zero hesitation."[13]

Such determination resonated with Gabriel, who shared it detail what it was like to awake later from the same procedure:

I woke up last December in a hospital bed and before even glancing toward my lap, the room spinning from anesthesia and my lungs partially collapsed from four and a half hours on surgical ventilation and hundreds—plural—of stitches and a 40-square-inch hole in my thigh where I'd been skinned down to the muscle, I could suddenly feel, in a way I could never have fathomed, that this was what being alive was. . . . For five days, I lay in a hospital bed without moving. No visitors: COVID. Every day, twice a day, someone came and injected anti-coagulating pig-intestine derivatives into my abdomen so I wouldn't die from a blood clot, my belly becoming a graveyard of needle-punched bruises.

Despite the difficult recovery process, Gabriel sometimes expressed joy that erupted in the form of singing. But, "at other moments, I was so overwhelmed by floods of repressed rage and grief that all I could do was open my mouth and start screaming." The nurse reassured Gabriel that such post-operative emotions are commonplace, saying, "The whole process is constant body horror."

Eventually, the physical and emotional tempest subsided. Seven weeks after the phalloplasty, Gabriel remarked, "I realized I couldn't remember the last time I'd thought about killing myself. The first story I ever wrote . . . was about committing suicide by walking into the Atlantic Ocean. I hadn't yet started kindergarten." And yet after the phalloplasty—despite surviving an obviously difficult childhood and being the victim of sexual violence as a woman—a sense of calm and relief gradually followed.

Like Gabriel, many people who elect to have surgeries attest that they're grateful for the decision. For example, Dr. Johanna Olson Kennedy conducted a study of nearly one hundred young people who had double mastectomies, and said, "Self-reported regret was near 0."[14] One limitation of this study, and many others like it, is that the follow-up research ended between one to five years post-operation. So if the young women received the operation at the age of thirteen (which some did), it meant that a fourteen-year-old had no regrets. Might the same teenager feel differently in her midtwenties when she wants to breastfeed her newborn and cannot? Furthermore, 28 percent of the young people either refused to reply to Olson Kennedy's survey or were lost to follow-up. If one of these individuals had committed suicide after the procedure, how would she reply to the researchers that she was not satisfied with the outcome of the surgery?

Even if surgery sometimes lessens dysphoria, the question must be raised: Is this the best standard of care? For example, if a person experiences body dysmorphic disorder and wishes to have a healthy limb amputated, could the surgical removal of the body part ease his dysphoria? It likely would. If a young anorexic woman is dysphoric about her weight, would a regimen of diet pills and liposuction perhaps make her feel less unhappy when she critiques herself in the mirror? Probably for a time. If a child feels dysphoric about school, would allowing him to drop out ease his anxiety? Without question! But is anyone convinced that any of these decisions are ultimately in the best interest of the individuals?

One large follow-up study of post-operative individuals concluded:

> Persons with transsexualism, after sex reassignment, have considerably higher risks for mortality, suicidal behavior, and psychiatric morbidity than the general population. Our findings suggest that sex reassignment, although alleviating gender dysphoria, may not suffice as treatment for transsexualism.[15]

Using a person's immediate feelings of relief as evidence to support irreversible bodily damage is bad medicine. After such a life-altering procedure, it can be difficult to objectively weigh the prudence of the decision. As one post-operative individual said, "I didn't really think about it because I was afraid that if I thought more about how this doesn't feel right, then I would realize that I was wrong, and I was afraid to realize that I was wrong because that would mean that I had made a horrible mistake. And that I had irreversibly changed certain aspects of my life."[16]

Because post-surgical depression is so common among those who attempt to transition, one social media trans influencer suggested that patients write themselves a letter of encouragement before surgery, "just so that your depression doesn't trick you into thinking it was a mistake, because it's not. You know that it's not."[17]

But perhaps the depression is worth listening to. Perhaps the restlessness is saying something meaningful that cries out for acknowledgment. After all, when most people awake after a typ-ical operation, they aren't fraught with depression or anxiety over whether they made the right decision.

For some individuals, feelings of regret and panic are immedi-ate. One recalled:

> I just like pretty much wish that I just never found out that like it [transitioning] was an option . . . I don't know what I was expecting, but it sure as hell wasn't this. I don't think people talk enough about how absolutely terrifying this surgery is and I wish I hadn't done this. I just kept going, "I want to go home. I want to go home. This was a mistake. I don't want to be here and I wish I hadn't done this." . . . I put so much money and time and effort into this, and knowing that it's irreversible and permanent and there's no going back.[18]

Many admit that the surgery didn't provide the relief they had anticipated. One patient remarked, "Phalloplasty for me has been a very traumatic experience. It's made me very suicidal. It's made me very depressed. It's made me feel very incomplete."[19] Similarly, Garrett recalled, "It felt like I had added something to my body that shouldn't have been there."[20] This only intensified a hyper-awareness toward his body, wondering if he could ever truly pass as a woman. He added, "It really made me hate my body a lot too because I'd always be like, 'Oh, my body looks so much like a man's,' which, like, duh. But it just made me really come to hate my body and so many facets of my body that I never hated before."

Meanwhile, other individuals report post-operative feelings of immediate euphoria. One woman remarked, "After every step that you take, every milestone, feels like a million bucks. When I got top surgery, I was elated. When I changed my name, I was elated. But when everything that I had set out to do was done, I still felt incom-plete."[21] Because no amount of hormones or surgery can change a person's sex, many describe their operations as a series of false summits, whereby the goal always seems close, but never within reach.

Such viewpoints aren't held merely by those who are unfairly labeled as "conservative transphobes." In fact, in 2016, President Obama's administration examined the possibility of allowing Medicaid Services and Medicare to cover the cost of gender surgeries. The resulting memo decided:

> Based on a thorough review of the clinical evidence available at this time, there is not enough evidence to determine whether gender reassignment surgery improves health outcomes for Medicare beneficiaries with gender dysphoria. There were conflicting (inconsistent) study results—of the best designed studies, some reported benefits while others reported harms.[22]

They added, "[T]he four best designed and conducted studies that assessed quality of life before and after surgery . . . did not demonstrate clinically significant changes or differences in psychometric test results after GRS [gender reassignment surgery]."[23]

Nonetheless, advocates of gender theory often cite a meta-analysis of twenty-eight studies that demonstrated that those who received surgeries "reported significant improvement in psychological symptoms." What often isn't mentioned is that the authors explained in the study that their results are based upon "Very low quality evidence."[24]

The prevailing assumption in culture is that individuals who are able to receive surgery will find relief, but the data shows that such an approach isn't working to solve the problem of dysphoria or suicide.[25] In fact, the longer the study and the more people who are included in it, the worse the outcomes are for the patient. Short-term studies aren't particularly illuminating when, according to the largest study on the subject, the increased mortality rate does not become apparent until about a decade after the surgery. Then, the mortality rate soars three times higher than the general population.[26]

Experimenting on children

According to the public health division of the state of Oregon, minors are forbidden to receive artificial tans. The statutes declare, "an entity doing business in this state as a tanning facility may not allow a person who is under 18 years of age to use a tanning device."[27] Therefore, any individual who appears under the age of 26 should "provide proof of their date of birth (DOB) and tanning operators are required to document the type of ID and the ID number on the client record." The only exception to this is when a minor has a written recommendation from his or her physician for the treatment of a medical condition.[28]

Meanwhile, the city of Portland believes that a twenty-year-old woman isn't old enough to responsibly decide if she want to get a small tattoo of a flower on her ankle.[29] If a tattoo parlor bends the rules and inks a person under twenty-one without parental consent, the business can lose its license. After all, the teenage brain has a very difficult time forecasting future outcomes of current behavioral choices, and this capacity won't be fully mature until individuals reach about twenty-five years of age.[30]

However, because the age of medical consent in Oregon is fifteen years old, girls can receive double mastectomies without parental permission.[31] In California, children who believe they are trans can have their breasts removed with parental permission at the age of twelve. Some states also will offer "gender-affirming" hysterectomies to sixteen-year-olds who feel dysphoric about having a uterus. Ironically, according to the National Women's Health Network, it is "incredibly unlikely" that any doctor would perform an elective hysterectomy on women under thirty-five years of age.[32] But if a woman identifies as trans, any number of "gender-affirming" doctors who promote their services on platforms like TikTok are willing to do so.

Many people assume that the debate raging over the topic of giving children and teens transgender medical intervention is between conservatives and liberals, between those on the "left" and the "right." However, there is fierce debate within the trans community over this topic as well, with some decrying it as an act of child abuse.

Meanwhile, others who do not identify as trans, such as Dr. Johanna Olson Kennedy, approve of thirteen-year-olds receiving double mastectomies. She reassures young people, "If you want breasts at a later point in your life, you can go and get them."[33] Dr. Patrick Lappert, a plastic surgeon, thinks otherwise. He remarked:

This is not a reversible procedure. The operation results in the permanent loss of the girl's ability to breastfeed. The breast mound can be reconstructed, as we do for women who have undergone mastectomy for cancer care, but what is being reconstructed is a breast mound, not a breast gland. The construct is not capable of producing nourishment for a baby.[34]

Nonetheless, Dr. Olson Kennedy argues that such interventions are vital:

So this idea that a fourteen, a fifteen-year-old would want a vagina if they identified as a girl is really not that out there. It's actually pretty understandable. Surgery, chest surgery for trans guys as minors is *critical*. . . . The difficulty of genital surgery is that it is surgical sterilization and people get super worked up about that. And that is the barrier that we have to overcome, and I think we're going to. But chest surgery is not that. It actually is a very easy, safe, relatively fast procedure that is absolutely life-saving.[35]

What's often overlooked is the millions of lives that are being erased by such procedures. Consider the impact of sterilization upon males alone. The average male has approximately two children in his lifetime.[36] In some countries, the average is as high as seven. However, if only 1,000 men receive "gender-affirming" sterilizations per year for one generation—and the global total is far higher than this—60,000 human beings will not come into existence because of their inability to procreate, and the 120,000 children they would have created will likewise not exist. Within five generations, approximately one million people will be missing. This is the result of only 1,000 male surgical sterilizations per year for one generation, and doesn't include females or the sterilizations induced by transgender medication.

The idea of having descendants, however, is hardly on the minds of young people. Nor is the thought of how infertility and bodily modifications might impact future relationships. Whereas half of adults who identify as trans desire to have children, when clinicians mention a future of sterility to young people who wish to transition, fewer than 3 percent seem to care.[37] It often isn't until many years after sterilization that the weight and permanence of the decision is felt, when many of their peers begin to start families. Years after one man's therapist unhesitatingly endorsed his decision to become infertile in an effort to affirm his transgender beliefs, he recorded his phone call with the therapist. In a rage, he confronted her to ask if she had studied the long-term psychological impact of the decision. She had not. He shouted, "I was mentally ill, and you let me dance in my delusion! And you would not tell me the truth. And now I'm infertile!"[38]

What such counselors and physicians overlook is that what might be seen as the cause of one's dysphoria at the age of fifteen can sometimes be the cure for it a decade later. One woman remarked, after pausing her transgender journey before surgery, "the self-hatred I had for my body was really resolved when I had a baby and they put this beautiful baby in my arms, and I looked at her and I thought, 'This is a pretty darn cool body I have.' And it was really the first time that I stopped having that dysphoria with my body."[39]

One can only imagine how many similar resolutions could be experienced if gender specialists promoted the inherent goodness of everyone's body. In the absence of such a mentality, surgeons become "service providers," expected to offer their skills on demand. For doctors such as Paul McHugh, who believe that doing so is "to collaborate with a mental disorder rather than to treat it,"[40] one quickly becomes a pariah.

But for those willing to compromise, significant profit awaits. According to economists, the market size of sex reassignment surgery in the United States alone is valued at more than $300 million and is projected to reach $1.5 billion by 2026.[41]

Dr. Michael K. Laidlaw explained:

Lupron monthly is US$775 alone. That's a $27,000 "pause button" at 5 years. Creating a pseudo-vagina is $25–30,000. Creating a pseudo-penis from arm skin flaps and forearm muscle and removing the ovaries and uterus can easily cost $30–40,000 and take multiple surgeries to complete. Not to mention complications and the need for repeat surgeries as Jazz Jennings has related. Multiply this together with the huge rise in cases documented or observed in Western nations and a major windfall is to be had.[42]

While "gender-affirming" physicians and pharmaceutical companies are positioned to reap the profits, many wonder where individuals can find the resources to afford lifelong medicalization. The California Insurance Commissioner believes that top surgery should be covered by insurance because it "corrects abnormal structures." Or, in the words of another advocate, it's "[l]ike fixing a birth defect."[43]

In other words, if a woman wishes to present in a less "womanly" way, by removing her breasts and injecting herself with testosterone, insurance ought to cover the expense. But what about the woman who is dysphoric about her body and wants to feel more "womanly"? Should insurance cover the cost of breast implants, liposuction, and facial reconstruction? Even if insurance does not cover either procedure, is there an ethical difference between the cosmetic enhancement of the body and the destruction of healthy body parts? While one might involve the vice of vanity, the other devalues the body.

Andrea Long Chu believes that individuals should be able to obtain medication and surgery, even if the person does not feel distressed about his or her gender. Andrea remarked, "And yet as things stand today, there is still only one way to obtain hormones and surgery: to pretend that these treatments will make the pain go away."[44] While this narrative has been unquestioned for some time, a coming tsunami of detransitioners are about to obliterate it.

Online groups comprised of tens of thousands of individuals who have halted their transition or begun to transition back to their sex are sounding the alarm through social media, testimonial videos, and online discussion forums.[45] They're reminding young people that if gender is so fluid, it's quite likely that individuals who wrestle with gender dysphoria, especially in their teens and twenties, could later identify as their biological sex and regret making unalterable physical changes. Detransitioners are also filing lawsuits against their former practitioners and are campaigning for future generations to receive a more balanced solution than the empty promises they had been given. In a survey of one hundred individuals who had medically or surgically transitioned, one of the most common reasons they offered for why they chose this path was, "I thought transitioning was my only option to feel better."[46] Detransitioners know that a better way exists, and many of them concur with Dr. Patrick Lappert, who remarked that this experiment "will likely be the greatest medical disaster of the last hundred years."[47]

12.

People who transition rarely express regret.

Studies have demonstrated that detransitioning is "exceedingly rare" and rates of regret for those who have transitioned are only 1 or 2 percent.[1] That's an incredible success, especially considering that the average regret rate for people who have knee replacement surgery is 20 percent![2]

In fact, one trans woman explained, "The so-called regret rate may not be actually a regret rate at all . . . because most people who detransition have been found to do so because of a hostile environment towards them being trans. So, they're not actually regretting it. It's just something they can't do right now because of the environment they're in."[3] If society wasn't so transphobic, "[W]e would see that Detransition rate drop even lower. . . . The important thing to say is that these people were never trans in the first place. . . . You don't stop being trans."[4]

Determining how many people express regret following their gender transition is not easy. Some transition only socially, while others do so medically or surgically. Meanwhile, some are dissatisfied with the cosmetic results of their surgery or hormonal treatments, but do not regret it. Others regret the choices, but still identify as trans. Still others have detransitioned in their identity and have ceased taking hormones but have not made any legal or surgical changes to undo their transition. For these reasons and more, it's inaccurate and simplistic to apply one statistic to all those who have explored various stages of transition.

But what about the claim that only 1 or 2 percent of all individuals who undergo reassignment surgery regret their choice? Studies that make such claims often lack validity due to four shortcomings:

First, there are no standardized measures for establishing results. For example, one of the most widely used statistics is that only 2.2 percent of individuals experience post-surgical regret.[5] However, this study counted only individuals who applied to change their legal documents to reflect their detransition. Carey Callahan, a female detransitioner said, "Moreover, that study defined a 'detransitioner' as someone who had changed their name and gender legally (an arduous process in Sweden at the time) and then had the motivation and money to go through the name change process in reverse, a standard so strict that I wouldn't be counted, and nor would 90% of the detransitioners I know."[6] Other surveys measure those who had surgical reversal procedures. But again, this would exclude most detransitioners.[7]

A second flaw that weakens the findings of many "low regret rate" studies is that they contain a small sample size. Some have as few as ten or twelve individuals.[8]

A third weakness of many of the studies is that they are based upon short follow-up times. Dr. Paul Rhodes Eddy noted, "The average timespan from a person's medical transition to taking steps to officially initiate detransition is somewhere between eight to eleven years."[9] However, many studies that show low rates of regret are conducted within five years of the operation, and some of them as little as five months.[10] Therefore, studies with shorter follow-up times will inevitably underestimate transition regret rates.

A fourth flaw is that these studies are often plagued by extremely high loss to follow-up rates. Many of the studies lost track of between 50 and 86 percent of the individuals![11] When determining how important this is to the validity of a study's findings, Dr. Joseph Dettori points out, "A good rule of thumb is that <5% loss leads to little bias, while >20% poses serious threats to validity. . . . One way to determine if loss to follow-up can seriously affect results is to assume a worst-case scenario with the missing data and look to see if the results would change."[12]

Richard Horton, the editor in chief of the medical journal *The Lancet* lamented that in recent years, there has been a significant downturn in the quality of modern scientific research. Speaking in general regarding this problem, he remarked, "Afflicted by studies with small sample sizes, tiny effects, invalid exploratory analyses, and flagrant conflicts of interest, together with an obsession for pursuing fashionable trends of dubious importance, science has taken a turn towards darkness. As one [person] put it, 'poor methods get results.'"[13]

Although it's difficult to determine an exact number of individuals who express post-surgical regret, it is generally agreed upon that somewhere between 60 and 90 percent of patients are satisfied with the results of their procedure.[14] But this still leaves a substantial subset of individuals who are dissatisfied. So, what's the motive behind minimizing the number and existence of detransitioners? One noted that detransitioners present a conundrum that's damaging to the revolutionary goals of gender theory:

- if they never actually had gender dysphoria then we need to be intensely scrutinizing the standard for diagnosing gender dysphoria
- if they did have gender dysphoria, but then it went away, we need to question the ethics of prescribing permanent bodily changes for what could be a temporary condition.[15]

Why detransition?

Just as people's motives vary as to why they choose to transition and to what degree they alter their bodies, those who detransition do so for a variety of reasons. It is often said that the majority do so because of persecution and the lack of support. However, surveys of detransitioners show that "[t]he three most commonly cited reasons for detransition among trans activists—financial concerns, lack of social support, and institutional discrimination were among the lowest, at 18%, 17%, and 7%—in fact, institutional discrimination was the lowest scoring category."[16]

On the other hand, one of the most common themes expressed by detransitioners is that the process never resolved their deeper issues. One woman explained:

"Being trans" on Tumblr was a fun distraction from the misery of my daily life. I still had next to no friends at my new school, I still had a bad relationship with my parents, I still hated my fat, but at least I could enter this alternate universe where I was a cool guy with lots of followers. It started being a lot less fun when I began pursuing transition in real life.[17]

Others shared similar sentiments:

It's become really clear in recent years that any sort of big problems that I thought I would fix by transitioning weren't really fixed.[18]

It was a waste of my money. It was a waste of my time. It was more time that I didn't do what I needed, which was [to] address my dissociative symptoms.[19]

Some realized after transitioning that their original motives were misguided attempts to grapple with their sexuality. One remarked, "My dysphoria was hatred of my body due to internalized misogyny."[20] In Newcastle, England, hundreds of young women have come forward, seeking help to detransition. What most of the women have in common is that they are either autistic or identify as lesbian.[21] Through a painful process of self-experimentation, they realized that they did not cease to be female just because they didn't fit the feminine mold. On the contrary, by attempting to pass as male, they were conforming to male stereotypes and reinforcing them.[22]

Meanwhile, others choose to detransition because they are dissatisfied with the results. One woman admitted, "Identifying as a male really made my dysphoria worse."[23] Another remarked that she knew if she continued trying to be a man, "I was going to give myself gender dysphoria eventually . . . which is really ironic."[24] Even after receiving chemical and surgical alterations to their bodies, many gaze into their mirrors each day with sorrow at a body that still disagrees with them.

The difficulty of detransitioning

When individuals begin to question whether they made the wrong decision to transition, they typically progress through a series of stages. Psychotherapist Stella O'Malley, who works with many such individuals, describes what she calls the "Arc of Detransition," which includes: Distress, Hope, Belonging, Euphoria, Expectation, Disappointment, Lost in Transition, Regret, Anger, and Detransition.[25]

For example, during the "Lost in Transition" stage, a man might think:

How am I supposed to go back? I didn't feel masculine enough before I took estrogen supplements and testosterone suppressing drugs. What am I supposed to do now that I feminized my body? How do I tell my co-workers? What do I say to my roommates? Some people don't even know that I'm male, and it was stressful enough the first time I tried to transition and pass. How are people going to look at me?

Such an individual is likely to feel overwhelmed, and it is therefore essential for families, friends, and faith communities to accompany him or her through the difficult transition. He or she may also wonder, "How can I make sense of the fact that so many people who cared for me during my darkest hours were helping me to hurt myself? How can I confront the pain of admitting that I did this to myself?" During such moments, one woman found solace in the fact that she wasn't the only one: "Knowing it's widespread throughout young millennials . . . and Gen Z helped me to have compassion for myself and not feel so stupid. A lot of us got sucked in."[26] Helena Kerschner concurred, "I feel like a cult survivor, a thousand percent. That cult robbed me of my adolescence."[27]

During the process of transitioning, individuals often find themselves alienated from family members and friends. In their place, they often discover a "gender-affirming" support system online or in their schools and communities. Should they detransition, they might fear being ostracized from the trans community and losing the only group that made them feel understood. The news of their decision might be difficult for their friends to hear, because it might make them question their own identity as trans.

Others within the trans community might argue that if a person is detransitioning, then he or she was never really trans in the first place. While this may feel invalidating, consolation can be found in accepting the truth of it. What they were in the first place—and will always be—is their given sex. Therefore, instead of wrestling with the idea of "Maybe I'm not really trans," they begin to accept "Maybe I'm not really the other sex."

While such social challenges can often be overcome in due time as the individuals seeks out new support networks, sometimes the more lasting obstacle to detransitioning is the effort that might be required to pass as one's own sex again. For a woman who has had a hysterectomy and the removal of her ovaries, she'll need hormonal supplements of estrogen for the rest of her life. Similarly, if a male's testes have been removed, he'll need testosterone supplements. He might also desire to have reconstructive surgery to his chest to reduce his enlarged breast tissue if he took estrogen. But for individuals who are already wearied by the toll of multiple surgeries and years of chemical treatments, they may feel that they've put their bodies through enough. Because the transition can be so difficult, some choose not to return to their biological sex but to identify as nonbinary, as a middle ground. One woman asked herself, "I'm not even going to pass as my own gender anymore?"[28]

Another lamented, "How do you go through yet another harrowing transition? What do you do? I've got no hair. I've got a beard . . . my body mutilated. How the hell do I go back to the Debbie that I was?"[29] The day she stopped taking testosterone, yet another woman said to herself, "I don't know if I'll ever look like a woman again. I don't know if I'll ever be seen as a woman again. But, regardless of the way other people see, me, I know that I need to do this for myself, not for anyone else. Not for society, not for men, not for trans folks."[30]

13.

Refusing to affirm a person's gender identity leads to suicide.

If a person identifies as trans, he or she should be affirmed in that identity and empowered to transition. When others refuse to do this, it causes unnecessary stress and anxiety to them. Gender identity is immutable, and that is why conversion therapy has been proven to be harmful and ineffective. Studies have shown that when parents and therapists try to change a person's gender, it doesn't work. Therefore, WPATH considers such "treatments" to not only be unsuccessful, but unethical.[1] On the other hand, research has shown that "There is no scientifically sound research showing negative impacts from providing gender-affirming care."[2]

No one chooses their gender identity; it's something they discover about themselves. What these individuals deserve is gender-affirmative care. As Julia Serano noted, "The only thing that has ever been shown to successfully alleviate gender dissonance is allowing the trans person to live in their identified gender."[3] Or, in the words of President Joe Biden, "To parents of transgender children, affirming your child's identity is one of the most powerful things you can do to keep them safe and healthy."[4]

The day before Yaeli Martinez took her life, her mother Abigail began feeling a pain in her chest accompanied by a premonition of sadness and anxiety about her daughter. Yaeli was a runaway who struggled with mental health issues, and years earlier had joined a trans advocacy group on her high school campus. The club informed Yaeli that if her mother would not support her transition, the state would pay for the transition procedures. All that needed to happen was for Abigail to lose custody of Yaeli.

Soon, the California's Department of Children and Family Services removed Yaeli and placed her into the foster care system. Each month, Abigail attended court hearings and begged for her daughter to at least be given a psychological evaluation because of her history of depression and suicidality. The judge denied her requests, and soon Yaeli began taking cross-sex hormones to manage her gender dysphoria.

One afternoon, after picking up her son from school, the young man asked his mother how she was feeling. Abigail replied, "I don't know. I'm just sad. I feel like I want to run away and scream but I don't know why." That night, she received a call that the police were searching for her daughter. Frantically, Abigail joined in the search until the authorities notified her that they had discovered her daughter's body on nearby train tracks. In tears, Abigail reflected, "You lose your mom, you're an orphan. You lose your husband, you're a widow. When you lose a child, there is no name and even when you breathe, it hurts."[5]

Stories like Yaeli's are tragically common within the transgender community. Parents and faith communities often clash with activists and schools regarding the best way to support individuals in such difficult circumstances. Trans advocates often paint those who disagree with gender theory as being hateful bigots, while those on the opposite side of the argument accuse trans advocates of being ignorant ideologues. What's often overlooked is that most people on both sides want the same thing: for individuals who experience gender dysphoria to be healthy and happy, free to live their most authentic life. However, they differ significantly in

what it means for a person to be his or her authentic self. Therefore, rather than vilifying the motives of those who hold opposing
viewpoints, a more fruitful approach is to allow the social science
to speak for itself.

When a person initially feels that their identity doesn't align
with their sex, the first stage of questioning is internal. Eventually,
if the discomfort persists, he or she begins to search for answers.
But because the topic can feel so mysterious and even shameful, the
investigative process typically begins alone, online. Online searches
for clues often lead to an anonymous community of other seekers
who find themselves at various stages of the same journey. For those
who are questioning their sexual identity, discussion forums and
social media influencers offer a smorgasbord of recommendations
that never would have been accessible prior to the internet.

Dr. Lisa Littman conducted a survey that revealed some of the
most common advice that young people received online:

> [H]ow to tell if they were transgender (54.2%); the reasons that
> they should transition right away (34.7%); that if their parents
> did not agree for them to take hormones that the parents were
> "abusive" and "transphobic" (34.3%); that if they waited to tran-
> sition they would regret it (29.1%); what to say and what not to
> say to a doctor or therapist in order to convince them to provide
> hormones (22.3%); that if their parents were reluctant to take
> them for hormones that they should use the "suicide narrative"
> (telling the parents that there is a high rate of suicide in trans-
> gender teens) to convince them (20.7%); and that it is acceptable
> to lie or withhold information about one's medical or psycho-
> logical history from a doctor or therapist in order to get hor-
> mones/get hormones faster (17.5%).[6]

One of the parents remarked, "The threat of suicide was huge
leverage. What do you say to that? It's hard to have a steady hand

and say no to medical transition when the other option is dead kid. She learned things to say that would push our buttons and get what she wanted and she has told us now that she learned that from trans discussion sites."[7]

Obviously, when any person makes a suicide threat, it must be taken seriously. Such an individual should be given an immediate and proper evaluation from a mental health professional. Unfortunately, when parents solicit the counsel of gender therapists, they often hear questions such as: "What would you rather have: A dead son or a live daughter?" In other words, "The only way to prevent self-harm is to accept that your child *is* trans and needs you to support the transition, whether it be social, hormonal, or surgical. As long as everyone goes along with this treatment pathway, the child will thrive."

This same story is promoted online to those questioning their identity as male or female. One woman, after having a hysterectomy and mastectomy at the age of twenty, said, "There's a very strong narrative that if you don't transition you are going to kill yourself. . . . I genuinely thought it was the only option."[8]

Some individuals and parents, upon reading such information, believe that social transitioning is the safest next step, to avoid self-harm. Unlike puberty blockers, cross-sex hormones, or surgery, social transitioning involves no medicalization. Some individuals may change their name, pronouns, attire, and restrooms. Some women, in order to appear less feminine, will wear a binder around their chest (which can cause permanent damage to one's breast tissue).[9] Sometimes, a person wrestling with gender dysphoria will opt for only a few of these changes and will then plateau, not desiring further steps to manage the dysphoria. Despite the popular narrative that social transitioning benefits gender dysphoric youth, evidence for the benefits of such an approach are lacking.[10] Rather, the key predictors of such a child's well-being are the quality of their peer relationships and family functioning.

While many people view social transitioning to be an exploratory season, research shows that it can be difficult to reverse, once initiated. The daily affirmation of a child's perceived gender has a solidifying effect on a child's belief system. Through a person's repeated imitation of the other sex, they become conditioned to be treated as such by others. But how is an individual to go back upon his or her declaration that their gender identity is something other than their sex? It takes an extraordinary amount of effort and risk to change one's name, pronoun, restrooms, and sports teams (if a person chooses to make all of those changes). Imagine going to such lengths, and then later changing one's mind and needing to declare to everyone: "Never mind." As a result, social transitioning is associated with persistence.[11]

If social transitioning could lead to persisting in one's declared gender identity, and this sometimes leads to the use of puberty blockers, cross-sex hormones, and surgery, one question remains: What is the long-term outcome for individuals who choose such a path?

Suicidality

According to the National Transgender Discrimination Survey, the suicide rate for those who identify as trans or nonconforming is an astonishing 41 percent.[12] Although some researchers question the accuracy of this statistic, and others have pointed out that the suicide rate of gender dysphoric patients is comparable to psychiatric patients in general, any population with a high suicidality deserves serious consideration.[13] Dr. Lappert observed, "That is an unimaginably high risk of death. There is nothing to compare with it. Returning war veterans with PTSD and rape victims each have about a 27% risk of suicide. It is startling to consider that the transgender person is suffering from emotional wounds that vastly surpass the effects of prolonged combat and rape."[14]

Following surgery, one might expect that these numbers would decrease. However, the largest study to date, conducted on thousands of individuals over a period of thirty years, demonstrated the opposite effect. The authors stated, "This study found substantially higher rates of overall mortality, death from cardiovascular disease and suicide, suicide attempts, and psychiatric hospitalizations in sex-reassigned transsexual individuals compared to a healthy control population."[15] They also noted, "Female-to-males, but not male-to-females, had a higher risk for criminal convictions than their respective birth sex controls."[16]

Following gender reassignment surgery, individuals became nineteen times more likely to commit suicide than the general population, and when the female-to-male transitioners are isolated, their suicide rate is a staggering forty times higher than the control group.

Although the study was not intended to demonstrate that surgery contributes to suicide rates, the authors noted, "Further, we cannot exclude therapeutic interventions as a cause of the observed excess morbidity and mortality."[17] So, although the study should not be used to argue that surgery leads to suicide, what's clear is that surgery does not sufficiently reduce the preexisting risk of self-harm. This is because underlying issues remain unaddressed and might be compounded by the bodily damage caused by the surgery. As endocrinologist Paul Hruz explained, "Yet gender affirmation, by failing to address underlying psychosocial needs, might possibly lead to a real increase in suicide."[18] There are other likely contributors as well, including the complexities of living post-transition and the ongoing hormonal interventions.

In response to the high rate of suicidality among the trans population, advocates of gender theory consider only one possible cause: transphobes. If only people were more accepting, the argument goes, those who identify as trans would not harm themselves with such tragic frequency. This proposal, known as the "social stress" hypothesis, is not without merit. Stigmatization, bullying, and rejection from families and faith communities would certainly contribute to feelings of hopelessness.[19] However, the study that reported the 41 percent suicide risk also noted, "The survey data did not allow us to determine a direct causal relationship between experiencing rejection, discrimination, victimization, or violence, and lifetime suicide attempts."[20]

Doctors Paul McHugh and Lawrence Meyer explain, "Studies show that while social stressors do contribute to the increased risk of poor mental health outcomes for these populations, they likely do not account for the entire disparity."[21] If the problem of suicidality and poor mental health outcomes could be resolved by creating a more culturally friendly environment for individuals who identify as trans, one would expect better results from more tolerant societies. But this is not the case, as can be seen from the dismal results in Sweden and the Netherlands.[22] Similarly, in the United States, Dr. Jay Greene pointed out, "Lowering legal barriers to make it easier for minors to undergo cross-sex medical interventions without parental consent does not reduce suicide rates—in fact, it likely leads to higher rates of suicide among young people in states that adopt these changes."[23]

The problem of poor mental health outcomes and suicide is largely the result of the fact that more than 90 percent of people who commit suicide have a psychiatric diagnosis.[24] Therefore, it is an oversimplification to blame intolerant cultures for the poor results of gender reassignment treatments. The core problem could be that legitimate underlying mental health issues are not being addressed.

In fact, there seems to be a deliberate effort to avoid such issues. In the words of Dr. Joanna Olson Kennedy, "It has to stop being . . . a mental health issue. The mental health piece of it comes from the way that the outside world responds to these young people."[25] During a presentation at the European Professional Association for Transgender Health, Aydin Olson-Kennedy, a female-to-male trans advocate who is espoused to Dr. Joanna, explained to gender clinicians that gender dysphoria might present itself as depression, anxiety, poor family relationships, feeling lonely, autism, and so on. In other words, gender dysphoria is the core issue, and if that's addressed, the other problems should resolve.[26]

Actually, the opposite is true: gender dysphoria is often one among other mental health issues and life challenges faced by such individuals. In her research of young people, Dr. Lisa Littman found that more than 60 percent of them "had one or more diagnoses of a psychiatric disorder or neurodevelopmental disability preceding the onset of gender dysphoria."[27] Some of the most common ones include major depressive disorder, specific phobia, adjustment disorder, autism, and anxiety. According to research of more than 1000 children and adolescents published by the American Academy of Pediatrics, psychological disorders were seven times higher among trans-believing youth *prior to any sign of gender dysphoria*. Psychological hospitalizations were between 22 and 44 times higher, reports of self-harm were between 70 and 144 times higher, and suicidal ideation was between 25 and 54 times higher—before any sign of gender dysphoria.[28]

Surgery and cross-sex hormones are not effective treatments for any of these comorbidities, and this is one reason why such procedures have not been effective in solving the problem of suicide (or gender dysphoria) among the transgender population.[29] The same could be said for chemical transitioning. Research by the largest gender clinic in the United Kingdom showed no decrease in suicide or self-harm among young people who took puberty blockers.[30] In fact, individuals who experience gender dysphoria have similar outcomes as those who have the same mental health issues without gender dysphoria. When the empty promises of gender medicine fail to materialize, many patients are left to conclude, as did the following twenty-two-year-old detransitioner, that "[t]he whole thing about transition being 'lifesaving' and making everything better was starting to not make sense in my mind."[31]

Many doctors who care for individuals who experience gender dysphoria are aware of this information and have met with stiff resistance upon raising such concerns within their institutions. Thirty-five psychologists resigned from the largest gender clinic in the UK because they were unable to properly explore underlying psychological factors.[32] Even trans advocates, such as Buck Angel, have expressed their opposition, arguing that fast-tracking young people into transitioning by telling them "You're gonna die if you don't transition" is "complete, total nonsense."[33] Or, in the words of endocrinologist Dr. William Malone, "Eventually the consequences of the application of this bad idea will be so evident that any except the extreme ideologues will be forced to accept what's happened."[34]

Therapy works

If social, medical, and surgical transitioning aren't the solution to gender dysphoria, what is the alternative? Despite the common objection that "conversion therapy" is harmful and ineffective, there are no reliable studies on "gender identity change efforts" for adults.[35] Some studies exist that show the harmful effects of attempting to coerce adults to change their sexual attractions. But a person's sexual attractions are not the same as his or her transgender beliefs. In addition, Dr. Paul Eddy points out, "[P]ro LGBTQ+ researchers have been reluctant to seriously investigate the efficacy of sexual orientation change efforts (SOCE) because of concerns about what conservatives would do with the findings."[36]

The term "conversion therapy" is a phrase loaded with rhetorical bias. Using it creates a false binary, that there are only two approaches to assisting individuals who experience gender dysphoria: to affirm them in their transition or to harm them by any other therapeutic means. Drs. Paul Eddy and Preston Sprinkle point out, "Any attempt to align one's internal sense of self with their body is considered to be a harmful 'conversion.' But this imports some profound anthropological assumptions into the meaning of *conversion*."[37]

They sum up the prevailing biased attitude toward the treatment of gender dysphoria:

> One *either* adopts the scientifically informed, attitudinally open-minded, and ethically kind and virtuous "affirmative" model that simply trusts the child's inner sense of self as offering the epistemologically privileged, and thus singularly reliable, truth of the matter. *Or* one adopts the (binary) alternative: the scientifically outdated, attitudinally narrow-minded and bigoted, and ethically uncaring and harmful "conversion therapy" model that coercively attempts to "change" the child's gender identity to fit with the therapist's own religiously or psychiatrically prejudiced gender norms. Now, cast in this mode, the rhetorical question woven within this binary narrative doesn't even have to be explicitly stated: *What thinking, competent, and even mildly decent therapist would ever choose anything other than the affirmative model?*"[38]

But as stated above, this is a false binary. For example, some who identify as trans are not interested in medical transitioning and might seek ways to manage dysphoria without medicalization. Some aren't interested in transitioning for a variety of reasons and many do not view a lifetime of hormonal treatments to be the only way to relieve their distress.

Those who promote the notion that "gender-affirmative" therapy is the only ethical pathway for treatment often make this claim based on the premise that gender is innate and unchanging. Yet at the same time, they strive to defend the narrative that gender is fluid. In the words of Kate Bornstein, "Gender fluidity is the ability to freely and knowingly become one or many of a limitless number of genders, for any length of time or rate of change."[39] Or, as

Julia Serano explained, "[T]he majority of the transgender people I know understand that our experiential gender is potentially fluid and often changes over time as we accumulate new experiences."[40] Therefore, if one's internal sense of gender identity isn't always fixed, why would it not be possible for therapists to assist clients to realign their identity with their sex?

Many psychologists have found counseling effective in this regard. This is not about dismissing the intensity and reality of one's dysphoric feelings. Rather, it involves taking a deeper look at the challenges being faced by the individual who is experiencing such feelings. Psychiatrist Susan Bradley noted that many who transition and reflect with regret upon their decision often say, "I wish somebody had understood me from a psychological point of view and didn't just take at face value that I thought this was the answer to how I was feeling."[41] Or, as Dr. Deborah Soh asks, "If a gender dysphoric person is not experiencing a mental health disorder, why do they need to transition to feel better?"[42]

Counseling has been proven to help individuals who experience gender dysphoria, in some cases to experience greater alignment to their biological sex.[43] It can involve therapy for coexisting psychological issues, parental counseling, talk therapy, and other forms of counseling. In a follow-up study by Dr. Kenneth Zucker and colleagues, of the twenty-five young women who had been treated by psychological interventions, gender dysphoria persisted in only three of the patients.[44]

Especially for children, for a long time the standard approach was "watchful waiting."[45] Although this term is easily misunderstood to imply passivity, it is not about withholding treatment. It's about seeking resolution to gender dysphoria in the least invasive means possible. In fact, Dr. James Cantor points out that "almost all clinics and professional associations in the world use what's called the *watchful waiting* approach to helping gender diverse (GD) children."[46] Despite this gentle approach that has become widely adopted by mental health professionals across the globe, Dr. Zucker, another proponent of this approach, was maligned by radical trans activists as a "transphobic doctor who supports repression and torture of gender-variant children."[47]

Unfortunately, in some places, laws forbid insurance companies to cover any therapy that seeks to align a person's identity with his or her sex.[48] In the United States, more than a dozen states have enacted laws that prohibit therapists from counseling with this as a desired outcome, at the risk of losing their license to practice. According to this mindset, the only forms of therapy that are affirming and supportive for individuals are the ones that approve of one's transition.

But in the words of Ryan Anderson, "It's an Orwellian abuse of language to say that helping a child be comfortable in his own body is 'conversion therapy,' but transforming a boy into a 'girl' is simply allowing the child to be 'her' true self."[49]

14.

Gender identity is innate.

It's hurtful and invalidating to claim that something would cause a person to be trans. Just as nothing causes cisgender individuals to identify with their biological sex, nothing causes a person to be trans. It's just who they are. They deserve to be appreciated and celebrated for having the courage to be their authentic selves, not psychologically dissected and erased. As Julia Serano remarked, "Unlike those cissexual researchers who find it fascinating and thought-provoking to ponder and pontificate on my existence, for me the question of why I am transsexual has always been a source of shame and self-loathing. . . . Eventually, I realized that dwelling on 'why' was a pointless endeavor."[1]

"I don't *want* to be a boy. I *am* boy." Parents often aren't sure what to think when their five-year-old girl makes such a declaration. She hasn't been influenced by YouTubers or activist groups, but she's adamant that she *is* male. Sometimes what young children mean by this statement is that they relate better to the other sex or enjoy doing the activities that are stereotypically performed by the other sex. But for some children, the feelings go deeper, and they persist. This is called early-onset gender dysphoria.

Other times, a person might not experience any feeling of incongruence between their sex and their identity until much later in life. What both individuals have in common is that if they seek guidance from a gender clinic, they're likely to hear the same newly created diagnosis: you *are* trans. Searching for contributing factors that might have played a role in one's gender dysphoria is considered insensitive because it implies that the individual might feel otherwise if their life had been different. The very idea of proposing psychological roots that might lay beneath one's transgender beliefs might cause an individual to feel invalidated instead of understood.

But what if a middle path could be struck? What if individuals could explore life experiences that may have impacted their sense of sexual identity without feeling shamed or invalidated? If such a path could be established, a few ground rules would need to be set. First, one would need to acknowledge that each person's experience of his or her body and identity is unique. For example, some people experience dysphoria inside-out (dysphoria of their identity first, and their body second), while others report outside-in (dysphoria of the body first, and identity next). Because each person's story is different, it is important that no one is made to feel dismissed because others do not share the same experience. Each person deserves to be heard. For this reason, taking a cookie-cutter or one-size-fits-all explanation to gender dysphoria is narrow-minded and harmful.

Also, rather than trying to pin down the origins of another's beliefs about gender entirely in nature or nurture, it's better to avoid both extremes and accept that each person is shaped in varying degrees by both factors. To be fair, it is unrealistic to believe that people who experience gender dysphoria are immune from having their sense of identity shaped by external experiences, personality traits, and personal choices. Such experiences, rather than invalidating a person's authentic self, can help all individuals to grow in self-knowledge.

Research shows that gender dysphoria is often one point of a constellation of challenges or mental health issues that individuals within the trans community battle. While it is true that gender dysphoria can cause anxiety and depression, a study published in *The American Journal of Psychiatry* showed that most individuals who experience gender dysphoria have another psychiatric disorder, and the gender-related distress is more often than not a symptom of the other mental illness.[2] They suffer from higher rates of autistic spectrum disorder, dissociative disorder, anxiety, depression, borderline personality disorder, schizophrenia, obsessive compulsive disorder, and ADHD.[3] Some have experienced significant amounts of trauma, and for these individuals, some clinicians believe that dissociating from one's body is a trauma response, a way of expressing distress.

When viewed through this lens, a desire to transition can sometimes be an adaptation, a way to recreate oneself to survive. Fluidity expresses resiliency. Consider the physical properties of water: Its strength is revealed by its ability to change shape when external forces act against it, so that it remains unbroken.

Regardless of what may be influencing an individual's shift in identity, the question to ask is: What is my gender dysphoria telling me? In asking this question, there's no intention of invalidating a person's experience, but precisely the opposite. Rather than offering a simplistic answer of "You're trans," and flattening all the layers and complexities that may be involved, listening to one's dysphoria with mercy gives the individual a chance to see where these clues may lead. Often, it is a road map toward deep healing. Taking this approach requires individuals to be brave enough to move beyond hatred for one's body to examine the stories or traumas that may have moved them toward transitioning as a survival mechanism. It's about having compassion for oneself rather than judgment.[4]

What's safe to say is that no one has all the answers. No one fully understands the causal pathways of the development of transgender beliefs, and no theory explains everything. But if people on all sides of the debate can listen to one another and learn, much progress could be made to offer better care for individuals who express distress in this area of life.

Below are a nearly a dozen different factors that can sometimes influence a person's sense of sexual identity. Rather than saying any of these things "cause gender dysphoria," it is more accurate to say that they could contribute to a person feeling dysphoric about his or her body. Some individuals might find that some of the factors resonate deeply with them, while others might not relate to any of them. The goal isn't to provide an exhaustive list, but to encourage individuals who experience gender dysphoria to listen with compassionate curiosity to their own story.

Stereotype anxiety

According to an article by Dr. Robert Leahy published in *Psychology Today*, "The average high school kid today has the same level of anxiety as the average psychiatric patient in the early 1950s."[5] Consider the societal pressure that young women experience to conform to an idyllic standard of womanhood: They're expected to be skinny (but healthy), irresistibly sexy (but modest), assertive (but submissive), and professional (but domestic). They endlessly compare themselves against filtered images of others online, often ending each day with their faces aglow in the dark of their rooms alone, scrolling through photos and videos of others who seem to have better lives, better bodies, better hair, and better relationships. Exhausted and often disappointed in themselves, they finally fall asleep much later than they should have, only to wake up hours later, reaching again for the screen that never fails to disappoint them. Overwhelmed and discouraged by their inability to measure up to stereotypical gendered expectations, many young women would rather opt out of the competition altogether. Abigail Shrier explained that "they sense a dangerous chasm lies between the unsteady girls they are and the glamorous women social media tells them they should be. Bridging that gap feels hopeless."[6]

Likewise, some young men question their sexual identity if they fall short of culture's masculine archetype. Or perhaps their interests and hobbies didn't align with typical stereotypical things that guys are "supposed" to be interested in. When individuals sense an incongruence between their personality and the societal expectations of their sex, it may feel easier to question if they were "born into the wrong body" rather than challenge rigid gender stereotypes.

Pope Francis noted, "Such rigidity, in turn, can hinder the development of an individual's abilities, to the point of leading him or her to think, for example, that it is not really masculine to cultivate art or dance, or not very feminine to exercise leadership."[7] But the solution isn't to change one's body or to eliminate sexual distinctions, but to avoid over-accentuations of it. The pope added, "I ask myself, if the so-called gender theory is not, at the same time, an expression of frustration and resignation, which seeks to cancel out sexual difference because it no longer knows how to deal with it. Yes, we risk taking a step backward. The removal of difference in fact creates a problem, not a solution."[8]

A healthier approach is to acknowledge that a person is not defined by his or her ability to conform to gender stereotypes. Dr. Deborah Soh shared, "I have always been male-typical, and to this day, despite looking very feminine, I still feel much more masculine. As a child, anytime I wore a dress, I remember feeling as though something was very wrong. My childhood friends were all boys because I was more interested in play fighting (and winning) than putting on lipstick and organizing tea parties."[9]

Nonetheless, she understood that her "tomboy" personality did not make her any less of a woman. Lacking such a stable sense of self, many young people become unnecessarily preoccupied with the question of gender. Some even find solace in the idea of being nonbinary. However, this only reinforces the myth of rigid gender stereotypes. How is a culture to overcome the problem of such stereotypes if the solution is to evacuate from sex altogether? Is there no room in the world for women who don't fit the mold of a super-feminine supermodel? Is it that unbearable for our culture to have men who don't personify stereotypical masculinity?

Because individuals who self-identify as nonbinary don't identify with either sex and find themselves somewhere in between or outside of these categories, they can be somewhat nomadic in their sense of self. Believing that humans can be something other than male or female is a recipe for restlessness. After all, it is impossible to arrive at a place that does not exist.

Internalized homophobia

Many detransitioners look back upon their experience with gender dysphoria and believe that their attempt to change their sexual identity was a misdirected attempt to navigate the complexities of their same-sex attractions. Helen Joyce explained that males who are sexually attracted to other males "are often highly gender non-conforming in childhood, and may develop gender dysphoria and a cross-sex identification if their culture is insufficiently accommodating."[10] Homosexual desires can be challenging to understand at a young age, and those who experience such urges might be unsure how to process them. Declaring oneself to be trans can sometimes feel like the solution.[11] In fact, one study showed that 41 percent of adolescents and young adults "expressed a non-heterosexual sexual orientation before identifying as transgender."[12]

For example, a young man who is attracted to other males and has struggled to ascend the hierarchical social structure of masculinity might find refuge in an identity that allows him to be more feminine. If he has been belittled by other males for his effeminate mannerisms, identifying as a woman might afford him the ability to attract some members of the sex that had bullied him.[13]

Attraction toward other males is known as androphilia, and it may also involve a longing to be desired as a woman.[14] Dr. Daryl Bem, a social psychologist, popularized a theory that within human sexuality, the exotic becomes the erotic.[15] In other words, humans are created to unite with the "other," and they desire to forge attachments to fulfill unmet needs. Some have theorized that if a male feels alienated from his own manhood, masculinity becomes the "other" to which he feels drawn. As a result, he may sexualize his need for masculine approval, acceptance, and affection. But if he is afraid to acknowledge his same-sex attractions, he might find that some of his unmet needs can be met by transitioning to a female identity.

While this may seem far-fetched to some, there are cultures in which it has become the norm. Take, for example, Iran. This Middle Eastern nation with strict regulations regarding gender roles and behavior surprisingly has the highest rate of sex reassignment surgeries in the world. The reason for this is not because the culture celebrates diversity. Rather, it's because homosexuality is punishable by death. If one surgically reassigns one's sex, he or she can avoid this penalty because their lifestyle appears heterosexual. As one woman remarked, "Transitioning to male would mean my attraction to girls would be 'normal.'"[16]

Sometimes, a similar prejudice is found within families. Although it is not common, some young men who experience same-sex attractions have found greater acceptance within their families after transitioning to a female identity, because then "they didn't have a gay son, they had like a straight daughter."[17] These forms of internalized homophobia contribute to some people undergoing hormonal and surgical alterations of their bodies. But as feminist Mary Lou Singleton remarked, "The medical transitioning of children is gay conversion therapy on steroids, literally."[18]

Sexual abuse

When a person experiences something as traumatic as sexual abuse, he or she often develops survival strategies to cope with the pain and avoid future trauma. Some of these strategies to escape pain are helpful, but others are misdirected. Dr. Lisa Littman explains, "A maladaptive coping mechanism is a response to a stressor that might relieve the symptoms temporarily but does not address the cause of the problem and may cause additional negative outcomes."[19]

One such example of a maladaptive coping mechanism after sexual abuse is to dissociate from one's body. For some, this is a way to distance oneself from negative memories. One young woman who was sexually assaulted her sophomore year of college said, "It absolutely contributed to just this feeling that I wanted to take my body off."[20] Another remarked, "I was deeply uncomfortable with my secondary sex characteristics, which I now understand was a result of childhood trauma and associating my secondary sex characteristics with those events."[21]

For others, dissociating from one's sex is a defense mechanism to become undesirable to those who might repeat the offense. One young woman, after having suffered sexual abuse, decided to gain weight and begin presenting as male. She said, "Nobody would bother me now."[22] Similarly, younger girls may disguise the evidence of their sexual maturation in order to feel safe in an unsafe world. One such girl made an internal vow after her abuse, saying, "I will never let that happen again. If I am a boy, that won't happen again."[23] Others desire to appear neither male nor female, finding a sense of safety in the ambiguity of existing somewhere in between. When a woman is wounded in such a deeply personal way, she may lose all interest in the idea of being sexually intimate with a man. In the absence of such attractions, she may conflate lack of sexual desire with questions about her identity.

Each person who experiences sexual trauma will respond in a unique way, and each deserves careful and compassionate treatment as they navigate through memories of the past and anxieties about the future. But the path to healing must eventually acknowledge that the abuse was not caused by one's body. To believe this is to absorb blame that belongs only to the abuser.

Bullying

In an article on treating children who experience gender dysphoria, Dr. Kenneth Zucker shared the story of Frank. Frank was bullied by an older brother, generalized his aggression to all other boys, and began primarily associating with girls. By the age of five, he expressed a desire to become female, stating that all his problems would go away if he were a girl. At the age of seven, Frank's parents brought him to a gender clinic because he said that he thought he was a girl.

Dr. Zucker's treatment plan for him involved helping him to recognize that there are many ways to be a boy, and that there are likely some other boys in his social setting who aren't like his brother. Exposing Frank to boys like himself could "help him to develop a more nuanced understanding of gender: that there are different ways to be a boy, that one does not have to be a girl as a fantasy solution to cope with his difficulties with his aggressive brother."[24]

Similarly, parents of a twelve-year-old girl who had been bullied for going through an early puberty reported that "as a result she said she felt fat and hated her breasts," but learned online that hating her breasts was a sign of being transgender.[25] When young people are not given healthy strategies to address rejection, insecurities, abandonment, and verbal wounds, they may absorb the scorn of those who mistreat them. One cannot blame them for considering gender transition as a path away from their pain. As one noted, "I was very impulsive. I was so desperate for a fix that when I first found out that transgender might be a thing, I kind of latched on to it. . . . The information that I got made it seem like I could change who I was."[26]

Trauma

As mentioned above, when individuals suffer a significant trauma in life, they may dissociate as a defense mechanism.[27] One young woman who had been bullied because of her same-sex attractions, and who experienced the death of her mother, explained why she initially decided to transition: "I also see a connection between my decision to transition and my mom's suicide. She killed herself when I was twenty and I started hormones about three months after she killed herself. We greatly physically resembled each other, and I think one of my motivations for changing my body is I wanted to differentiate myself from her."[28]

Another young woman who witnessed the murder of her mother deduced from the experience that she would be safer and stronger as a man. The idea of becoming stronger is a common theme among some young women who aim to transition. In the words of Alex, "I have my imaginary world and that's one of my coping strategies. When I'm feeling down or depressed, I'll kind of like go into my imaginary world, and in my imaginary world I am a guy. I have a flat chest. I'm strong."[29] Similarly, when Kathy Grace was young, she remembers watching her father abuse her mother and internalized the message that women are hated, vulnerable, and weak.[30] For her, establishing a masculine gender identify offered her protection from being victimized.

In one study of children and teens who visited a gender clinic in Australia, 98 percent of them had experienced adverse childhood events before developing transgender beliefs. The researchers found an average of five traumas per child, most of which occurred within the family. They noted that because it can be difficult to untangle gender dysphoria from comorbid factors such as anxiety, depression, and sexual abuse, "Our results suggest the need to bring into play a biopsychosocial, trauma-informed model of mental health care for children presenting with gender dysphoria."[31]

Pornography

Although many people assume that nearly all pornography is consumed by males, current studies show that approximately three of four women have viewed it within the past six months.[32] However, more than 80 percent of the most popular porn videos involve the violent degradation of women.[33] When young girls witness adult women being humiliated, objectified, and abused, it is understandable that they might feel disgusted and afraid of sexual intimacy. When they see impossible standards of sexualized beauty, they are likely to devalue their own attractiveness.

How might these things relate to a young woman's sense of gender? In a survey of one hundred detransitioners, 71 percent of women who medically or surgically transitioned said that they did so because "[i]t made me uncomfortable to be perceived romantically/sexually as a member of my natal sex/natal gender."[34] A young women who experiences a significant amount of anxiety regarding her sexuality and identity might fixate on the possibility of becoming another gender as a method of curbing her anxious thoughts. It becomes an escape from sexism, objectification, and societal or romantic expectations.

Pornography can also trigger and exacerbate gender dysphoria by introducing images that otherwise would never have been seen. Those who spend countless hours immersed in online pornographic content eventually stumble upon genres of porn that they had never expected or imagined, including trans content. The toxic cocktail of curiosity, shame, and arousal might lead them to seek out more of the same. But when the fog of sensuality dissipates and they're left alone in their disappointment, they're likely to wonder why they felt such fascination for something they never initially desired.

Family dynamics

Although many children who experience gender dysphoria come from stable and loving homes, research shows that parents of gender dysphoric children often exhibit high levels of psychopathology.[35] When a parent's mental health is unsound, children can form insecure or anxious attachments to them. Similarly, gender dysphoric young people are more likely to report coming from a family structure other than living with their biological mother and father.[36] But if children do not form healthy bonds with their parents, they miss an important step in establishing their own sense of sexual identity, and may form insecure or disorganized attachment patterns.[37] For example, one study showed that three out of four boys who experience gender dysphoria exhibit an insecure attachment to their mothers.[38]

Various situations can contribute to unhealthy attachments related to gender dysphoria.[39] One is when parents hope for their baby to be a sex other than the one they receive. If this is expressed to a child, he or she may internalize the parent's disappointment regarding his or her sex. Sometimes the child is the sex that the parent had hoped for, but wasn't what they had expected. For example, as a little girl, Heather Skriba enjoyed playing with action figures and camouflage, which created tension between her and her father. He said to her, "I always wish that I had a daddy's girl as a daughter." Heather recalled:

> What that communicated to my eight-year-old heart was like I'm not the daughter that my dad wants. Being around my version of femininity brings my dad pain, like it's defective, it's not good enough, and I internalized that as my identity, as my value. So that caused me to develop a lot of social anxiety, a lot of insecurity, a ton of self-hatred.[40]

Later, she realized after trying to transition that it wasn't just a hatred and discomfort about her sexual identity, it was a discomfort in who she was as a person. In her words, "It wasn't just, 'I don't like being a woman,' it was like 'I don't like being me.' . . . At the end of the day it was like this tired, lonely, really hurt little girl who just needed love."

Another common scenario is when a child perceives that their sibling of the other sex receives more attention and love. A child might conclude from this that his or her sex is an obstacle to being loved. In the case of one three-year-old boy whose sister had special needs and required additional care, the boy wanted to become female, and declared, "Mommy and daddy, you don't love me when I'm a boy."[41]

Walt Heyer, who transitioned to a female identity as an adult and detransitioned eight years later, recalled that as a child, his grandmother fawned over him whenever she dressed him as a girl, but never affirmed him as a boy. Eventually, he brought the dress home from her house and would put it on when no one was around, to "maybe get those same feelings back that grandma would make me feel."[42] He said it was a "marvelous distraction for a while,"[43] but his underlying issues remained unaddressed. Walt was later diagnosed with a dissociative disorder that originated in the sexual abuse he suffered from his uncle and the confusion caused by the grandmother who cross-dressed him.

Body image distress

Body dysmorphic disorder is a mental health condition in which a person spends an inordinate amount of time and energy obsessing over his or her physical imperfections. This condition is distinct from gender dysphoria, and the presence of one diagnosis rules out the other. Whereas body dysmorphia tends to focus on one part of the body, gender dysphoria is more generalized. However, one can experience traits of both conditions.

Struggles regarding body image predominantly, although not exclusively, affect females and involve persistent feelings of inadequacy tied to anxiety. Although nearly all adolescent females sometimes feel uncomfortable with their bodies, some experience profound levels of distress. One shared about her desire to receive top surgery, "You have to understand that this is something that like from the day that I began puberty I've just longed for, with never a day that I liked my chest, and never a day that I thought it was great to have."[44] Another observed, "I think women may be more likely to locate suffering and take out forms of pain and suffering on their bodies."[45]

For some, the goal is to become male. One remarked, "I was born a female, and I decided, Oh, this sucks. I want to be a guy."[46] Others, however, aren't interested in identifying into manhood; rather, their desire is to opt out of womanhood. For both, the body often becomes the target of one's angst. Because complex struggles such as depression, self-loathing, and anxiety can be difficult to battle against, it can be alluring to lock onto the idea that one's body is the problem. With a clear target now within one's sights, a young woman might feel that she's no longer fighting a ghost. If she can pinpoint her unhappiness on her body, she might feel temporarily liberated from needing to address the elusive deeper issues. One might even begin to retroactively assign the body as the sole origin of one's distress, thus becoming preoccupied with it. After all, it's much easier to admit that you don't like your body when the deeper reality might be that you don't like yourself.

Ben, a detransitioned woman, had a friend who struggled with body dysmorphia unrelated to her sexual identity. The friend discovered a therapist who successfully treated her by using cognitive behavioral therapy and dialectical behavioral therapy. When she asked her gender therapist if they could try some of the same methods to help relieve her gender dysphoria, the counselor was baffled by the request and instructed her to just keep it together until she could get her cross-sex hormones.[47] Thankfully, many counselors who assist people who struggle with gender dysphoria realize that these methods are often very helpful for them as well.[48]

Autism

Although only 1 percent of the general population is autistic, 42 percent of those who identify as transgender or nonbinary meet the criteria for an autism diagnosis.[49] Autism is often characterized by rigid, black-and-white thinking patterns, and a difficulty or discomfort with nuance. Individuals on the autistic spectrum often exhibit a deep fixation and focus on a particular idea or activity, and may express strong anxiety about any interference with the subject of interest. They may struggle with a lack of insight into their own feelings and wrestle with the social challenges of not fitting in with others. Because of their social limitations, they often find online communication easier than face-to-face interactions.[50]

It isn't difficult to see how some of these characteristics might predispose an adolescent who is uncertain about her place in the world to fixate on gender transitioning as a simplistic solution to the complex challenges of her life.

Autogynephilia

After taking cross-sex hormones and preparing for gender reassignment surgery, James Shupe decided that he could never pass as a woman, and began pushing to have the government officially recognize his sex as nonbinary. In 2016, he became the first American to do so, when an Oregon judge declared his status, enabling him to be granted a new birth certificate that stated that his sex was "unknown."

However, in 2019, James reclaimed his legal status as male. In an article entitled, "I Was America's First 'Nonbinary' Person. It Was All a Sham," he explained that he eventually realized that his sexual confusion was better explained by the fact that he was sexually abused and beaten as a child, experienced post-traumatic stress disorder after nearly two decades of service in the military, and experienced a condition known as autogynephilia.[51]

The term "autogynephilia" is a Greek term coined by psychiatrist Dr. Ray Blanchard, meaning "love of oneself as a woman."[52] It could manifest as a desire to dress in a seductive manner, to experience the physiological functions of a woman's body, to possess female body parts, to engage in stereotypical female behavior, or to experience sexual acts as a woman. Although it is distinct from gender dysphoria—and classified differently in the DSM—it is not unrelated. Men who experience autogynephilia are not necessarily dysphoric about their own body as much as they are aroused by the thought or sight of themselves having a female body. This, however, can lead to questioning one's sexual identity if the internalized shame they feel leads them to conclude that they're in the wrong body.

Autogynephilia sometimes originates when a young man begins privately exploring the world of cross-dressing. Julia Serano explained that as a young man, womanhood seemed unknowable and fascinating to him:

> The idea that cross-dressing can be a continual process of demystification [of women] very much resonates with my personal experiences. . . . As a teenager who was dealing with sexual attraction for the first time, I found it hard not to conflate my desire to be female with my sexual attraction for women. And in this respect, feminine accoutrements—whether clothing, cosmetics, or other accessories—became highly symbolic of both.[53]

Although autogynephilia often evolves from cross-dressing into an obsession with the eroticization of oneself in a female manner, this phase isn't always permanent. Sometimes this theme pervades the early stages of experimentation, but wanes over time as one begins to think of oneself as a woman in a non-sexual context.[54] Interestingly, men who experience autogynephilia are often hyper-masculine in their external presentation, interests, and occupations.

Blanchard's research on the subject has been met with hostility by some in the trans community, who do not relate to the experience. Others who may relate to it might feel that it reduces their identity to a sexual fetish. In the words of psychologist Dr. J. Michael Bailey, "an explanation based on autogynephilia may be experienced as a narcissistic injury."[55]

However, others such as Anne Lawrence defend the work of Blanchard, saying that after discovering his research, Anne finally felt understood and less alone and stigmatized. Lawrence felt that the typical transgender narrative did not apply to him and coined the phrase "men trapped in men's bodies."[56] He explained that autogynephiles are "men who love women and want to become what they love."[57] From his perspective, autogynephilia is about the fantasy of femininity rather than the daily identification with the feminine.

Interestingly, there does not seem to be a female equivalent to autogynephilia. Blanchard noted that some women experience arousal at the thought of being a gay man, but this is not nearly as common as autogynephilia in men.[58] What seems to be more common among women is the opposite and inversion of autogynephilia: asexuality among women. Or, one might say, "anti-gynephilia." If autogynephilia is a male's desire to become the object of his own lust, it could be proposed that the female counterpart is to escape from being the object of lust. If autogynephilia inclines a man to become the object of his desire, asexuality inclines some woman to find refuge in becoming undesirable.

Rapid-onset gender dysphoria

In 2018, researcher Dr. Lisa Littman published a study of parental reports of adolescents who suddenly exhibited signs of gender dysphoria without any childhood history of the condition. The research drew an immediate vitriolic reaction, and Littman was accused of "transphobic baseless fearmongering." Claims were made that her research had methodological flaws and was "infested with ignorant parents."[59] Her job at the Rhode Island Department of Health was terminated, and Brown University removed its press release promoting the study and apologized. Meanwhile, the publisher of her paper, *PLoS One*, announced it would conduct a review of the paper and issue a correction. Seven months later, they issued the "correction" . . . and changed none of her findings. Littman remarked, "I am somewhat bemused to see that I've been characterized as placing 'ideology over scientific rigor'—presumably for not parroting ideological points articulated unscientifically."[60]

What was so controversial about Littman's paper was the introduction of a new term known as rapid-onset gender dysphoria (ROGD). Whereas early-onset gender dysphoria applies to children, RODG (although not a formal diagnosis) describes the modern phenomenon of adolescent females suddenly reporting gender dysphoria, without any signs of preexisting childhood gender dysphoria.

In her research, Littman noticed a distinct pattern emerge among these young people. The typical subject was a teenage female who came from an upper-middle-class white family with progressive parents. Most were part of a friend group where one or more came out as transgender around a similar timeframe. They had little or no experience in real-life dating relationships but spent a significant amount of time on social media, absorbing a flood of ideologies without a foundation of lived experience. They spent hours each day reading blogs, participating in online discussion forums, and watching social media influencers. Untethered from reality and living in an online world where theoretical concepts abound, they found a sense of community, identity, and mission. As one young woman noted, "The internet is the best place you can go to if you're like scared about talking to anyone. . . . That's how I found out I was trans. It was from a YouTube video."[61] Mary Eberstadt explained, "the new virtual gender communities offer what in-person communities used to: connections, an audience, a sympathetic ear, and a relational answer to the question: *Who am I?*"[62]

Helena Kerschner, who detransitioned and now tries to help other young people reconsider their plans to transition, recalled the dangers she found online: "You also have that overt kind of brainwashing that happens that encourages you to reinterpret everything in your life as a sign of gender dysphoria." She added that the message given online is that "Your life is going to be so much better if you transition.

You are trans. The reason you don't fit in with other girls is because you're trans. So, it's really this big, complicated stew of unreality that young people fall into when they're just scrolling all day on social media and don't have pushback."[63]

Another significant trait shared by these young women was that 62 percent of them "had one or more diagnoses of a psychiatric disorder or neurodevelopmental disability preceding the onset of gender dysphoria."[64] The three most common were major depressive disorder, specific phobia, and adjustment disorder. A significant number had experienced trauma, struggled to handle negative emotions, and often felt overwhelmed by strong emotions while going to great lengths to avoid feeling them. Many parents also reported that their children had high expectations that transitioning would solve problems in various areas of life. Many were unwilling to work on basic mental health issues before obtaining gender reassignment treatments.

Before coming out as trans, many were high academic achievers. However, following the announcement of their trans identity, their parental relationships deteriorated, their grades dropped, their range of interests in life narrowed, and their mental well-being worsened.[65]

The significant range of commonalities reported by parents about these young women combined with the exponential rise in gender dysphoria led to Littman theorizing that "social contagion" was a factor, in the form of imitation, conformity, and mimicry. This phenomena, which could be considered a psychogenic epidemic, often impacts adolescent females, who tend to be more susceptible to such social influences. She noted, "certain beliefs could be spread by peer contagion, including the belief that a wide range of symptoms should be interpreted as gender dysphoria (and proof of being transgender) and the belief that transition is the only solution to relieve distress."[66] In fact, many who detransitioned agreed with the statement: "Someone told me that the feelings I was having meant that I was transgender, and I believed them."[67]

One reason why Dr. Littman's research met with such hostility within the trans community was that some who experienced gender dysphoria felt minimized by it. The very idea of "rapid-onset" gender dysphoria felt invalidating, as if they never had such feelings before discovering social media or an LGBT club on campus. And indeed, for those who experienced childhood gender dysphoria, the ROGD explanation is not a good fit. But it's not intended to be a one-size-fits-all explanation. Rather, one must recall that human experiences are as unique as each human person.

There's no need to discard the concept of ROGD because it doesn't apply to everyone. In fact, much of the research uncovered by Littman should be concerning to anyone interested in the well-being of individuals who experience gender dysphoria. For example, she noted: "For parents who knew the content of their child's evaluation, 71.6% reported that the clinician did not explore issues of mental health, previous trauma, or any alternative causes of gender dysphoria before proceeding and 70.0% report that the clinician did not request any medical records before proceeding."[68]

According to detransitioners, this is a universal problem because gender clinics often present only one pathway forward for individuals who express discontent with their sexual identity (and rarely communicate effectively with patients' own medical providers). As one patient recalled, the basic message was that transitioning is the answer: "Don't you ever try to love who you are, as you are. Never learn to do that."[69] There was never a deep discussion to help individuals distinguish what they needed from what they wanted, and the only way to be authentic was to make social, hormonal, or surgical alternations. Anything less is considered inauthentic and repressive.

But what if transitioning is a form of repression? What if gender "affirmative" care deprives people of the opportunity to develop strategies to address core psychological issues by making the body a false target of intervention? If so, then this would not only delay healing, but would make it more difficult later in life.

As Littman reported:

> Promoting the affirmation of a declared gender and recommending transition (social, medical, surgical) without evaluation may add to the harm for these individuals as it can reinforce the maladaptive coping mechanism, prolong the length of time before the AYA [adolescent or young adult] accepts treatment for trauma or mental health issues, and interfere with the development of healthy, adaptive coping mechanisms.[70]

If this is true, then many gender clinics around the world are missing countless opportunities to help their clients to address and heal serious issues that may need clinical intervention. Such individuals are being deprived of viable strategies to live in their bodies.

Although some trans activists eschew such a theory, considering it repressive and narrow-minded, the Dutch—who pioneered the process of transitioning—are now promoting what they call the "Modified therapeutic model." This focuses on exploring developmental factors that may have led to a patient's dysphoria. Unfortunately, not many clinics in the United States recommend this work be done prior to transition.

The Dutch, however, understand that this approach is not a transphobic minimization of the distress that some individuals experience in their bodies. Nor is it a promise that when core needs are met, gender dysphoria will disappear. Rather, it's a truly human approach that invites and challenges individuals to consider a bigger picture of what it means to be made whole.

15.

You should use whatever pronoun a person prefers.

Using a person's pronoun and chosen name is a basic courtesy and a simple way to show that you respect that individual. Refusing to do so is deliberately antagonistic and transphobic. It communicates a clear message that your prejudices are more important than another person's feelings and their sense of safety. As Michelle Mann remarked, "This creates a hostile environment that supports the oppressive belief that people existing out of the gender binary shouldn't or do not exist."[1]

Few topics within the realm of gender theory elicit as much of a fiery debate as the topic of one's pronouns. In 2015, the New York City Commission on Human Rights declared that civil penalties up to $250,000 can be imposed upon anyone who intentionally refuses to use a person's pronouns, such as zi or hir.[2] In Wisconsin, a thirteen-year-old was charged with sexual harassment for not using the preferred pronouns of they/them for a classmate.[3]

To acclimate students to university life, many colleges provide guides to their students to help them properly use preferred pronouns such as ae, per, xe, zie, sie, ey, ve, tey, and e. During orientation, incoming freshmen might hear a classmate remark, "My preferred pronouns are it and fae," and not understand what this means. Therefore, the University of Wisconsin offers their students a "How-To Guide" on using pronouns that gives examples of how to use these terms in a way that is grammatically sound. For instance, "Xe laughed at the notion of a gender binary. They tried to convince xem that asexuality does not exist."[4] Meanwhile, the University of Washington recommends that students avoid speaking of pronouns being "preferred" because this suggests that "a person's pronoun is optional."[5]

While some might consider pronouns to be a matter of personal choice that ought to be respected and accepted as a common courtesy, little thought is given to those who feel violated and coerced by such requirements. For example, in court, should a woman who has been sexually assaulted be required to refer to her male rapist as "she" on a witness stand? Refusing to comply could have serious ramifications. Julia Beck, who identifies as a lesbian feminist, was accused of violence and kicked off the Baltimore mayor's LGBT Commission. Her crime? Using male pronouns to refer to a convicted male rapist who identifies as transgender and prefers female pronouns. The inmate sexually assaulted two women in a female prison, after requesting to be transferred there because of his declared gender identity.[6] Ironically, the man who led the inquisition against Julia Beck also identifies as a lesbian.

To avoid offending others, most people simply use whatever names and pronouns a person chooses. More often than not, they do so not because they feel any deep conviction about the truth of transgender ideology, but because they simultaneously wish to be courteous, abide by social expectations, and avoid being labeled a bigot. Others, however, shake their heads and roll their eyes about the matter, considering it an absurdity that anyone should be coerced to adopt such neologisms.

Many within the trans community feel dismissed and invalidated by such an attitude, though. In the words of Michelle Mann, if you've misgendered someone, you ought to have a "kind and empathetic apology prepared . . . and affirm the person who has been hurt by your mistake. Instead of getting defensive, you should own up to your mistake and express regret. . . . You might have to talk with the person you accidentally misgendered afterward to check if they're okay and if they need you to do something further. . . . [telling them] 'I'm terribly sorry, I didn't use your preferred pronouns earlier. I'll make sure to be more careful in the future.'"[7] When you meet someone for the first time, she adds, "The best thing you could do would be to say something like, 'Hello! I am Violetta, and I use the pronouns she/her. How may I refer to you?'"[8]

Such elaborate apologies, however, sometimes backfire. After being accidentally "misgendered," one woman recalled that the group of people went to great lengths to apologize for their mistake, assuring her that they felt terrible for their oversight, adding that it was wonderful that she had discovered her true self and was living authentically. She recalled, "It was ridiculous. It was no big deal, and a simple, 'Oh, okay. Sorry about that,' would have been fine. That's what started me thinking that transgenderism is stupid."[9] One detransitioner remarked, "I would look at somebody and be like, 'I don't even know what their sex or gender is because I haven't asked them their pronouns yet.' I was so brainwashed."[10]

Although many do not share the sentiments of these women, the fact remains that "misgendering" is a topic that requires a careful balance of clarity and charity. Consider the act of "deadnaming." This is when someone insists upon calling another by his or her birth name, and not the person's chosen name that reflects his or her transgender beliefs. For example, imagine if a man named Andrew underwent social, hormonal, and surgical changes to present as female. At work, this individual's coworkers had no idea that the person they had always known as Rachael used to be named Andrew. However, one employee uncovered the fact and insisted upon using Andrew's birth name in public. Even those who disagree with gender ideology should understand that this would likely cause the person unnecessary distress. A more charitable approach would be to assume the person would prefer to keep such personal information about the past private. Besides, any hopes of building a bridge of friendship would be incinerated by such a lack of sensitivity.

With that having been said, imagine the case of a twelve-year-old girl who comes home from school and announces to her parents that she's trans, she's changing her name, and she wants her parents to adopt her new set of pronouns and buy her a binder until she can afford top surgery. What is the most loving response? Should the parents unquestioningly follow her lead so that she can lead her most "authentic" life? Here, a case could be made that the more charitable approach would be to listen to the young woman with sincerity while lovingly challenging her transgender beliefs. In other words, holding the daughter with one hand, holding on to reality with the other, and refusing to let go of either.

In this case, using the child's preferred pronouns might appear to be an act of kindness but would be a form of false compassion that perpetuates a delusion that ultimately is not in the best interest of the daughter. If the parents unhesitatingly affirm the daughter's new declared gender identity, they are confirming her belief that she's living in the wrong body. As Abigail Shrier said, once this belief system becomes fixed, "her given body can only be an endless source of disappointment to her."[11]

These two scenarios show that these delicate questions should be considered on a case-by-case basis. In severe cases where not referring to a person's new name could make a relationship impossible, it may be more pastorally effective to avoid using their previous name—or perhaps use an agreed-upon nickname—to prevent the destruction of the relationship. If the use of certain pronouns causes a person profound psychological distress, perhaps one could avoid using pronouns altogether.

Therefore, some bishops recommend that "[t]he faithful should avoid using 'gender-affirming' terms or pronouns that convey approval of or reinforce the person's rejection of the truth."[12] Some might retort that such a refusal is uncharitable. Michelle Mann considers it to be "rude and harassing" not to use one's preferred pronouns and argues that such intolerance makes individuals more likely to commit suicide because "it makes them feel incredibly invalidated when their pronoun set isn't acknowledged and honored."[13]

If using a person's new pronouns or name could make them feel affirmed and loved, why would any Christian refuse to do so? One reason is that if refusing to use a person's set of preferred pronouns would make them feel suicidal, it's a fair indication that there are much deeper issues going on in the individual's life that may need attention. Obviously, if a person is in such a fragile state, one needs to act in a compassionate manner and avoid triggering unnecessary distress in them. One man who experiences gender dysphoria noted, "If you're not going to accept someone's pronouns, then you need to find ways to try a lot harder to listen, meet them where they are at, and show that you want to get to know them and love them."

However, to unhesitatingly endorse everyone's preferred pronoun is to overlook that words express more than courtesy and inclusion. Language can convey sentiments of kindness, but it can also be used to sculpt ontology and anthropology. Words should express the truth of the person, and to change a person's pronouns is to call into question the very nature of what it means to be male and female. According to postmodern thought, language doesn't need to describe reality because it has the power to shape it. This is why it has been said that "All social engineering is preceded by verbal engineering."[14]

If parents address their daughter by male pronouns, it endorses the idea that sex can be divorced from one's identity and conveys the falsehood that she isn't her sex. This contradicts the truth of the sexual unity of the human person. What might have been intended as an act of charity—to use a new set of pronouns—reinforces a false identity. Therefore, using incorrect pronouns could be harmful to children and to others, who might think that a person's sexual identity is subjective and malleable.

If parents want to affirm the truth of their daughter's identity and help her to embrace her authentic self, they will lovingly help her to accept her whole being, including her body. They will help her to see that she doesn't need to hurt her body to be her authentic self. Nor does she need to fit into a rigid box defined by gender stereotypes. Rather, she can bear God's image to the world in a unique and personally distinct way. If the parents hold fast to these beliefs and refuse to use their daughter's new pronouns, it might create immediate tension and resentment. However, it could be argued that if they do not hold fast to the truth and speak it in love to their daughter, she's likely to feel much greater resentment toward them later in her life, for having failed to challenge her beliefs. Odds are, many people will use any set of pronouns she wishes to adopt, but very few will love her enough to question these changes.

When having a conversation with someone, whether it be a child, coworker, or friend, regarding the use of one's preferred pronouns, perhaps the best approach would be to say something such as:

You know I love you and care about you, and that I would never want to do something to hurt you. But you also know that I would never want to lie to you. I understand that it's important to you that I use the pronouns you mentioned to me. However, if I were to do that, I would feel like I'm not being truthful to you. If it's helpful, I would be willing to avoid using certain names or pronouns, since you have shared how hurtful it is to hear those. I hope that you don't reject me because of my viewpoints, and that you agree with me that the world is a big place, with lots of room for people who might not agree with one another, who can still love and respect each other. I hope you can still choose to accept me as a friend, even though we might not see eye-to-eye on this issue. I still think we have a lot to learn from each other.

By taking this approach, you are placing into the other person's hands the freedom to accept your diversity or to exclude you from their life. Hopefully, with all the emphasis on inclusion and tolerance in today's culture, he or she will reciprocate your openness to maintain a friendship despite your different viewpoints.

16.

Trans people should be free to compete in sports, use restrooms, and enter public spaces that align with their gender identity.

It's unfair to discriminate against trans athletes. Research of sports medicine demonstrates that there is "no direct or consistent research suggesting transgender female individuals (or male individuals) have an athletic advantage at any stage of their transition"[1] But even if they did, Lia Thomas rightly remarked, "It's not taking away opportunities from cis women, really. Trans women are women, so it's still a woman who is getting that scholarship or that opportunity."[2]

It's also unjust to force trans people to use the restroom that does not align with their gender identity. Being barred from public facilities that correspond with a person's gender causes unnecessary distress to individuals who simply need to use the bathroom or have a place to stay for the night. These people are not there to abuse children; they simply want to live ordinary lives without drawing attention to themselves.

In 2022, Lia Thomas—who had competed on the men's swim team at the University of Pennsylvania for three years without significant success—shattered the women's Ivy League record in the

100 free, beating out Yale's Iszac Henig (who also swims in the female division, but identifies as male). Henig explained, "As a student-athlete, coming out as a trans guy put me in a weird position. I could start hormones to align more with myself, or wait, transition socially and keep competing on a women's swim team. I decided on the latter."[3]

Although no one questioned Henig's right to swim with women while identifying as a male, a firestorm of debate ensued over Lia's victories. The NCAA defended Lia's right to compete, while others, such as Olympian Caitlyn Jenner (formerly Bruce Jenner), argued that Thomas's presence in the pool with women was unfair, would kill women's sports, and is "not good for the trans community."[4]

As similar controversies erupted across the globe, female athletes who expressed their discontent about taking second place to such opponents were belittled as sore losers and transphobes. They were told that they need to quit overreacting; that the presence of a few trans athletes would not signal the end of women's sports. However, the difficulty isn't resolved because of the relatively small number of athletes who identify as trans. For example, in three years of competitions against two male runners who identified as female in Connecticut, nearly one hundred girls failed to move on to the next level of competition because they finished behind them.[5] Furthermore, when a male competes as a female, he often removes a woman from the opportunity to compete.

Some of the consequences of men competing as women are more severe than the difference between a gold and bronze medal or missing out on a scholarship. Within the field of mixed martial arts, Fallon Fox, who identifies as a female, vanquished Tamikka Brents in two minutes, broke her eye socket, and left her with a concussion and seven staples in her head. After recovering from the injuries, Tamikka said, "I've fought a lot of women and have never felt the strength that I felt in a fight as I did that night. I can't answer whether it's because she was born a man or not because I'm not a doctor. I can only say, I've never felt so overpowered ever in my life and I am an abnormally strong female in my own right. Her grip was different, I could usually move around in the clinch against other females but couldn't move at all in Fox's clinch." Rumors spread that Fallon Fox had broken two women's skulls, and Fox tweeted, "For the record, I knocked two out. One woman's skull was fractured, the other not. And just so you know, I enjoyed it."[6]

Some might retort that combat sports are inherently dangerous, and those who compete in mixed martial arts are aware of the risks involved. However, combat sports often have a dozen or so different weight classes, ranging from strawweight to super heavyweight. On the day before opponents face one another in the octagon, they weigh in to ensure that they aren't one pound above their respective weight class (or half a pound for championship bouts). If they miss weight, they could be disqualified from competition. For a title match, they become ineligible to win the belt, even if their opponent should choose to continue with the fight.

Therefore, if a 265-pound heavyweight fighter weighs more than eight ounces above his weight class, this unfair advantage renders him ineligible to become a champion. For biological realities such as weight, age, or height, there is no psychological identity that overrides it. Because there's no such thing as being trans-weight, a heavyweight fighter cannot identify into a different weight class to annihilate smaller opponents and take home their paychecks. Because it's impossible to be trans-age, a thirty-year-old Little League coach cannot identify as an eleven-year-old and relieve the starting pitcher when his team is falling behind. However, if a man identifies as a woman, then regardless of any athletic advantage this might afford him, it is considered transphobic to question his "right" to compete against women.

Everything in sports—from the size and age of the athletes to their equipment and uniform fabric—is standardized to ensure that one opponent is not given an unfair advantage over the other. One USA swimming official, who resigned over the controversy regarding Lia Thomas, pointed out that "if a swimmer was wearing an illegal swimsuit, we would tell the swimmer 'Go change your swimsuit. That's not the right fabric. It's giving you an advantage.'"[7]

But is there an objective athletic advantage to being male? Yes. Men, on average, have 36 percent more muscle mass than women.[8] They also have greater aerobic and anaerobic capacity, slow and fast twitch muscle fibers, and a larger heart.[9] Their bones are shaped differently and are stronger than women's.[10] Because of women's decreased ligament strength in comparison to males, females are five times more likely to rupture their ACL.[11] Studies of grip strength also show that 95 percent of men produce greater force than 90 percent of females.[12]

Many of these advantages are because the adult male body has been marinated for decades in levels of testosterone that are approximately ten times higher than a woman's.[13] In order to attempt to offset this advantage, the International Olympic Committee required that male athletes who identify as women take testosterone-suppressing drugs to bring their levels down to 10 nanomoles of testosterone per liter of blood for at least a year prior to competition. But since the average woman has between 0.5 to 2.4 nanomoles per liter, a male's level of testosterone after suppression is still between four and twenty times higher! Even after a year of testosterone suppression, the typical male athlete only loses about 5 percent of lean body mass, muscle area, and strength.[14]

This also does not account for the fact that testosterone levels fluctuate. Prior to competition, a man's testosterone levels will spike in a manner that is more pronounced than in female athletes.[15] Regardless of an athlete's testosterone level on the day of competition, the physiological superiority of the male is largely due to the impact of experiencing puberty as a male, which cannot be reversed.

If testosterone alone could mitigate the differences between male and female athletes, women who identify as males would be flooding into male-dominated sports by taking testosterone supplements. But regardless of how much testosterone is injected into a woman, she will typically be unable to compete with male athletes at the same division. However, when a woman takes testosterone while transitioning, she becomes more likely to defeat the other female athletes.[16]

The objective biological differences between men and women explain why in 2017, nearly 800 high school boys beat the women's world record in the 100-meter sprint, and why the woman's world record 400-meter race is bested more than 15,000 times per year by men and boys.[17] It explains why Serena and Venus Williams were surprised, when they claimed that no man ranked outside of the top 200 in the world could defeat them, and an unknown but cocky, cigarette-smoking German tennis player who was nearing retirement volunteered for the challenge. Karsten Braasch said he prepared for the match with a few cocktails and a round of golf, and then defeated Serena 6–1 and Venus, 6–2. Serena remarked, "I didn't know it would be that difficult. I played shots that would have been winners on the women's circuit and he got to them very easily."[18]

Nonetheless, as the Williams sisters demonstrate, women are capable of extraordinary athletic feats. However, women can't display their talents if they're being beaten by average male athletes. There's no need to think any less of their accomplishments because they're not competing against males, though. This would be like devaluing the career of an undefeated boxer because he never fought an opponent who weighed ten pounds more than he did.

Although the debate over sports and gender identity is often framed around the subject of "trans athletes," this isn't the real issue. The issue is men competing in women's sports. During competition, athletes do not compete against the internal sense of identity of the other person, but against the other person's body. Therefore, in the spirit of true sportsmanship, one must admit that at least in the world of athletics, being female matters more than feeling female.

Bathroom wars

Few issues regarding trans rights are as polarizing as the topic of bathrooms. When North Carolina's legislature passed House Bill 2, requiring individuals to use the restroom that corresponds with the sex indicated on their birth certificate, major business such as the NBA, NCAA, and PayPal responded with economic sanctions, estimated to cost the state nearly 4 billion in revenue.[19]

Opponents of the bill decried the injustice of forcing an individual who identifies as trans into the restroom of his or her biological sex. This point needs to be considered. Imagine the case of a man who has spent the past twenty years of his life presenting as a female. He has undergone numerous surgeries including a penectomy and breast implants, he dresses in a feminine manner, and looks entirely female. Would parents of young boys feel more comfortable if he used the men's restroom? Should he use public showers intended for males? How safe and comfortable would this person feel in such an environment? One individual who wrestled with this remarked, "I wouldn't dare use a public toilet because I'd find either violent men or women who wished an encounter with a violent man on me."[20]

Or what about people such as Audrey Mason-Hyde, who remarked, "[T]here are mostly no toilets for people like me, who don't identify within the gender binary, and that toilets are just another way we categorize people."[21] These questions and daily challenges aren't often considered by those who haven't spent a moment of their lives wrestling gender dysphoria.

On the other side of the debate are females who have no desire to see or be seen by a male in locker rooms, spas, and bathrooms. In response to such an objection, trans activist Chase Strangio replied, "[W]hen a transgender woman uses a women's restroom there are still zero men—biological or otherwise—in that restroom. This is straightforward: Transgender women are women; transgender men are men."[22] Such a rebuttal doesn't quell the concern of parents who have no desire to have their children exposed to individuals of the other sex in various stages of undress.

Although nearly all individuals who identify as trans would simply like to use the facilities and get on with their day, granting males access to female spaces opens a door for sexual predators to potentially abuse women and children. Well over one hundred such cases have already been reported.[23] Many parents and women ask, "If a person who is male but identifies as female is unsafe in a male restroom, what makes the females safe when a male enters their space? Why is it necessary to make women feel unsafe to make men feel safe?"

For example, consider the difficulties faced by women's shelters. Many of these exist to provide a haven for women who are escaping domestic abuse. One sex abuse victim who suffered from post-traumatic stress disorder filed a human rights complaint in Toronto after being forced to share a room with a man who identified as a woman.[24] In California, nine women from a homeless shelter filed a sexual harassment lawsuit because they were forced to share a shower with such an individual.[25] Because the Department of Housing and Urban Development has redefined sex to include gender identity, such shelters cannot discriminate against men who seek admission to such shelters if they identify as female.[26] Should battered women be forced to choose between homelessness and sharing a room with a man? On the other hand, should homeless or abused men who present as female be forced to use shelters and showers for men?

The debate isn't likely to subside any time soon, and perhaps the best solution is to provide additional services and unisex or private restrooms to anyone who might wish to use them. That way, the privacy and safety of women and children are respected, while individuals who identify as trans are not forced to enter spaces that make them feel unsafe and uncomfortable. After all, making reasonable accommodations in a spirit of Christian charity does not require one to endorse all of gender theory.

In the meantime, it's helpful to remember that not all individual who identify as trans feel the same way about public policy issues. Remembering this will be critical for respectfully walking with people who experience gender dysphoria. All too often, such individuals are treated as a caricature for broader cultural and political debates. The less Christians do that, the better, when it comes to engaging real people.

Prisons

Whereas women who wish to leave a shelter to avoid the above situations can leave the facility, women who are incarcerated have no such choice when male inmates are admitted to their prison based upon their declared gender identity as female. Unfortunately, men who "transition" to women do not take on the lesser criminal tendencies of females. They are six times as likely to commit crime as women, and they retain the same rates of sexual violence as men.[27] In fact, research into prisoners in England and Wales who identify as trans revealed that 48 percent of them were incarcerated for a sexual offense.[28]

Hundreds of male prisoners have applied to transfer into women's prisons, and as their requests are being granted, the results of the experiment have been tragically predictable. Demitrius Minor is one of twenty-seven males in a female prison who identify as female. While serving a thirty-year sentence for killing his foster father, he impregnated two inmates.

Stephen Wood is a sex offender, burglar, rapist, and pedophile who took the name Karen White, but received no hormonal or surgical changes to appear female. He based his gender identity solely upon his internal sense of self and therefore applied to be transferred to a women's prison. The petition was granted, and he subsequently raped two female prisoners.[29] He's now serving a life sentence in a men's prison.

In Scotland, an inmate from a male prison was transferred to a women-only facility because he identified as female. After some time in the women's prison, he reidentified as a man. Because the prison officials were slow to determine how to handle his request, the prisoner became frustrated and angry, threatening to rape other prisoners and staff. Finally, the request was granted, and the man soon identified as a woman again. Upon being released, he committed suicide. Rohna Hotchkiss, a prison governor in Scotland who witnessed the debacle, remarked, "It was a tragedy, a deeply disturbed person. And instead of having their genuine psychological issues dealt with, they were left to say that it's because I can't be a woman . . . a man . . . a woman."[30]

While it's obvious that such situations pose a grave threat to incarcerated women—many of whom have already suffered abuse from men—what is often overlooked is that male prisons are likely to be dangerous places for inmates who identify as trans. One can imagine how such an individual, who has no ulterior motive of assaulting women, might wish to be transferred to a less hostile environment. For this reason, many penal systems are likely to adopt some of the changes already being made in England, such as separate prisons or dedicated units within prisons for such individuals.[31] Such measures ought to be considered for the well-being of all prisoners. Because many prison systems lack such accommodations, Lierre Keith, the founder of Women's Liberation Front, remarked, "It is a vicious violation of women's basic human rights to put convicted rapists in women's prisons and teenage boys in girls' locker rooms."[32]

Classification of Crimes

Another dilemma that arises when nature is contested is the classification of crimes. If a man who identifies as a woman assaults a woman, did a man or a woman commit the offense? In the UK, classification is based upon one's declared gender identity rather than one's sex.[33] As a result, the crimes of males are now being attributed to females, resulting in an unprecedented surge of "women" assaulting women and children.

Professor Kathleen Stock offered a sampling of the headlines that have appeared in the UK:

"Gang of women repeatedly stamp on man's head in 2am brawl at Leicester Square underground station"; "Sheffield woman found with over 1,000 indecent images of children hauled before the court"; "Woman who once shoved policeman onto Tube tracks jailed for spitting at officer"; and "Woman who 'bragged about being a pedophile' approached boys at Remembrance event."[34]

Similarly, headlines in Massachusetts announced, "Woman gets 30 years for child sex abuse."[35] But a woman did no such thing. Rather, the man who received this sentence had previously lobbied on social media for citizens to vote yes on a veto referendum that would allow individuals who identify as trans to use the locker rooms and bathrooms of their choosing. He wrote, "I am human just like you. I deserve the same rights as you do. I am transgender. Not a criminal. I shouldn't be stripped of my rights, vote yes on #3 this Tuesday! I will not be erased!"[36]

If anything is being erased, it's the reputation of women. According to UK prison statistics, one woman realized that "Of all the sex offenders behind bars (in men's or women's prisons) who identify as women, well over two-thirds are male."[37] Such absurdities are the inevitable result of believing that human nature is malleable.

In mathematics, if a small miscalculation is made at the beginning of a long equation, the resulting error will be compounded exponentially. In the same manner, when the evident nature and simple truth of masculinity and femininity is dismissed, the cultural consequences will be undeniable and cataclysmic. Therefore, the best argument against gender theory is to consider the inevitable outcome of embracing it.

Helen Joyce explained:

Think what would have to happen if gender identity were truly to supplant sex, right across society. Everyone would have to stop caring whether other people were male or female, and instead concern themselves only with identities. Women would undress in front of males as comfortably as in front of females, provided those males identified as women. No other consideration would count—not religion, modesty, trauma or anything else. An Orthodox Jewish woman would willingly receive an internal examination from a male doctor, and a rape victim would pour her heart out to a male crisis counsellor—again, provided those males identified as women. Everyone would be open to sexual partners with any combination of primary and secondary sexual characteristics, provided they had the "right" identity. Anyone who said they could desire only certain combinations would be regarded as a bigot, or perhaps a pervert. I doubt any mammalian species could live like this.[38]

17.

Parents and educators ought to affirm any child who identifies as trans.

When parents and communities fail to accept and welcome gender diverse children, they do great harm to these individuals. Studies show that when trans individuals are rejected by their families, they are more likely to become homeless, engage in sex work, and attempt suicide.[1] Gender dysphoria is hard enough to battle even while you're surrounded by those who support you. It becomes unbearable when those who claim to love you don't affirm your identity.

Your child says she's trans. Now what? Many parents are frightened that if they don't affirm the child's declared gender identity, they could lose their child. In fact, some trans activists openly discuss how they train family court judges to view parental hesitation as a form a "medical neglect."[2] As a result, some parents can lose custody of their children if they don't consent to hormones and surgery.[3] Therefore, what should you do if your child claims to be trans? If you don't affirm her proclaimed gender identity, are you rejecting her?

First off, here's what *not* to do: Don't freak out, be dismissive, tell her it's just a phase, try to win a debate, convince her she's immature, or remind her that the frontal lobe of her brain isn't fully developed. Upon reading this, some parents might think,

"Okay, I already managed to do all of that during our first conversation, and now she's locked in her room with her earphones on, not answering the door, and probably staring at her cellphone screen again. Any suggestions for damage control?"

When the dust settles, approach her gently and say, "I want to apologize. I'm sorry I didn't handle that very well. I honestly wasn't sure what to think or what to say. Do you mind if I could try to listen again?" Although teenagers often have a short attention span when listening to their parents, they have a surprisingly long one when parents offer a sincere apology. Nonetheless, if she spouts off a snarky reply, give her a pass this time. Let her air her grievances.

Should she be willing to reengage in a conversation, here are ten tips for your initial discussions:

One: Express gratitude that she has shared this information with you. Odds are, these feelings have been brewing in her mind for quite some time, but she was afraid to talk to you about them. She might have privately navigated through stages of initial awareness about her gender dysphoria, followed by waves or confusion, shame, exploration, self-rejection, resignation, and acceptance. For her to confide in you more deeply about where she's at in this process, she'll need to feel safe.

Two: Express reverent curiosity. By the time she talks to you about this, she has probably spent countless hours learning about the subject online and discussing it with others. If you don't understand concepts or terms she uses, invite her to explain what she means by them. If some of them strike you as absurd, unscientific, or theologically unsound, now is not the time to debate. Listen and learn what she's thinking. If you show her that you're willing to listen to her, in due time she'll value what you have to say in return. If she's open to sharing with you some of the sources where she's learned about the topic of gender, take the time to explore what they are saying, so you can better understand what she's thinking. In time, as she sees that you're willing to learn more about what matters to her, she may be open to reviewing resources you could share with her, that charitably call into question some of the ideologies she may have internalized.

Three: Be empathetic. Don't try to disprove her feelings. Rather, find places where you agree and might be able to affirm her ache or discontent. You could say, "I can see why you would feel constrained by the way the world expects people to fit into stereotypes. That makes sense." Although you might not agree on what it means for her live as her "authentic self," you can affirm her desire to live authentically. You could also affirm that this must be difficult to experience and acknowledge that you realize she didn't choose to feel this way. It's possible to validate her feelings without validating her reasoning, beliefs, and ideology. You could add, "I can see this has been very hard on you. I hear what you're saying, and I want to help. Thank you for trusting me with this."

Four: Rather than interrogating her, ask thoughtful questions. For example, "Can you tell me more about this? I want to understand." "What can I do for you?" "What has it been like to tell me about this? It must have taken courage." As your conversations deepen with time, you might be able to gradually map out the history of conflicts she has felt with her sexual identity. For example, "When did you start feeling this way?" "What was happening in your life at that time?" "When does the discomfort feel most intense?" For some individuals, gender dysphoria is like a white noise always playing in the background of their lives. For others, it fluctuates in intensity, and certain things such as formal attire and events (where individuals are expected to dress in a strictly masculine or feminine way) could trigger dysphoria. Another female recalled, "I felt the most dysphoric in my teenage years just in my bedroom."[4] As you learn more about her experiences, you can discover ways to avoid triggering some of the distress.

Five: Don't debate her memories, even if they seem embellished. Parents of gender dysphoric teens often note that their child often reinterprets their childhood history through a transgender lens. Rather than trying to disprove her recollection, listen to her perception.

Six: Be humble. If she points out some of your flaws and the hurts that you have caused, own what you can without blame-shifting. Seek forgiveness where it is needed. Often, parents worry that if they admit blame, they empower their children to hold things against them. The opposite is true. When children witness authentic vulnerability, they learn from example that ownership of one's shortcomings is a trait to be emulated.

Seven: Remind her that she is loved. Reaffirm that you will never leave her, no matter what. Explain that God loves her unconditionally as well. Perhaps you could take this moment to also apologize on behalf of the Church if she has ever been alienated by members of her faith community. Reassure her that God loves her, that He desires a personal relationship with her, and that the Church is her home. Assure her of your prayers and encourage her to have a genuine prayer life as well.

Eight: Listen for deeper motives. Drs. Yarhouse and Sadusky write:

What motivates their gender atypical behavior varies. Teens may engage in atypical expression to manage gender dysphoria, reduce anxiety about body image, express a sense of "true self," experience sexual arousal, seek entertainment, or respond to boredom. Moreover, some teens do appear to be in a search for identity and community.[5]

Each person's motivation is their own. But by listening well, you can gradually discover that there are often motives that run much deeper than simply the profession, "I'm trans." What might appear on the surface to be a feeling of inadequacy could have a layer of shame beneath it, and self-hatred at the core. Insofar as these or other deeper factors surface, try to help them distinguish how they feel from who they are. Your unconditional love will help her to explore difficult emotions such as resentment, anger, hurt, and self-loathing, so that the deeper unmet needs can be addressed with healthy strategies.

Nine: Don't pull away from your child. The topic of gender can cause so much relational friction that some parents opt for a "flight" response, hoping the difficulty will spontaneously resolve if they ignore it long enough. One young woman recalled that as she was wrestling with the idea of gender, she felt as if she were being pushed in a "confused and desperate head space" by her parent's isolated attitude toward her. Speaking of her mother, she wished that she "would have shown a bit more understanding and asked me some questions and talked to me like I was a human being going through a struggle rather than a problem to be solved."[6] So, rather than viewing her as a problem to be solved, consider her to be a mystery to be gradually revealed. According to existing research on the well-being of LGBT-identifying young people, the best predictor of their well-being over time is the quality of their relationship with you, their parents.[7]

Ten: Buy yourself time. You could say, "To be honest, this is a lot for me to understand. But I can tell that this really matters to you, and so I want you to know that I take this seriously because of that. I need some time to process our conversation and learn more about this." Telling her that you need time enables you to avoid making any major decisions or promises (other than love) in your initial conversations. It allows you time to strategize how to help them manage their dysphoria in the least invasive manner possible. Further, it models the type of thoughtful discernment around complexity that you hope your child would emulate.

After the conversation

When the conversation is finished, it's time for you to get to work. Here are fifteen strategies to deploy that will help to keep communication open and maximize the chances that she'll rethink what she's learned about gender theory (if that has played a role in her disclosure).

One: Don't beat yourself up. Many parents turn inward and begin blaming themselves or displace their negative emotion onto their child. Find a good support network that will be there for you. When you find this network, then you will be in a better place to think: "Instead of trying to merely fix my daughter, are there some things that need to be fixed at home? Does my marriage need work? Am I willing to go to counseling to address that? Are there wounds in my life that haven't been healed or addressed, that might have contributed to difficult dynamics within the family?" Take an honest assessment of what might need improvement at home and restructure your family life to create more room for family dinners, vacations, and recreation time together.

Two: Unplug. New limits need to be established on screen time for the entire family. Although it's obvious that teens spend too much time on screens, a fair case can be made that the same is often true of the parents. Each family must discern what's right for them because a radical and immediate disconnect might not always be the best approach. Ideally, you want to be able to critically engage with the content, rather than merely banning it. Therefore, a good place to start would be to install accountability filters on all the devices, so you know what websites are being viewed. You might also need to remove some of the social media accounts that could be exacerbating your child's dysphoria and impose a curfew on her phone so that it goes to bed in your room at night instead of hers. These changes are likely to cause friction, but you cannot retreat from what needs to be done for the sake of avoiding conflict.

It's also important to monitor their screen time because social media influencers often groom young people to believe that their parents don't love them if they don't endorse the child's plans to transition. Teens are often more trustful of individuals they meet online than those they interact with on a daily basis. But if the child forms a bond with an online community and then declares his or her identity as trans, they may feel a greater obligation to persist in that identity, even when they begin to have doubts about it.

Three: Get outside. If your family is going to spend less time on screens, fill that empty time with outdoor activities and prioritize times of family connection. Getting away gives the family a moment to step away from the intensity of the debates. Also, when children spend more time engaged in three-dimensional play, camping, physical labor, and works of service, they are better able to connect with their bodies than if they spend endless hours immobile on a screen, taking on the roles of various avatars. When children spend time outdoors, they are surrounded with the inherent goodness of nature and the solidity of reality, where all things are created good (including them). Even when they engage in fantasy play outdoors, they're immediately confronted with the reality of natural laws that cannot be denied. They cannot fly, and thus they learn to reconcile fantasy from reality regarding the limits of the human body. However, no such limits exist when one's face is aglow with the endless possibilities offered online.

Four: Encourage socialization. If your child is young, set up play days with other children. Even if she prefers the activities that are more often performed by boys, with enough interaction with other children, she will discover that she's not the only one with different interests. It's essential for her to connect with them and experience their similarity. It's also good if these activities aren't stereotypically masculine or feminine. For example, it's helpful for dads to cook or sew with a son who might be interested in such hobbies, or for mothers to build a fort or play sports with a gender dysphoric daughter. In doing so, they can demonstrate that gender atypical interests are not an indication of one's identity.

If your daughter is beyond the age where you can set up enjoyable play days for her, encourage her to spend time with good friends, and do what you can to foster positive relationships with other young females. Aim not simply to condemn the friends who you think are a poor influence but to extend invitations or set up social activities for the friends that you feel might have a more positive impact on her life. This will help to offset the tendency of many teens who experience gender dysphoria to establish their closest relationships virtually with online communities.

Five: Find a good counselor instead of a gender clinic. Such institutions typically offer only one pathway of treatment for gender dysphoria, and it's not to explore deeper issues or reconnect with one's body. Many gender clinics also fast-track children towards medical transition, with or increasingly without parental consent—and sometimes without parental knowledge. Instead, find a therapist who is experienced in treating gender dysphoria who understands that irreversible medical and surgical intervention is not the way professionals should care for individuals who experience psychological challenges. But before setting up an appointment for your child, interview the potential therapist to assess his or her approach to working with gender dysphoric children. Ask them if they believe someone can be born into the wrong body, if they believe that some kids are trans, or if they would sometimes encourage transitioning in response to gender dysphoria. For recommended resources, see chastity.com/gender.

Six: Learn about gender theory. Those who experience gender dysphoria often feel as if no one truly understands them except for others who identify as trans. Don't let this be the case in your home. Study the topic and the stories of those who experience gender-related distress from their own perspectives. Learn more about pediatric endocrinology, theology, psychology, and gender. Then, as your relationship with your child hopefully deepens and you're able to have more substantial conversations, you can ask her thought-provoking questions. For example, Maria Keffler suggests, "Can you give me a definition of transgender that doesn't rely on sex-role stereotypes?"[8]

Also, be prudent about how you use the information you discover. For example, giving a young woman statistics on the side effects caused by cross-sex hormones or puberty blockers might not be persuasive because she might abhor her body. Again, for recommended resources to learn more about gender, go to chastity.com/gender.

Seven: Research their school. Many teachers, clubs, schools—and entire school districts—promote gender theory beginning in pre-K and continue indoctrinating the children through high school. The resources inform students that loving parents are the ones who support their child's transition. If the child lacks a "supportive" home environment, and his or her parents don't love their child enough to support their declared gender identity, the school is often prepared to fill this void with a cadre of affirming allies who will usher the child through the various stages of transition. If any of this is happening at your child's school, it's time to sound the alarm to other parents and perhaps find a new school.

Eight: Fill the void. Changing schools is likely to be a difficult transition for your child, so do what you can to find ways to fill the void that the previous community had filled, so she can discover how many people love her enough to tell her the truth about the goodness of how she has been created. Many detransitioners recall that the communities that had affirmed their desire to transition sometimes felt like a cult, demanding rigid adherence to gender theory, loyalty to the cause, and suspicion and demonization of outsiders. As a result, they can exhibit a vociferous reaction to anyone who might question their identity. This can make it very difficult for them to believe that others can simultaneously disagree with them and love them.

At other times, the child might welcome such a change of environment and thrive within it. Especially if the student has already identified as trans and is considering the possibility of detransitioning, changing schools affords her the opportunity of a new beginning. It also avoids the awkwardness of detransitioning in her previous social circles and being branded as inauthentic or indecisive.

Nine: Move. Sometimes, changing a school doesn't suffice. Many families have decided to take extreme measures to relocate the family to another state to create an altogether fresh environment. Although this isn't necessary for every family, those who have made the decision often say that it was just what they needed to reset.

Ten: Be patient. The process of accompanying your child on this journey is more of a marathon than a sprint. As a result, be reasonable in your expectations. Should your child choose to desist from her identity as trans, it's likely to take time and be more of a process than a declaration. Sometimes a child will show signs of improvement and then boomerang back into the identity. In the event that she desists, let it go. One detransitioner expressed gratitude about how her mother never held this experience against her. She noted, "As firm as she was, she also no longer brings up or harps on that period in my life now that it's over, which has helped our relationship so much because I am very embarrassed about ever thinking I was non-binary and she doesn't have a grudge about it. Since then, we've been able to connect over being women."[9]

But even if your child persists in her transgender beliefs, identifies as trans into adulthood, questions your love, and pulls away from you, don't give up or stop loving her. Continue to extend holiday invitations, birthday wishes, and notes of congratulations for important life events. God's love for your child is unconditional, and yours is as well.

Eleven: Learn to compromise. Accompanying a child who is experiencing gender dysphoria requires parents to strike a balance of standing in the truth while exercising compassion. So, if your child is adamant that she wants you to use her new name, see if you're able to agree with her on a nickname that prevents her from experiencing the distress she feels about her birth name, but doesn't require you to endorse her renunciation of her sex.

If you have a young child who is experimenting with cross-sex behavior, sometimes it's more effective to ignore the behavior while affirming behavior that corresponds with the child's sex. If your daughter is uncomfortable wearing dresses, it's best not to force her into one. If your son enjoys theater, dance, or other activities that some cultures might consider to be stereotypically female, here's a thought: Go to the plays and cheer for him! Encourage him to have the courage to burst through artificial gender norms as the man God created him to be. This will help him to realize that his identity as a male is not defined by what the culture says is manly.

Twelve: Don't make every conversation about gender. Instead, make sure that most of your conversations are not about the subject. Sometimes, when a child is experiencing gender dysphoria, they spend an inordinate amount of time obsessing over the possibility of transitioning and evaluating the effectiveness of the steps they've already taken. Therefore, do what you can to lead conversations in new directions, talking to them about their hobbies, goals, academics, world events, and so on.

Thirteen: Be respectful. When you do have conversations regarding the trans community, be charitable. There's no need to speak in a condescending way about other people, no matter how different their beliefs might be from yours. Doing so will immediately shut down any potential for a fruitful dialogue.

Fourteen: Take care of yourself. The process of accompanying a child who experiences gender dysphoria can be mentally and emotionally exhausting for the parent. Parents often waver between feelings of self-blame, anger, helplessness, and anxiety. If their child persists into adulthood with transgender beliefs, parents grieve the loss of the hopes they once had for their child. Therefore, it is essential that parents seek out fellowship, community, counseling, guidance, exercise, adequate rest, recreation, and so on. At chastity.com/gender you can find networks of other parents for support.

Fifteen: Storm heaven. While there are psychological and socio-logical factors at play that can influence a child's sense of his or her sexual identity, parents cannot overlook the spiritual element of the situation. Pray and fast for your child, because children some-times build up a wall so high that you need to go up to heaven to reach them. Seek the intercession of other prayer warriors in your family and community as well. Also, take advantages of the sac-raments and sacramentals, such as praying the Rosary or blessing the house with Holy Water.

Finally, offer up the suffering you have experienced during this trial as a prayer for your child—and for other families experienc-ing the same struggle. As one priest said:

> [T]he money to buy souls is suffering, accepted with love. . . . Suffering is a goldmine to exploit for saving souls, for helping missionaries, for being a hidden apostle. What happiness it is to be able to suffer when we cannot act! . . . The Lord has given us a field to work, and we must irrigate it with tears falling from the winepress of sorrow, in order that it may be fruitful.[10]

Educators, pastors, and youth leaders

Although teachers, priests, and youth ministers could use many of the above principles intended for parents, leaders within schools and churches face their own unique set of pastoral chal-lenges. Youth ministers ask, "What do we do when a boy in the youth group won't go on the retreat if he's forced to be a part of the male-small group sessions?" What's a teacher to do if a child and her parents—who are attorneys—insist that the school accommodate their request to use her new name and preferred pronouns? Or, what about the priest who has a teenage boy in his parish who wants to be confirmed with a female confirma-tion name? Each of these leaders genuinely care for children, but often aren't sure what do to without compromising the truth or alienating the child—and perhaps his or her entire family—from the Church.

While some situations have clear answers, many require prayerful discernment to form creative and reasonable accommodations. For example, in the case of the boy who wants to attend the retreat without being included in the boys' small group, perhaps the youth minister can have co-ed small groups instead of ones that are segregated by sex. If the Church is going to create a welcoming environment for individuals who are gender nonconforming, the Church cannot wait until such individuals are "done" with their dysphoria before they are invited to sit in the pews. If that's the case, they're likely never to come. In the same respect, leaders have an obligation to the other children who have been entrusted to them to avoid causing unnecessary confusion regarding their understanding of being made male and female.

The first step in creating a warm welcome is to accept the fact that Christians have much to learn about this subject. The Church does have answers, and ones that are eternally true, good, and beautiful. But when it comes to the pastoral care of individuals who experience gender dysphoria, there's much work to be done. Some churchgoers might spend one hundred hours hearing news about transgender issues for every one minute that they spend talking to someone who identifies as trans. These numbers need to be inverted because both parties have a great deal to learn from each other.

As one young woman named Kat said, "I didn't need a know-it-all Christian. I needed a Christian who desired to know *me*, and who had the humility to admit that they didn't have it all figured out."[11] Preston Sprinkle remarked, "Some people might enjoy being instructed by a person who seems to have all the right answers—a two-legged Google with a mouth that never seems to shut. But I think most people are like Kat. They want to know the truth, but they want to find it with a friend."[12]

This posture of humility is not a style that one adopts, however. It's an acknowledgment of reality. This is why Dr. Mark Yarhouse recommends to pastors that if they have a member of the congregation who identifies as trans (or someone who is considering joining the church), they should invite him or her out for coffee, and say, "It seems like I'm meeting you at about chapter seven or eight of your life, but I haven't had the opportunity to hear about chapters one through six, but I'd like to."[13]

With this having been said, it should be clarified that offering a warm welcome does not mean that parishes and intuitions of Catholic education can endorse or promote gender theory. They cannot, because it is based on a false understanding of what it means to be human, and therefore will not lead to true human flourishing in this life or the life to come. Therefore, dioceses, churches, and schools have a responsibility to formulate policies that clearly explain the Church's teaching to parents, faculty members, parish staff members, students, and parishioners.

For schools, this means more than offering a quick Q & A session on the topic of gender in a high school theology class. It requires a continuous curriculum that teaches authentic Catholic anthropology, preferable rooted in the Theology of the Body. It also requires that school leadership prayerfully discern the employment of every staff member—and not only in the religion department—to ensure that they not only believe what the Church teaches but live out that teaching in their own vocations. It would also require that the school clearly outline their policies in the student and parent handbooks, so that anyone who chooses to attend the school would know in advance where the school stands on issues such as bathroom usage, pronoun usage, and the use of one's baptismal name (or at least a name that does not contradict the reality of one's sex). For examples of such policies, visit chastity.com/gender.

Finally, leaders and educators would also do well to assess the language they use. Because language has evolved dramatically in the last few years, teachers often slip into the habit of adopting terminology that undermines Church teaching without realizing it. Leaders who employ such terms unwittingly give credence to gender theory. Here are six ways Christians ought to be more precise with the language they adopt:

One: When discussing the topic of gender, a teacher might speak about someone being a "biological male." But are there males who aren't biological ones? This is as redundant as it would be to speak of a four-sided square, as if there are some squares that have three or five of sides. It should suffice to speak of one who *is* male. Anything more obfuscates reality.

Two: Some people assume that there's no harm in using the term "cis" as a prefix or adjective to describe one's sex. Again, this is redundant. The prefix is a newly minted adjective, coined to facilitate the idea that a cis male is one kind of male, and a trans male is simply another way of being male. But to concede this point is to concur that some females are males, which is untrue.

Three: Consider the problem with using terms such as "assigned" female at birth. If a person's sex is assigned by an external authority, then why couldn't it be reassigned by someone who has more authority, such as the individual herself? While the terms could be useful within a clinical setting for certain individuals who have disorders of sexual development, it's misleading to generalize all individuals as having been "assigned" a sex. Likewise, it's problematic to speak of someone who is "born male," because this subtly undermines the fact that one's sex was determined before birth, recognized after delivery, and will remain stable for all eternity.

Four: When leaders and teachers slip into the habit of universally adopting anyone's preferred pronouns out of a false sense of compassion, they immerse themselves into another's delusion instead of lovingly holding firm to reality and gently drawing others back toward it. Even when the individual is not around, when leaders adopt incorrect pronouns, they foster an intellectual milieu that is untethered from reality. However, sometimes it is most prudent to find agreeable nicknames or avoid gendered language to maintain the possibility of accompanying an individual through what is likely to be an already distressful time of life.

Five: The idea that a person can "transition" from male to female is false. This would be like saying a person can transition from human to fish. While a person can certainly swim, no one can transition into something that they are not. Therefore, regardless of how many medications or operations a man receives, he cannot transition to a woman. It is unloving to lead people to believe that this is possible. Granted, there is some utility in using the term when describing actions that a person has taken to present as the other sex, but care must be taken to avoid giving the impression that such actions create an actual transition.

Six: Rather than referring to a person as "trans," it is more accurate to refer to him or her as someone who "identifies as trans" or who experiences gender dysphoria (if that is true). If religious leaders and educators begin adopting the idea that certain individuals "are trans," it does not merely affirm that some individuals experience a discord between their sex and their identity. Rather, it affirms that this discord *is* the identity of certain people. But the Church does not believe that some people are inherently *cis* and others are *trans*. Rather, all people are beloved children of God, and *that* is the deepest truth of one's identity.

Taking a loving and logical approach to the delicate subject of gender isn't easy. But it helps to keep in mind that the job of educators and pastors isn't merely to defeat infernal ideologies, but to care for those who have been impacted by them. As Dr. Mark Yarhouse wrote, "Most people who are gender dysphoric are not trying to deconstruct norms regarding sex and gender. They're just trying to survive."[14] He adds, "Most are not meaning to participate in a culture war; most are casualties of the culture war."[15]

18.

If you struggle with gender dysphoria, you should accept that God made you trans.

The last thing that individuals who experience transgender inclinations need is to feel rejected by God. A large Pew Research survey of individuals who identified as LGBT showed that "religious affiliation is a significant predictor of LGBT individuals' happiness."[1] Therefore, faith communities have an obligation to affirm the gender identity of such people and welcome them without trying to "fix" them. God doesn't make mistakes, and trans individuals shouldn't be made to feel like second-class citizens in their churches.

When you write a book, you want to have all the answers. The trouble with this topic is that no one does. Those who experience transgender inclinations often feel like a mystery even to themselves, and those who care about them often feel at a loss for how best to walk with them in love. Perhaps the reason why so little progress has been made forging connections between faith communities and those who identify as trans is that the two parties spend so little time listening to each other.

Many who experience gender dysphoria are afraid to disclose their feelings to others, out of a fear of how they might react. This is an understandable concern, considering that some people think that gender dysphoria isn't something that Christians experience.

They have a caricature in their minds of what "trans people" look like and cannot fathom that they probably sit with some of them every Sunday without realizing it. As a result, those within the trans community often feel invisible. While most prefer the idea of passing, many of them are at different stages in their journey, and some haven't taken the first step toward transitioning. This can be especially painful because one of the deepest yearnings of the human heart is to feel seen.

If you find yourself in this situation, how can you open up to others about your struggle? One recommendation might be to ask someone you trust, "Is it okay if I talk to you about something that's really weighing on me?" By posing this question, you're inviting the listener to respond with sensitivity, and you'll hopefully receive a welcoming reply. Since the terminology of gender theory is often perplexing to those who haven't spent significant time researching it, it's often best to describe your feelings and experiences rather than beginning with a declaration such as "I'm nonbinary." If that is language you use to talk about your experience, it may be helpful to explain what about that language has resonated with you, as time goes on. But for now, try to let them know what you need and give them time to digest the information.

Examples of what you need may be, "I need space after I share this, so I would ask that you not bombard me with a bunch of questions right away, even though I am sure you have some." You may need them to bring it up again, or you may ask that they wait until you initiate another conversation. You may need the person to respect your privacy, and ask them not to confide in others, since it is your story to tell.

If you pour out your heart and the other doesn't respond as you had hoped, try not to jump to the conclusion that he or she does not love you. Also, be prudent about who you share this information with, as some people can be trusted more than others. In the same respect, be careful about trans advocates who lead you to believe that those who love you the most—your parents—cannot be trusted if they don't endorse what you believe. Disagreement isn't a sign of hate; it's an indication that someone loves you enough to be honest with you.

You might also want to discern the quantity of people you tell, not merely their quality. Announcing your declared gender identity to everyone on social media might create such a whiplash of reactions that its wisest to be discerning about when and who you tell. Also, many detransitioners have reported that the more public and outspoken they were about their transgender identification, the more challenging it was to socially detransition.

Managing dysphoria

One of the most important keys to enduring any trial is to find the right support system. One woman who struggled with being female recalled, "Feeling like we couldn't be women, being cut off from other women is one of our deepest wounds and healing it means finally finding common ground and community with other women."[2] In your quest to find the right community, one sign that a group is wrong for you is if they lead you to believe that you might need to make medical alterations to your body in order to be your authentic self. They might sincerely care about you, but if they don't know what's truly best for you, their advice is as useful as receiving heart surgery from a person who hasn't been to medical school but has the best intentions. Instead, if you're open to counseling, find a good therapist who shares your faith and knows how to help you strive for wholeness and holiness.

Also, be patient with yourself. Often, a sense of urgency for change leads individuals to make irreversible, life-changing decisions. But every attempt to alter the way in which the body reveals one's sexuality obscures the signs of one's true identity. Your feelings matter, so give yourself time to process them. Jesse Hinty, a member of the Pique Resilience Project, shared why she pushed forward through the steps of her transition:

> I think I had this complex of wanting to prove myself as authentic, regardless of any sense of doubt that was creeping in. . . . The feeling of wanting to prove myself completely overrode any thought of "Hmm, maybe I should slow down or like maybe I should think about this a little bit harder." I just wanted to feel validated . . . like my dysphoria experience mattered.[3]

Your dysphoria does matter, and this is precisely why you should be curious about it. Perhaps there's more to your dysphoric feelings than your body. As you explore this possibility, don't place unnecessary pressure on yourself to conform. For example, if you're female, you don't need to embrace all things stereotypically feminine and go shopping for pink dresses in order to be a follower of Christ. Go at your own pace. You also do not have to have all the answers to your questions about gender before approaching God. God's idea of following Him is not: "Get yourself together and then you're welcome in my house." If Christians had to wait until they were perfect before approaching God, churches would be empty—with the exception of those who were delusional about their own perfection.

When individuals who wrestle with their sexual identity force themselves to fit into certain cultural stereotypes of masculinity and femininity, it often makes matters worse. They might assume that in order to please God, they need to conform immediately to an invisible mold of what society wants them to be. But imagine if Saint Joan of Arc believed this! She would never have shattered the cultural norm that women can't be military leaders. France, then, would have lost at the battle in Orléans in 1429, and England might have conquered her nation. She exemplifies why it's so important to look to God rather than the world to obtain our sense of self. After all, God is not interested in putting anyone into a mold, because sainthood is the full bloom of the human personality.

Therefore, if a young woman today has interests that don't conform to the expected pattern of femininity, this doesn't make her male or nonbinary. It makes her a 100 percent female and 100 percent herself. After all, there are many ways to be a man and many ways to be a woman. One detransitioner, who reminisced about what she wished she knew during the process of transitioning, said, "If I could go back I would tell myself that I didn't have to be a certain way to be a woman . . . you don't have to change the way that your body looks."[4] In other words, your sexual identity does not need to be earned, proved, felt, or even fully understood. It only needs to be received.

Although this may be easier said than done, one way to work towards acceptance is to try to engage in activities that make you feel good about your body. This might involve exercise, sports, dance, hiking, etc. The point is to step away from negative thinking patterns and try to discover something that feels right about your body. Physical achievements can sometimes lead to a healthy sense of admiration for the abilities of one's body, rather than a constant devaluation of it.

Walking with God

Sometimes a person can do all the prayer and counseling in the world, and yet the distress they feel about their body never fully resolves. They might wonder, "What am I doing wrong? Why isn't God listening to me? Why won't he take this away? What if this never changes? What does hope look like for someone like me?" Fr. Jacques Philippe recommends that during times of suffering, we should ask ourselves:

What attitude does God want me to have toward this situation? The point is to move from "Why?" to "How?" The real question isn't "Why is this happening to me?" but "How should I live through these things?" How am I called to face this situation? What call to growth is being made to me through this? That question will always get an answer.[5]

Sometimes the wound that we feel separates us most from God is the door through which he enters our lives. One individual who wrestled with his sexual identity remarked:

Mostly I try to remember that God is meeting me with his perfect love in every moment no matter what. And every moment is an opportunity for me to love the people in my life. It can be really hard when I feel like gender dysphoria is a cruel and unbreakable curse that literally keeps me up at night because I am not comfortable in my own skin.

If you think about it, there's no one who knows your distress other than God. He alone sees your heart and the anguish you have felt. He understands that those who identify as trans have unique sufferings, as do those who are considering the idea of detransitioning. One such man asked himself:

Should I do this? If I do this, where am I going to go? What am I going to do? I have this whole lifestyle. I have breasts. I have all these things. I have clients. I have clientele. I have men waiting on me. I need to pay my bills. What am I going to do if I do this? And those thoughts got louder, and louder, and louder, and louder, and I could hear . . . God's voice just telling me to come to Him, just come to Him, Trust Him. Just trust me, I'll handle it.[6]

If you feel that you're uncertain of what God is asking you to do, or what would happen if you followed his voice, imagine what you would do if you felt trapped in a fog. No matter how dense the cloud might be, you could always look at your feet and see the path. In the same way, God will always reveal to us what he calls us to do in the present moment. Therefore, if regrets about the past or anxieties about the future cloud your vision, God desires to meet you in the present moment. He knows that half of every cross is the mystery of it. But in the midst of that uncertainty, He says to you, "I don't need you to understand. I need you to trust."

The world often believes that suffering is meaningless and that if something is difficult, it must be bad. Therefore, the goal should always be to find the quickest way to remove it. Such a reaction is understandable. For example, Saint Paul experienced an unnamed, excruciating suffering and wrote, "Three times I begged the Lord about this, that it should leave me, but he said to me, 'My grace is sufficient for you, for my power is made perfect in weakness' (2 Cor. 12:8–9). Speaking of this passage, Saint Augustine remarked:

> So when we are suffering afflictions that might be doing us either good or harm, we do not know how to pray as we ought. But because they are hard to endure and painful, because they are contrary to our nature (which is weak) we, like all mankind, pray to have our afflictions taken from us. At least, though, we owe this much respect to the Lord our God, that if he does not take our afflictions away we should not consider ourselves ignored and neglected, but should hope to gain some greater good through the patient acceptance of suffering. For my power is at its best in weakness.[7]

It's also helpful to recall Jesus's posture toward unwanted suffering. In his agony in the garden, he made his distress known to the Father, imploring three times, "My Father, if it is possible, let this cup pass from me; yet, not as I will, but as you will" (Matt 26:39). When the cup was not removed, his prayer did not end. Rather, he spoke to His Father using the Psalms. Although many of the Psalms are prayers of thanksgiving, victory, and praise, one third of all the Psalms are songs of lamentation.

As a spiritual exercise, if you wish to encounter God in a unique way, choose one of these and pray it three times.[8] First, offer the prayer from your own heart to the Father. Then, pray it a second time slowly, imagining Christ offering the same prayer during His Passion, when He was betrayed, judged, stripped, beaten, humiliated, and crucified. Then, pray it one final time, uniting your prayer with Christ, praying together to the Father. The point here is to speak with God about your feelings of alienation from Him and others. There's no need to bury your negative emotions, because prayer is not a time for putting on a religious mask. It's the time when all of our masks can drop and you can be alone with Him who loves you.

In uniting your suffering to Christ, you become an unrepeatable reflection of God. During the Last Supper, and at every Mass, one hears the prayer "This is my body, given up for you." In a profound way, Christians who experience distress about their own bodies can offer a similar prayer to God. In a unique way, they are able to live out the Mass by accepting their bodies as a gift from God the Father and returning it to Him as an offering, in imitation of His Son, through the power of the Holy Spirit.

Walking with God in this way might bring about deep healing in ways that you might have never thought needed healing. Sometimes, gender dysphoria can resolve as deeper wounds are addressed. Other times, the discomfort persists. One fifty-seven-year-old who still struggles with it at times said that the biggest problem he has in his relationship with God is that "I restrict how much of His love I receive."[9]

Thanks be to God, a person's holiness does not depend upon the absence of gender dysphoria. In fact, the Old Testament speaks of individuals who were eunuchs. These were castrated males who were looked down upon within ancient Judaism. However, Isaiah prophecies that when the Messiah comes, God will "give them a name better than sons and daughters" (Isaiah 56:3–7). Granted, it's not a perfect parallel for those who might identify as trans, but there's no question that these individuals would have experienced no small amount of dysphoria about their bodies in their own way.

Like them, your witness of faith, hope, and love is needed in the Church. You have been created to make a gift of yourself, and God knows that you have a story to offer the world that He has entrusted to no one else. Part of your story involves loving your enemy, even if you feel that your enemy is your own body. But keep in mind that loving does not require liking. Rather, it is an act of the will to do what is best for the other, and to avoid harming what God has entrusted to you. This may be difficult, but there is only one key that can unlock the vault of limitless grace that God wishes to provide for you: trust.

What does this look like? In the words of one remarkable individual who wrote to me:

What does a saint with gender dysphoria look like? I don't know. But I know that I should aspire to be a saint and I have gender dysphoria. And my version of sanctity may not look like anyone else's. When dysphoria overwhelms me, I try to remind myself that I am already the bride of Christ and destined to be His bride for eternity.

Although one's body can feel like a curse, the gift of one's sexuality as male or female is a blessing from a loving Father. Such a claim might cause you to feel anger toward God for how He created you, but don't be afraid to talk to Him about those emotions. He will listen to you. And if you are willing to listen to Him, he might say with love, "You were not born into the wrong body. You were born into the wrong culture—a culture that told you that you need to hurt your body in order to be your authentic self. It's the culture that needs to be reconstructed, not you."

Listen to
Jason's Podcast!

GOT QUESTIONS? GET ANSWERS.

WATCH VIDEOS
GET RELATIONSHIP ADVICE
LAUNCH A PROJECT
READ ANSWERS TO TOUGH QUESTIONS
FIND HELP TO HEAL FROM THE PAST
LISTEN TO POWERFUL TESTIMONIES
SHOP FOR GREAT RESOURCES
SCHEDULE A SPEAKER

Endnotes

Introduction

1   Jesse Singal, "When Children Say They're Trans," *The Atlantic*, July/August 2018.
2   Gabriel Mac, "My Penis, Myself," *New York* magazine (December 20, 2021).
3   Cf. A. Haas et al., "Suicide Attempts among Transgender and Gender Non-Conforming Adults: Findings of the National Transgender Discrimination Survey" (New York: American Foundation for Suicide Prevention / Los Angeles: Williams Institute, 2014).
4   Cf. E. Wilson et al., "Transgender Female Youth and Sex Work: HIV Risk and a Comparison of Life Factors Related to Engagement in Sex Work," *AIDS and Behavior* 13:5 (2009), 902–913.
5   "Tranzformed—Finding Peace with Your God Given Gender," https://youtu.be/Ebodf8rWpv4.
6   Lauren Booker, "What it means to be gender-fluid," CNN.com (April 13, 2016).
7   Cf. University of Essex, "Working with Schools and Colleges: Trans Inclusion Guidance," https://www.essex.ac.uk/-/media/documents/study/outreach/transgender-guidance.pdf.
8   "Please list some of the infinite number of genders," https://www.whatdotheyknow.com/request/please_list_some_of_the_infinite.
9   Edith Stein, *Finite and Eternal Beings* (Washington, D.C.: ICS Publications, 2002), 507.
10   Pope John Paul II, "Third General Conference of the Latin American Episcopate," Puebla, Mexico: The Holy See (January 28, 1979).

1. Each person has their own gender identity.

1   Cf. "Gender-Affirming Care and Young People," https://opa.hhs.gov/sites/default/files/2022-03/gender-affirming-care-young-people-march-2022.pdf.
2   Cf. Human Rights Campaign, "Glossary of Terms," https://www.hrc.org/resources/glossary-of-terms.
3   Cf. Lexico, "Gender," https://www.lexico.com/definition/gender.
4   Cf. D. Haig, "The Inexorable Rise of Gender and the Decline of Sex: Social Change in Academic Titles, 1945–2001," *Archives of Sexual Behavior* 33:2 (April 2004), 87–96.
5   J. Money, "An Examination of Some Basic Sexual Concepts: The Evidence of Human Hermaphroditism," *Bulletin of Johns Hopkins Hospital* 97:4 (October, 1955), 301–319.
6   Money, "An Examination of Some Basic Sexual Concepts," 301–319.
7   John Money, preface, in John Money & A. A. Ehrhardt, *Man and Woman, Boy and Girl. Gender Identity from Conception to Maturity* (Northvale, NJ: Jason Aronson, 1972).
8   Cf. Kate Millett, *Sexual Politics* (New York: Avon Books, 1970), 54.
9   World Health Organization, "Gender and health," https://www.who.int/health-topics/gender#tab=tab_1.
10   "Live Debate w/Trans Activist," https://www.youtube.com/watch?v=7mamVI4UPYQ.
11   "Meet The WORST 'Groomer' LGBT Teachers On TikTok," https://youtu.be/a-hjYD9U54M.
12   "Transgender Women Aren't 'Women,'" https://youtu.be/LZOZY6A62XY.
13   Fionne Orlander, https://twitter.com/FionneOrlander/status/1062728906304827392 (November 14, 2018).
14   "The Truth About Trans Kids, From Trans Adults," https://youtu.be/f8GtmWxKbO8
15   Buck Angel, https://twitter.com/BuckAngel/status/1209236297140834304 (23 December 2019).
16   "The Truth About Trans Kids, from Trans Adults," https://youtu.be/f8GtmWxKbO8.
17   "Transgender Women are MEN," https://www.youtube.com/watch?v=q-U4P8VdOso.
18   Abigail Favale, "The Eclipse of Sex by the Rise of Gender," *Church Life Journal* (March 1, 2019).
19   "Our Trans Loved Ones: Questions and Answers for Parents, Families, and Friends of People Who Are Transgender and Gender Expansive," PFLAG (2015), 18, https://www.pflag.org/ourtranslovedones.
20   Cf. DSM-5, (Washington, D.C.: American Psychiatric Publishing, 2013), 450.
21   DSM-5, 452.
22   Lawrence S. Mayer, and Paul R. McHugh, "Sexuality and Gender Findings from the Biological, Psychological, and Social Sciences," *New Atlantis* 50 (Fall 2016), part 3.

23   S. Müller, "Body Integrity Identity Disorder (BIID)—Is the Amputation of Healthy Limbs Ethically Justified?," *American Journal of Bioethics* 9:1 (January 2009), 36–43.

24   Julia Serano, *Whipping Girl* (Berkeley: Seal Press, 2016), 216.

25   DSM-5, 454.

26   Cf. A. Flores et al., *How Many Adults Identify as Transgender in the United States* (Los Angeles: Williams Institute, 2016).

27   Cf. J. Herman et al., *Age of Individuals Who Identify as Transgender in the United States* (Los Angeles: Williams Institute, 2017), 2; B. Wilson and A. Kastanis, "Sexual and Gender Minority Disproportionality and Disparities in Child Welfare: A Population-based Study," *Children and Youth Services Review* 58 (2015), 12; M. Johns et al., "Transgender Identity and Experiences of Violence Victimization, Substance Use, Suicide Risk, and Sexual Risk Behaviors among High School Students—19 States and Large Urban School Districts, 2017," *Morbidity and Mortality Weekly Report*, (January 25, 2019).

28   Cf. Richard Orange, "Teenage Transgender Row Splits Sweden as Dysphoria Diagnoses Soar by 1500%" *Guardian*, February 22, 2020.

29   Cf. Gordon Rayner, "Minister Orders Inquiry into 4,000 Percent Rise in Children Wanting to Change Sex," *Telegraph* (September 16, 2018); "Thousands of 'Trans' Teens Want to DETRANSITION... (Women, Lesbians, Homophobia)," https://www.youtube.com/watch?v=bHOASkcG-zY&t=151s; "Referrals to GIDS, financial years 2010-11 to 2021-22," https://gids.nhs.uk/about-us/number-of-referrals/.

30   Cf. K. Zucker, "Gender Identity Disorder in Children and Adolescents," *Annual Review of Clinical Psychology* 1 (2005), 467–92; K. Drummond et al., "A Follow-up Study of Girls with Gender Identity Disorder," *Developmental Psychology* 44 (2008), 34–45; M. Wallien and P. Cohen-Kettenis, "Psychosexual Outcome of Gender-dysphoric Children," *Journal of the American Academy of Child and Adolescent Psychiatry* 47 (2008), 1413–1423; T. Steensma et al., "Desisting and Persisting Gender Dysphoria after Childhood: A Qualitative Follow-up Study," *Clinical Child Psychology and Psychiatry* (2011), 499–516; D. Singh, "A Follow-up Study of Boys with Gender Identity Disorder" (PhD dissertation; University of Toronto, 2012); T. Steensma et al., "Factors Associated with Desistence and Persistence of Childhood Gender Dysphoria: A Quantitative Follow-up Study," *Journal of the American Academy of Child and Adolescent Psychiatry* 52 (2013), 582–590; T. Steensma, "From Gender Variance to Gender Dysphoria: Psychosexual Development of Gender Atypical Children and Adolescents" (PhD dissertation; VU University-Amsterdam, 2013); J. Ristori and T. Steensma, "Gender Dysphoria in Childhood," *International Review of Psychiatry* 28:1 (2016), 13–20; B. Abel, "Hormone Treatment of Children and Adolescents with Gender Dysphoria: An Ethical Analysis," *Hastings Center Report* 44:4 (2014), S23–27; P. Eddy, *Reflections on the Debate Concerning the Desistance Rate among Young People Experiencing Gender Dysphoria*, Center for Faith, Sexuality & Gender, June 2021; P. McHugh, P. Hruz, and L. Mayer, "Brief of Amici Curiae in Support of Petitioner, *Gloucester County School Board v. G.G.*," Supreme Court of the United States, No. 16-273 (January 10, 2017), 12.

31   James M. Cantor, "Transgender and Gender Diverse Children and Adolescents: Fact-Checking of AAP Policy," *Journal of Sex & Marital Thera*py (2019), 307–313.

32   Cf. Jaime M. Grant et al., "Injustice at Every Turn: A Report of the National Transgender Discrimination Survey" (Washington, D.C.: National Center for Transgender Equality and National Gay and Lesbian Task Force, 2011), 28.

33   Cf. J. Herman et al., "2015 U.S. Transgender Survey," National Center for Transgender Equality, 99,100.

34   Cf. I. Nolan et al., "Demographic and Temporal Trends in Transgender Identities and Gender Confirming Surgery," *Translational Andrology and Urology*, 8:3 (June 2019).

35   Cf. Aaron S. Breslow et al., "Toward Nonbinary Nuance in Research and Care: Mapping Differences in Gender Affirmation and Transgender Congruence in an Online National U.S. Survey," *Transgender Health* 6:3 (2021), 157; Denton Callander et al., "The Complexities of Categorizing Gender: A Hierarchical Clustering Analysis of Data from the First Australian Trans and Gender Diverse Sexual Health Survey," *Transgender Health* 6:2 (2021).

36   Michelle Mann, *Not "Him" or "Her"* (n.p.: n.p., 2021), 3.

37   Abigail Shrier, *Irreversible Damage* (Washington, D.C.: Regnery Publishing, 2020), 7.

38   David Haig "The Inexorable Rise of Gender and the Decline of Sex: Social Change in Academic Titles, 1945–2001," *Archives of Sexual Behavior* 33:2 (April 2004), 93.

39   John F. Oliven, *Sexual Hygiene and Pathology: A Manual for the Physician and the Professions* (London: Pitman Medical Publishing Co., 1965).

40   John Finley, *Sexual Identity* (Steubenville, OH: Emmaus Road, 2022), xix.

41   "TED Talk: Ending Gender by Scott Turner Schofield," https://youtu.be/TWubtUnSfA0.

42   Twitter.com, @ana_litical.

43   Anonymous, "Experience: I Regret Transitioning," *Guardian*, February 3, 2017.

44   Cf. Congregation for Catholic Education, *Male and Female He Created Them* (Vatican City, 2019), 11; *Ratalio Finalis* (October 2015), 58.

45   As quoted in Margaret Hartmann, "The History of Pink for Girls, Blue for Boys," *Jezebel*, April 10, 2011; J. Magalty, "When Did Girls Start Wearing Pink?," *Smithsonian*, April 7. 2011.

46   Ryan Anderson, "Neither Androgyny nor Stereotypes: Sex Differences and the Difference They Make," *Texas Review of Law & Politics* 24:1 (March 19, 2020).

2.   Gender is a social construct.

1   Christina Hoff Sommers, "You Can Give a Boy a Doll, but You Can't Make Him Play with It: The Logistical and Ethical Problems with Trying to Make Toys Gender-Neutral," *The Atlantic*, December 6, 2012.

2   R. Fabes et al., "The Relations of Children's Emotion Regulation to Their Vicarious Emotional Responses and Comforting Behaviors," *Child Development* 65 (1994), 1678–1693.

3   Cf. Anne Moir and David Jessel, *Brain Sex* (New York: Random House, 1991), 18.

4   Cf. Louann Brizendine, *The Female Brain* (New York: Morgan Road Books, 2006), 17.

5   Cf. Deborah Blum, *Sex on the Brain*, (New York: Penguin, 1997), 68.

6   Cf. Leonard Sax, *Why Gender Matters* (New York: Random House, 2017), 19.

7   Barbara and Allen Pease, *Why Men Don't Listen & Women Can't Read Maps* (New York: Broadway Books, 2001), 70.

8   Cf. Leonard Sax, "Sex Differences in Hearing: Implications for Best Practice in the Classroom," *Advances in Gender and Education* 2 (2010): 13–21.

9   Cf. L. Ruytjens et al., "Functional Sex Differences in Human Primary Auditory Cortex," *European Journal of Nuclear Medicine and Molecular Imaging* 34:12 (December 2007), 2073–2081; S. Ikezawa et al., "Gender Differences in Lateralization of Mismatch Negativity in Dichotic Listening Tasks," *International Journal of Psychophysiology* 68:1 (April 2008), 41–50; J. Beech and M. Beauvois, "Early Experience of Sex Hormones as a Predictor of Reading, Phonology, and Auditory Perception," *Brain and Language* 96:1 (January 2006), 49–58.

10   A. Shaqiri et al., "Sex-Related Differences in Vision Are Heterogeneous," *Scientific Reports* 8:1 (May 14, 2018), 7521.

11   Cf. Israel Abramov et al., "Sex & Vision I: Spatio-Temporal Resolution," *Biology of Sex Differences* 3:20 (2012).

12   Cf. Marek Glezerman, *Gender Medicine* (New York: Overlook Press, 2016), 28.

13   Cf. A. Thompson and D. Voyer, "Sex Differences in the Ability to Recognise Non-Verbal Displays of Emotion: A Meta-Analysis," *Cognition and Emotion* 28:7 (2014), 1164–1195; R. Levant et al., "Gender Differences in Alexithymia," *Psychology of Men & Masculinity* 10:3 (2009), 190–203.

14   Glezerman, *Gender Medicine*, 231.

15   Cf. B. Montagne et al., "Sex Differences in the Perception of Affective Facial Expressions: Do Men Really Lack Emotional Sensitivity?" *Cognitive Processing* 6 (2005), 136–141.

16   John Paul II, *Letter to Women*, 12.

17   Cf. P. Sorokowski et al., "Sex Differences in Human Olfaction: A Meta-Analysis," *Frontiers in Psychology* 10:242 (2019), 1.

18   Cf. J. Diamond et al., "Gender-Specific Olfactory Sensitization: Hormonal and Cognitive Influences," *Chemical Senses* 30:1 (2005), i224–i225; P. Dalton et al., "Gender-Specific Induction of Enhanced Sensitivity to Odors," *Nature Neuroscience* 5 (2002), 199–200; N. Boulkroune et al., "Repetitive Olfactory Exposure to the Biologically Significant Steroid Androstadienone Causes a Hedonic Shift and Gender Dimorphic Changes in Olfactory-Evoked Potentials," *Neuropsychopharmacology* 32 (2007), 1822–1829.

19 Cf. A. Oliveira-Pinto et al., "Sexual Dimorphism in the Human Olfactory Bulb: Females Have More Neurons and Glial Cells Than Males," *PLOS One* (November 5, 2014).

20 Brizendine, *The Female Brain*, 87.

21 Cf. Brizendine, *The Female Brain*, 97.

22 Rachel Nuwer, "The Smell of Newborn Babies Triggers the Same Reward Centers as Drugs," *Smithsonian*, September 24, 2013.

23 Anne Moir and David Jessel, *Brain Sex* (New York: Random House, 1991), 18; Cf. D. McGuiness, "Sex Differences in Organization, Perception, and Cognition," *Exploring Sex Differences*, eds., B. Lloyd and J. Archer (London: Academic Press, 1976), 123–155.

24 Cf. H. Frenzel et al., "A Genetic Basis for Mechanosensory Traits in Humans." *PLOS Biology* 10 (2012).

25 Cf. L. Fedigan and S. Zohar, "Sex Differences in Mortality of Japanese Macaques: Twenty-One Years of Data from the Arashiyama West Population," *American Journal of Physical Anthropology* 102 (1997), 161–175.

26 Cf. Dick Swaab, *We Are Our Brains* (New York: Penguin Books, 2014), 58; M. Hines, "Sex-Related Variation in Human Behavior and the Brain," *Trends in Cognitive Sciences* 14 (2010), 448–456; J. Hassett et al., "Sex Differences in Rhesus Monkey Toy Preferences Parallel Those of Children," *Hormones and Behavior* 54 (2008), 359–364.

27 Cf. S. Kahlenberg and R. Wrangham, "Sex Differences in Chimpanzees' Use of Sticks as Play Objects Resemble Those of Children," *Current Biology* 20 (2010), R1067–R1068; E. Lonsdorf et al., "Boys Will Be Boys: Sex Differences in Wild Infant Chimpanzee Social Interactions," *Animal Behavior* 88 (2014), 79–83.

28 Cf. J. Higley, "Aggression," in), *Primate Psychology*, Dario Maestripieri, ed. (Cambridge, MA.: Harvard University Press, 2003), 17–40.

29 Cf. A. Nordenström et al., "Sex-Typed Toy Play Behavior Correlates with the Degree of Prenatal Androgen Exposure Assessed by CYP21 Genotype in Girls with Congenital Adrenal Hyperplasia," *Journal of Clinical Endocrinology & Metabolism* 87 (2002), 5119–5124; Cf. Swaab, *We Are Our Brains*, 59.

30 Cf., Blum, *Sex on the Brain*, 184; J. Udry et al., "Androgen Effects on Women's Gendered Behaviour," *Journal of Biosocial Science* 27:3 (July 1995), 359–368; E. Chapman et al., "Fetal Testosterone and Empathy: Evidence from the Empathy Quotient (EQ) and the 'Reading the Mind of the Eyes' Test," *Social Neuroscience* 1 (2006), 135–148; F. Purifoy and L. Koopmans, "Androstenedione, Testosterone, and Free Testosterone Concentration in Women of Various Occupations," *Social Biology* 26 (1979), 179–188.

31 Cf. Glezerman, *Gender Medicine*, 75; P. Celec et al., "On the Effects of Testosterone on Brain Behavioral Functions," *Frontiers in Neuroscience* 9 (February 17, 2015), 5.

32 DSM-5, 457; Cf. L. Gooren, "The Biology of Human Psychosexual Differentiation," *Hormones and Behavior* 50 (2006), 589; Thomas E. Bevan, *The Psychobiology of Transsexualism and Transgenderism: A New View Based on Scientific Evidence* (Santa Barbara, CA: Praeger, 2014), 111–115.

33 Cf. M. Gershoni and S. Pietrokovski, "The Landscape of Sex-Differential Transcriptome and Its Consequent Selection in Human Adults," *BMC Biology* 15:7 (2017).

34 F. Mauvais-Jarvis, "Sex and Gender: Modifiers of Health, Disease, and Medicine," *Lancet* (August 22, 2020), 565; Cf. A. Arnold, "A General Theory of Sexual Differentiation," *Journal of Neuroscience Research* 95 (2017), 291–300.

35 Cf. J. Becker et al., "Strategies and Methods for Research on Sex Differences in Brain and Behavior," *Endocrinology* 146 (2005), 1650–1673; A. Matsumoto, ed., *Sexual Differentiation of the Brain* (New York: CRC, 1999).

36 Mauvais-Jarvis, "Sex and Gender: Modifiers of Health, Disease, and Medicine," 566.

37 Cf. Glezerman, *Gender Medicine*, 27.

38 Cf. R. Loomes et al., "What Is the Male-to-Female Ratio in Autism Spectrum Disorder? A Systematic Review and Meta-Analysis," *Journal of the American Academy of Child & Adolescent Psychiatry*, 56 (2017), 466–474.

39 Mauvais-Jarvis, "Sex and Gender: Modifiers of Health, Disease, and Medicine," 576.

40 Mauvais-Jarvis, "Sex and Gender: Modifiers of Health, Disease, and Medicine," 567.

41 Cf. Glezerman, *Gender Medicine*, 107; V. Caso et al., "Antiplatelet Treatment in Primary

and Secondary Stroke Prevention in Women," *European Journal of Internal Medicine* 23 (2012), 580–585.

42 Cf. H. Whitley et al., "Sex-Based Differences in Drug Activity," *American Family Physician* 80:11 (2009), 1254–1258; Institute of Medicine, Committee on Understanding the Biology of Sex and Gender Differences, *Exploring the Biological Contributions to Human Health: Does Sex Matter?*, ed. Theresa M. Wizeman and Mary-Lou Pardue (Washington, D.C.: National Academies Press, 2001), Executive Summary, 1.

43 Cf. Glezerman, *Gender Medicine*, 102,

44 M. Ferretti et al., "Account for Sex in Brain Research for Precision Medicine," *Nature* 569 (May 2019), 7754.

45 Mauvais-Jarvis, "Sex and Gender: Modifiers of Health, Disease, and Medicine."

46 Cf. Glezerman, *Gender Medicine*, 22.

47 Cf. D. Stroumsa et al., "The Power and Limits of Classification—A 32-Year-Old Man with Abdominal Pain," *The New England Journal of Medicine* 380 (May 16, 2019), 1885–1888.

48 Blum, *Sex on the Brain*, xvii.

49 Finley, *Sexual Identity*, 171.

50 Cf. Glezerman, *Gender Medicine*, 145.

51 Cf. John Paul II, TOB 21:3.

52 Cf. Blum, *Sex on the Brain*, 65.

53 Cf. Blum, *Sex on the Brain*, 105.

54 Yitzhak Koch, as quoted in Deborah Blum, "Is Mother's Milk Key to Child's Growth, Future?" *Sacramento Bee*, July 8, 1996, A-1.

55 Cf. F. Hassiotou et al., "Maternal And Infant Infections Stimulate a Rapid Leukocyte Response in Breastmilk," *Clinical and Translational Immunology* 2:4 (April 2013), e3.

56 "Golding's Introduction to Lord of the Flies," https://www.youtube.com/watch?v=vYnfSV27vLY.

57 As quoted in Kate Heron, "You Too: Selling Men on Gender Equality," *Literary Review of Canada*, March 2019.

58 Edith Stein, *Essays on Women*, vol. 2, *The Collected Works of Edith Stein* (Washington, D.C.: ICS Publications, 1996), 132.

59 As quoted in Dale O'Leary, The Gender Agenda (Lafayette, LA: Vital Issues Press, 1997), 201.

3. Some people are trans.

1 Most Rev. Michael F. Burbidge, "A Catechesis on the Human Person and Gender Ideology."

2 "Trans Woman Reacts to Lia Thomas INFURIATING Transphobes," https://youtu.be/ozigPNCnY5c.

3 "Gender euphoria," https://www.youtube.com/watch?v=9s3OlhQIZzM.

4 Kaylee Korol, "Trans tip number 2! Everyone seems to forget this!," Instagram, June 12, 2019.

5 Judith Butler, *Gender Trouble* (New York: Routledge, 1990), xx.

6 Levi Hord, "The Radical Truths of Transgender Studies," TEDxWesternU," https://www.youtube.com/watch?v=2f92jeAYuD4.

7 Cf. Hord, "The Radical Truths of Transgender Studies."

8 Favale, *The Genesis of Gender*, 42, 43.

9 "Trans-Racial? British Man Gets Cosmetic Surgery to Become Korean," https://youtu.be/zPByNY64iIQ.

10 "This Man Will Do Anything to Become More Like a Parrot!, Ripley's Believe It or Not," https://youtu.be/dVvrDbWpsKA.

11 Deborah Soh, *The End of Gender* (New York: Threshold Editions, 2020), 149.

12 Kai Shappley, *A Trans Girl Growing Up In Texas*, https://youtu.be/cuIkLNsRtas.

13 Cf. Josef Pieper, *The Human Wisdom of St Thomas: A Breviary of Philosophy from the Works of St Thomas Aquinas* (San Francisco: Ignatius Press, 2002).

14 Pope John Paul II, *Gratissimam Sane*, 19.

15 Robert George, "Gnostic Liberalism," *First Things*, December 2016.

16 *Gratissimam Sane* 19.

17 Cf. John Paul II, TOB 19:4.

18 Cf. John Paul II, TOB 14:4; 20:5.

19 Christoph Cardinal Schönborn, preface, Pope John Paul II, *Man and Woman He Created*

Them (New York: Pauline Books and Media, 2006), xxiv–xxv.

20   Cf. Michelle Cretella, "Dr. Cretella on Transgenderism: A Mental Illness Is Not a Civil Right," TFP Student Action (Nov. 15, 2017).

21   Alex Stedman, "Alexis Arquette, Actress and Sister to Patricia and David Arquette, Dies at 47," Reuters, September 11, 2016.

22   John Paul II, TOB 32:1; 15:1.

23   John Paul II, TOB 48:5.

24   John Paul II, TOB 26:4.

25   Karol Wojtyla, *God is Beauty* (Quarryville, PA: Theology of the Body Institute, 2021), 70.

26   John Paul II, *Dominum et Vivificatem*, 59.

27   John Paul II, *Crossing the Threshold of Hope* (New York: Knopf, 1994), 209.

28   *Gaudium Et Spes*, 36.

29   G. K. Chesterton, *Heretics* (United States, Simon and Brown, 2012), 109.

30   Cf. John Paul II, TOB 8:1, 13:2.

31   Cf. Margaret McCarthy, "Gender Ideology and the Humanum," *Communio* 43 (Summer 2016), 294.

32   Pope Francis, *Laudato Si*, 155.

33   Cf. John Paul II, TOB 14:5

34   Edith Stein, "The Ethos of Women's Professions," in *Essays on Women*, (Washington D.C.: ICS Publications, 1996), 50.

35   Abigail Favale, "The Eclipse of Sex by the Rise of Gender," *Church Life Journal* (March 1, 2019).

36   John Paul II, TOB 27:4.

37   John Paul II, TOB 29:4.

38   John Paul II, TOB 28:4.

39   Luce Irigaray, *An Ethics of Sexual Difference*, trans. Carolyn Burke and Gillian C. Gill (Ithaca, NY: Cornell University Press, 1993), 5.

40   John Paul II, TOB 18:4; cf. "Letter on the Collaboration of Men and Women in the Church and in the World," Congregation for the Doctrine of the Faith (2004), 12.

4.   Sex is assigned at birth.

1   Declaration of Deanna Adkins, M.D., U.S. District Court, Middle District of North Carolina, Case 1:16-cv-00236-TDS-JEP, 6, 7.

2   V. Shteyler et al., "Failed Assignments—Rethinking Sex Designations on Birth Certificates," *New England Journal of Medicine* 383:25 (December 2020): 2399–2401.

3   "Hey Doc, Some Boys Are Born Girl," Decker Moss at TEDxColumbus, https://youtu.be/nOmstbKVebM.

4   Cf. L. Sax, "How Common Is Intersex?," *Journal of Sex Research* 39:3 (2002), 174–178.

5   Margaret McCarthy, "Gender Ideology and the Humanum," *Communio* 43 (Summer 2016), 288.

6   Paul McHugh, "Brief of Amicus Curiae," *R.G. & G.R. Harris Funeral Homes, Inc. v. Equal Employment Opportunity Commission*, 2014, https://www.supremecourt.gov/DocketPDF/18/18-107/113262/20190822151939369_TO%20PRINT%2019-8-22%20Dr.%20Paul%20McHugh%20Amicus%20Brief%20FINAL.pdf.

7   Soh, *The End of Gender*, 7.

8   Julia Mason MS MD, @JuliaMasonMD1, Twitter, December 17, 2020.

9   Selective Service System, SSS.gov, "Who needs to register?"

10   Cf. "Phenotypic Plasticity and the Evolution of Gender," *Integrative and Comparative Biology* 53:4 (October 2013); D. Policansky, "Sex Change in Plants and Animals," *Annual Review of Ecology and Systematics* 13 (1982), 484.

11   Cf. Blum, *Sex on the Brain*, 17.

12   Cf. Blum, *Sex on the Brain*, 16.

13   Cf. R. R. Warner and S. E. Swearer, "Social Control of Sex Change in the Bluehead Wrass, Thalassoma bifasciatum (Pisces: Labridae)," *Biological Bulletin* 181 (1991), 199–204.

14   Cf. C. Collin and J. Shykoff, "Outcrossing Rates in the Gynomonoecious-Gynodioecious Species Dianthus sylvestris (Caryophyllaceae)," *American Journal of Botany* 90:4 (April

1, 2003), 579–585; University of Lincoln, "New Research Sheds Light on Why Plants Change Sex," *ScienceDaily* (blog), January 10, 2017, https://www.sciencedaily.com/releases/2017/01/170110094606.htm.

5. Intersex people prove that sex is not binary.

1   Cf. A. Fausto-Sterling, "The Five Sexes: Why Male and Female are Not Enough," *The Sciences* (March/April 1993), 20–25.

2   Cf. M. Blackless et al., "How Sexually Dimorphic Are We? Review and Synthesis," *American Journal of Human Biology* 2 (March 12, 2000), 151–166; Anne Fausto-Sterling, *Sexing the Body: Gender Politics and the Construction of Sexuality* (New York: Basic Books, 2000).

3   Cf. Makiyan Z, "Systemization of Ambiguous Genitalia," *Organogenesis* 12 (2016), 169–182; P. Lee et al., "Global Disorders of Sex Development Update since 2006: Perceptions, Approach and Care," *Hormone Research in Paediatrics* 85 (2016), 159.

4   Cf. L. Sax, "How Common Is Intersex?" *Journal of Sex Research* 39:3 (2002), 174–178.

5   L. Sax, "How Common Is Intersex?," 174–178.

6   Cf. L. Sax, "How Common Is Intersex?," 174–178.

7   Cf. L. Sax, "How Common Is Intersex?," 174–178.

8   L. Sax, "How Common Is Intersex?," 174–178.

9   Cf. Sax, "How Common is Intersex?," 174–178; I. Hughes et al., "Consensus Statement on Management of Intersex Disorders," *Pediatrics* 118:2 (2006), 488–500.

10   M. Blackless et al., "How Sexually Dimorphic Are We?," 151.

11   Anne Fausto-Sterling, *Sexing the Body: Gender Politics and the Construction of Sexuality* (New York: Basic Books, 2000), 31.

12   Cf. Helen Joyce, *Trans* (London: Oneworld Publications, 2021), 189.

13   Cf. Intersex Society of North America, "Congenital Adrenal Hyperplasia (CAH)."

14   Cf. S. Berenbaum, "Gendered Peer Involvement in Girls with Congenital Adrenal Hyperplasia: Effects of Prenatal Androgens, Gendered Activities, and Gender Cognitions," *Archives of Sexual Behavior* 47:4 (2018), 915–929; S. Berenbaum and E. Snyder, "Early Hormonal Influences on Childhood Sex-Typed Activity and Playmate Preferences," *Developmental Psychology* 31(1995), 31–42; S. Berenbaum and M. Hines, "Early Androgens Are Related to Childhood Sex-Typed Toy Preferences," *Psychological Science* 3 (1992), 203–206; A. Servin et al., "Prenatal Androgens and Gender-Typed Behavior: A Study of Girls with Mild and Severe Forms of Congenital Adrenal Hyperplasia," *Developmental Psychology* 39 (2003), 440–450; M. Hines, "Sex-Related Variation in Human Behavior and the Brain," *Trends in Cognitive Science* 10 (2010), 448–456.

15   Cf. M. Hines, "Prenatal Endocrine Influences on Sexual Orientation and on Sexually Differentiated Childhood Behavior," *Frontiers in Neuroendocrinology* 32 (2011), 170–182.

16   Ryan Anderson, *When Harry Became Sally* (New York: Encounter Books, 2018), 90.

17   Cf. M. Özdemir et al., "Ovotesticular Disorder of Sex Development: An Unusual Presentation," *Journal of Clinical Imaging Science* 9 (2009): 1.

18   Özdemir et al., "Ovotesticular Disorder of Sex Development," 4.

19   Karol Wojtyla, *Love and Responsibility* (San Francisco, Ignatius Press, 1993), 47.

6. Some people have the brain of one sex but the body of the other.

1   Katherine Wu, "Between the (Gender) Lines: Science of Transgender Identity," Harvard University Science in the News, blog, December 2016, http://sitn.hms.harvard.edu/flash/2016/gender-lines-science-transgender-identity/.

2   Cf. Antonio Guillamon et al., "A Review of the Status of Brain Structure Research in Transsexualism," *Archives of Sexual Behaviors* 45:7 (October 2016), 1615–1648; M. Diamond, "Transsexualism as an Intersex Condition," Pacific Center for Sex and Society (May 20, 2017); R. Fernández et al., "Molecular Basis of Gender Dysphoria: Androgen and Estrogen Receptor Interaction," *Psychoneuroendocrinology* 98 (December 2018), 165.

3   Jessica Herthel and Jazz Jennings, *I am Jazz* (New York: Dial Books, 2014).

4   J. N. Zhou et al., "A Sex Difference in the Human Brain and Its Relation to Transsexuality," *Nature* 378 (1995), 66–70.

5   Curt Suplee, "Possible Transsexual Brain Trait Found," *Washington Post*, November 2, 1995.

6   J. N. Zhou et al., "A Sex Difference in the Human Brain and its Relation to Transsexuality," 70.

7   H. Hulshoff, "Changing Your Sex Changes Your Brain: Influences of Testosterone and Estrogen on Adult Human Brain Structure," *European Journal of Endocrinology* 155 (2006), 107–114.

8   Mark Yarhouse, *Understanding Gender Dysphoria* (Downers Grove, IL: InterVarsity Press, 2015), 73.

9   F. Kruijver et al., "Male to Female Transsexuals Have Female Neuron Numbers in a Limbic Nucleus," *Journal of Clinical Endocrinology & Metabolism* 85:5 (May 2000), 2034–2041.

10   Cf. G. Rametti, et al. "White Matter Microstructure in Female to Male Transsexuals Before Cross-Sex Hormonal Treatment. A Diffusion Tensor Imaging Study," *Journal of Psychiatric Research* 45 (2011), 199–204.

11   Cf. Kranz GS, et al. "White Matter Microstructure in Transsexuals and Controls Investigated by Diffusion Tensor Imaging," *Journal of Neuroscience* 34:46 (2014): 15466–15475.

12   Cf. E. Santarnecchi et al., "Intrinsic Cerebral Connectivity Analysis in an Untreated Female-to-Male Transsexual Subject: A First Attempt Using Resting State fMRI," *Neuroendocrinology* 96:3 (2012), 188–193; I. Savic and S. Arver, "Sex Dimorphism of the Brain in Male-to-Female Transsexuals," *Cerebral Cortex* 21:11 (2011), 2525–2533.

13   Lawrence S. Mayer, and Paul R. McHugh, "Sexuality and Gender Findings from the Biological, Psychological, and Social Sciences," *New Atlantis* 50 (Fall 2016), Part 3.

14   L. Mayer and P. McHugh, "Sexuality and Gender Findings from the Biological, Psychological, and Social Sciences," *New Atlantis* 50 (Fall 2016), Executive Summary.

15   "Gender Dysphoria in Children," American College of Pediatricians (November 2018).

16   McHugh, "Brief of Amicus Curiae."

17   Cf. Mohammad Reza Mohammadi and Ali Khaleghi, "Transsexualism: A Different Viewpoint to Brain Changes," *Clinical Psychopharmacology and Neuroscience* 16:2 (2018), 136–143.

18   Cf. J. Gu, R. Kanai, "What Contributes to Individual Differences in Brain Structure?," *Frontiers in Human Neuroscience* 8 (2014), 262.

19   S. Stagg, "Autistic Traits in Individuals Self-Defining as Transgender or Nonbinary," *European Psychiatry* 61 (September 2019), 17–12.

20   Cf. L. Hare et al., "Androgen Receptor Repeat Length Polymorphism Associated with Male-To-Female Transsexualism," *Biological Psychiatry* 65:1 (2009), 93–96; R. Fernández, "The (CA)n Polymorphism of ERβ Gene is Associated with FtM Transsexualism," *Journal of Sexual Medicine* 11:3 (March 2014), 720–728.

21   Cf. E. Santarnecchi et al., "Intrinsic Cerebral Connectivity Analysis in an Untreated Female-to-Male Transsexual Subject: A First Attempt Using Resting State fMRI," *Neuroendocrinology* 96:3 (2012), 188–193; Savic and Arver, "Sex Dimorphism of the Brain in Male-to-Female Transsexuals," 2525–2533.

22   Cf. Savic and Arver, "Sex Dimorphism of the Brain in Male-to-Female Transsexuals," 2525–2533.

23   Cf. Milton Diamond, "Transsexuality Among Twins: Identity Concordance, Transition, Rearing, and Orientation," *International Journal of Transgenderism* 14:1 (2013), 24–38.

24   Larry Cahill, "An Issue Whose Time Has Come: Sex/Gender Influences on Nervous System Function," *Journal of Neuroscience Research* 95: 1-2 (January/February 2017), Spc1, 1–791.

25   Cahill, "An Issue Whose Time Has Come," 12–13.

26   Kristie Overstreet PhD, "Why Are Many Doctors Scared of Transgender Patients?, TEDxLivoniaCCLibrary," https://www.youtube.com/watch?v=7tG3LWxWZxg.

27   Margaret M. McCarthy, *Sex and the Developing Brain*, 2nd ed. (San Rafael, CA: Morgan & Claypool, 2017).

28   Larry Cahill, "A Half-Truth Is a Whole Lie: On the Necessity of Investigating Sex Influences on the Brain," *Endocrinology* 153 (2012), 2542.

29   Cf. Louann Brizendine, The Male Brain (New York: Harmony Books, 2010).

30   Lisa Elliot, "Bad Science and the Unisex Brain," *Nature* 566 (February 28, 2019), 453.

31   M. Ferretti et al., "Account for Sex in Brain Research for Precision Medicine," *Nature* 569 (May 2019), 7754.

32   Cf. M. Hines, "Sex-Related Variation in Human Behavior and the Brain," *Trends in Cognitive Science* 14:10 (2010), 448–56; M. Hines, "Gender Development and the Human

Brain," *Annual Review of Neuroscience* 34 (2011), 69–88; McCarthy, *Sex and the Developing Brain*; Marianne J. Legato, MD, ed., *Principles of Gender-Specific Medicine: Gender in the Genomic Era*, 3rd ed. (Amsterdam: Academic Press, 2017).

33   Cf. Larry Cahill, "His Brain, Her Brain," *Scientific American* (October 1, 2012).
34   Cf. M. Ingalhalikar et al., "Sex Differences in the Structural Connectome of the Human Brain," *Proceedings of the National Academy of Sciences of The United States of America* 11:2 (2003), 823–828; Larry Cahill, "Fundamental Sex Difference in Human Brain Architecture," *Proceedings of the National Academy of Sciences of the United States of America* 111:2 (2014): 577–578.
35   Cf. Glezerman, *Gender Medicine*, 64.
36   Cf. B. Shaywitz, et al. "Sex Differences in the Functional Organization of the Brain for Language," *Nature* 373 (2004), 607–609.
37   Cf. D. Kent et al., "Sex-Based Differences in response to Recombinant Tissue Plasminogen Activator in Acute Ischemic Stroke," *Stroke* 36 (2005), 62–65.
38   Cf. B. and A. Pease, *Why Men Don't Listen & Women Can't Read Maps*, 65.

7.   The idea of a rigid gender binary is the result of Western colonialism.

1   E. Towle and L. Morgan, "Romancing the Transgender Native: Rethinking the Use of the 'Third Gender' Concept," in Stryker and Whittle, *Transgender Studies Reader* (New York: Routledge, 2006), 666, 672.
2   Towle and Morgan, "Romancing the Transgender Native," 672.
3   Towle and Morgan, "Romancing the Transgender Native," 672.
4   Janis Walworth, *Transsexual Workers: An Employer's Guide* (Los Angeles: Center for Gender Sanity, 1998), 89.
5   Cf. A. Agrawal, "Gendered Bodies: The Case of the 'Third Gender' in India," *Contributions to Indian Sociology*, 31 (1997), 292; Kessler and Wendy McKenna, *Gender: An Ethnomethodological Approach* (New York: Wiley, 1978), 29; Don Kulick, *Travesti: Sex, Gender, and Culture among Brazilian Transgendered Prostitutes* (Chicago: University of Chicago Press, 1998); Marjorie Garber, *Vested Interests: Cross-Dressing and Cultural Anxiety* (New York: Routledge, 1992), 11, 71.
6   Towle and Morgan, "Romancing the Transgender Native," 672.
7   Cf. Adnan Hossain, "Beyond Emasculation: Pleasure, Power, and Masculinity in the Making of Hijrahood in Bangladesh" (doctoral dissertation, University of Hull, UK).
8   Cf. Serena Nanda, *Gender Diversity* (Long Grove, IL: Waveland Press: 2014), 31.
9   Cf. Atindriyo Chakraborty, "Manusmriti and the Judiciary–A Dangerous Game," CounterCurrents.Org, July 27, 2000.
10   Cf. *Manu Smriti* in Sanskrit with an English translation at https://www.indiadivine.org/content/files/file/644-manu-smriti-in-sanskrit-with-english-translations-pdf/.
11   As quoted in Joyce, *Trans*, 36.
12   Joyce, *Trans*, 176.
13   Nanda, *Gender Diversity*, 13.
14   Cf. Nanda, *Gender Diversity*, 19.
15   Nanda, *Gender Diversity*, 23.
16   Nanda, *Gender Diversity*, 123.
17   Cf. C. Epple, "Coming to Terms with Navajo 'Nádleehí': A Critique of 'Berdache,' 'Gay,' 'Alternate Gender,' and Two-Spirit,'" *American Ethnologist* 25/2 (1998), 267–290; E. Moral, "Qu(e)erying Sex and Gender in Archaeology: A Critique of the 'Third' and Other Sexual Categories," *Journal of Archaeological Method and Theory* 23:3 (2016), 788–809.
18   Cf. Kulick, *Travesti: Sex, Gender, and Culture among Brazilian Transgendered Prostitutes*.
19   Nanda, *Gender Diversity*, 47–48.
20   Cf. Nanda, *Gender Diversity*, 51–56.
21   Nanda, *Gender Diversity*, 96.
22   Br. Malachy Joseph Napier, CFR, "True Identity or Ideology? Catholic Anthropology and Gender Ideology," (thesis, Saint Joseph's Seminary, Dunwoodie, 2020).
23   Cf. M. Kay Martin and Barbara Voorhies, as quoted in *Female of the Species* (New York: Columbia University Press, 1975), 23.

24 Towle and Morgan, "Romancing the Transgender Native," 666, 681.
25 In-flight press conference of His Holiness Pope Francis from the Philippines to Rome, January 19, 2015.

8. More people are coming out as trans only because society has become more accepting.

1   *Passionate Inanna,* Enheduanna.
2   City of God VII, 26.
3   City of God XVI, chapter 8.
4   Karl Marx and Frederick Engels, *The Communist Manifesto*, trans. Samuel Moore, vol. 6, *Karl Marx and Frederick Engels, Collected Works* (London: ElecBook, 1998), 32.
5   Frederick Engels, *The Origin of the Family, Private Property and the State* (New York: International Publishers, 1942), 58.
6   Engels, *The Origin of the Family, Private Property and the State*, 50.
7   Engels, *The Origin of the Family, Private Property and the State*, 65.
8   Engels, *The Origin of the Family, Private Property and the State*, 66.
9   Engels, *The Origin of the Family, Private Property and the State*, 67.
10 Kate Bornstein, *Gender Outlaw: On Men, Women, and the Rest of Us* (New York: Routledge, 1994), 115.
11 Simone de Beauvoir, *The Second Sex* (New York: Vintage Books, 2021), x.
12 Cf. Louis Menand, "Stand by Your Man," *New Yorker*, September 18, 2005.
13 Jean-Paul Sartre, *Existentialism Is a Humanism*, trans. Carol Macomber (New Haven, CT: Yale University Press, 2007), 22.
14 Simone de Beauvoir, *The Second Sex*, 8.
15 "Simone de Beauvoir Explains 'One is Not Born, but Rather Becomes, a Woman,'" https://youtu.be/Aekr9sLbVhQ.
16 Alice Schwarzer, *After the Second Sex: Conversations with Simone de Beauvoir* (New York: Pantheon, 1984), 40.
17 Simone de Beauvoir, *The Second Sex*, 147.
18 Simone de Beauvoir, *The Second Sex*, 301.
19 Céline Leboeuf, "One Is Not Born, But Rather Becomes, a Woman: The Sex-Gender Distinction and Simone De Beauvoir's Account of Woman," in *Feminist Moments: Reading Feminist Texts*, eds. K. Smits and S. Bruce (London: Bloomsbury Academic, 2016).
20 Simone de Beauvoir, *The Second Sex*, 21.
21 Judith Butler, *Gender Trouble* (New York, Routledge: 1990), 151–152.
22 Michel Foucault, "Nietzsche, Genealogy, History," in *Language, Counter-Memory, Practice: Selected Essays and Interviews*, ed. D. F. Bouchard (Ithaca, NY: University Press; 1977), 153.
23 Sandra Lee Bartky, as quoted in *Gender Trouble*, endorsement page.
24 "Judith Butler: Your Behavior Creates Your Gender: Big Think," https://youtu.be/Bo7o2LYATDc.
25 Cf. Butler, *Gender Trouble*, 200, 201.
26 Butler, *Gender Trouble*, 34.
27 "Who Is Afraid of Gender?," Prof. Judith Butler: https://youtu.be/cqc3uCold08.
28 Butler, *Gender Trouble*, xv, 190.
29 Judith Butler, "Sex and Gender in Simone de Beauvoir's Second Sex," *Yale French Studies* 72 (1986), 35.
30 Cf. Butler, *Gender Trouble*, 203.
31 Butler, *Gender Trouble*, 136.
32 Butler, *Gender Trouble*, 9.
33 Butler, *Gender Trouble*, 192–193
34 Susan Faludi, "Death of a Revolutionary," *New Yorker* (April 15, 2013).
35 Manifesto of the Communist Party, *Marx/Engels Selected Works*, vol. 1 (Moscow: Progress Publishers, 1969).
36 Shulamith Firestone, *The Dialectic of Sex* (New York: Farrar, Straus and Giroux: 1970), 12.
37 Firestone, *The Dialectic of Sex*, 11.

38   Firestone, *The Dialectic of Sex*, 30.

39   Firestone, *The Dialectic of Sex* 4.

40   Firestone, *The Dialectic of Sex*, 10, 13.

41   Firestone, *The Dialectic of Sex*, 93.

42   Faludi, "Death of a Revolutionary."

43   Firestone, *The Dialectic of Sex*, 180.

44   Firestone, *The Dialectic of Sex*, 175.

45   Firestone, *The Dialectic of Sex*, 29.

46   Firestone, *The Dialectic of Sex*, 185.

47   Firestone, *The Dialectic of Sex*, 208.

48   Firestone, *The Dialectic of Sex*, 187.

49   Firestone, *The Dialectic of Sex*, 215.

50   Firestone, *The Dialectic of Sex*, 215–216.

51   Judith Butler, *Undoing Gender* (New York: Routledge, 2004), 157.

52   "Lettre ouverte à la Commission de révision du code pénal pour la revision de certains textes régissant les rapports entre adultes et mineurs," 1977; Cf. Abigail Favale, *The Genesis of Gender*, 76 –77.

53   Favale, *The Genesis of Gender*, 77.

54   Kate Millett, "The Feminist Time Forgot," *Magazine*/Journal, 1998.

55   Faludi, "Death of a Revolutionary."

56   Faludi, "Death of a Revolutionary."

57   Faludi, "Death of a Revolutionary."

58   Julia Serano, *Whipping Girl* (Berkeley, CA: Seal Press, 2007), 30.

59   Serano, *Whipping Girl*, 29.

60   Serano, *Whipping Girl*, 227, 239.

61   Pope Francis, *Amoris Laetitia*, 54.

62   Butler, *Gender Trouble*, xiv

63   *Women in Christ: Toward a New Feminism*, ed. Michelle M. Schumacher (Grand Rapids, MI: William B. Eerdmans Publishing Co., 2003), 63.

64   Firestone, *The Dialectic of Sex*, 15.

65   Favale, "The Eclipse of Sex by the Rise of Gender."

66   Joseph Cardinal Ratzinger, *The Ratzinger Report* (San Francisco: Ignatius Press, 1985), 95–96.

67   Address of His Holiness Benedict XVI on the Occasion of Christmas Greetings to the Roman Curia, Clementine Hall (December 21, 2012).

68   Marc Barnes, "A Conservative Trans Dilemma," New Polity, https://newpolity.com/blog/a-conservative-dilemma.

69   Angela Franks, "Humanae Vitae in Light of the War Against Female Fertility," *Church Life Journal* (July 24, 2018).

70   Butler, *Gender Trouble*, xi.

71   Butler, *Gender Trouble*, xi.

72   Kyle Lukoff, "Call Me Max" (New York: Reycraft Books: 2019), 5.

73   Cf. Jodie Patterson, "Raising Penelope, My Transgender Son," Refinery29, November 16, 2015.

74   Cf. Mary Kay Linge and Jon Levine, "Over $200K Being Spent on Drag Queen Shows at NYC Schools, Records Show," *New York Post*, June 11, 2022.

75   Cf. Sam Merriman, "Children Are Being 'Brainwashed' by TikTok Videos on 'Cool' Trans Surgery Viewed 26 Billion Times, Campaigners Claim," DailyMail.com, December 25, 2021.

76   "University of Southern Maine Students Demand Professor Be Replaced for Saying Only Two Sexes Exist," Foxnews.com, October 7, 2022.

77   Cf. Diana Glebova, "Irish Teacher Imprisoned for Continuing to Teach after Refusing to Use 'Gender-Neutral' Pronouns," Nationalreview.com, September 6, 2022.

78   Cf. 1995 Beijing Conference, 1996 International Bill Gender Rights, 2007 Yogyakarta Principles, 2020 *Bostock vs. Clayton County*.

79   Cf. Murphy, Heather, "Always Removes Female Symbol from Sanitary Pads," *New York Times*, October 22, 2019.

80   Upton Sinclair, *I, Candidate for Governor: And How I Got Licked* (1935; repr. Los Angeles: University of California Press, 1994), 109.

81 Cf. Joyce, *Trans*, 12, 15.
82 Cf. "Through Science to Justice: Magnus Hirschfeld and Germany's LGBT Rights Movement by Natasha Pagel," https://youtu.be/DOzfYbgq-UI.
83 Stephen Whittle, "A Brief History of Transgender Issues," *Guardian*, June 2, 2010; cf. Joyce, *Trans*, 14, 17.
84 "LGBT Studies: How the Nazis Destroyed the Work of Magnus Hirschfeld," https://youtu .be/QU-WVjwJPNk.
85 Cf. Joyce, *Trans*, 20.
86 Cf. R. Green, "The Three Kings: Harry Benjamin, John Money, Robert Stoller," *Archives of Sexual Behavior* 38:4 (August 2009), 610–613.
87 "The Sexes: Prisoners of Sex," *Time*, January 21, 1974, 64.
88 John Colapinto, *As Nature Made Him* (New York: Harper Perennial, 2006), 26.
89 Colapinto, *As Nature Made Him*, 27.
90 Colapinto, *As Nature Made Him*, 27.
91 Colapinto, *As Nature Made Him*, 28.
92 "Sexes: Attacking the Last Taboo," *Time*, April 14, 1980.
93 Colapinto, *As Nature Made Him*, 30.
94 Colapinto, *As Nature Made Him*, 34.
95 Colapinto, *As Nature Made Him*, 33.
96 Cf. J. Money, "Matched Pairs of Hermaphrodites: Behavioral Biology of Sexual Differentiation from Chromosomes to Gender Identity," *Engineering and Science* 33 (1970), 34–39.
97 "The Sexes: Biological Imperatives," *Time*, January 8, 1973.
98 Colapinto, *As Nature Made Him*, 87.
99 Colapinto, *As Nature Made Him*, 91.
100 Colapinto, *As Nature Made Him*, 107.
101 J. Money and P. Tucker, *Sexual Signatures: On Being a Man or Woman* (Boston: Little, Brown, 1975), 95.
102 Colapinto, *As Nature Made Him*, 179.
103 Colapinto, *As Nature Made Him*, xvii.
104 Cf. M. Diamon and K. Sigmundson, "Sex Reassignment at Birth: A Long Term Review and Clinical Implications," *Archives of Pediatrics and Adolescent Medicine* 151 (March 1997).
105 Paul R. McHugh, "Surgical Sex: Why We Stopped Doing Sex Change Operations," *First Things*, November 2004.
106 Paul McHugh, "Transgender Surgery Isn't the Solution," *Wall Street Journal*, June 12, 2014.
107 J. Meyer, and D. Reter, "Sex Reassignment: Follow-Up," *Archives of General Psychiatry* 36: (1979), 1010, 1012.

9. Puberty blockers are a safe, effective, and reversible way to pause puberty.

1 "Johanna Olson, MD Talks About Research on Transgender Youth," https://www.youtube. com/watch?v=jjtRJsC16HE.
2 Cf. A. DeVries et al., "Puberty Suppression in Adolescents with Gender Identity Disorder: A Prospective Follow-Up Study," *Journal of Sexual Medicine* 8 (2011), 2276–2283; R. Costa et al., "Psychological Support, Puberty Suppression, and Psychosocial Functioning in Adolescents with Gender Dysphoria," *Journal of Sexual Medicine* 12 (2015), 2206–2214; J. Turban et al., "Pubertal Suppression for Transgender Youth and Risk of Suicidal Ideation," *Pediatrics* 145: 2 (2020).
3 "I Am Leo, Transgender Documentary," https://youtu.be/Nysd3h4ZtIs.
4 S. Giordano, "Lives in a Chiaroscuro: Should We Suspend the Puberty of Children with Gender Identity Disorder?," *Journal of Medical Ethics* 34:8 (2008), 583.
5 Cf. Michael Biggs, "The Tavistock's Experiment with Puberty Blockers," Department of Sociology and St. Cross College, University of Oxford (version 1.0.1), July 29, 2019; P. Cohen-Kettenis and S. van Goozen, "Pubertal Delay as an Aid in Diagnosis and Treatment of a Transsexual Adolescent," *European Child & Adolescent Psychiatry* 7 (1998), 246–248.
6 P. Cohen-Kettenis et al., "Treatment of Adolescents with Gender Dysphoria in the Netherlands," *Child and Adolescent Psychiatry Clinics of North America* 20 (2011), 689–700.

7   Cf. Jaime Stevens et al., "Insurance Coverage of Puberty Blocker Therapies for Transgender Youth," *Pediatrics* 136:6 (December 2015), 1029–1031.

8   *Growing Up Trans* (full documentary), *Frontline*," https://youtu.be/uIuS-48tSpE.

9   Sara Solovitch, "When Kids Come in Saying They Are Transgender (Or No Gender), These Doctors Try to Help," *Washington Post*, January 21, 2018.

10 Jordan Crimson "The Gender Affirmative Model: APA Publishes Groundbreaking Book on Care for Trans and Gender Expansive Youth," Spectrum South (June 2018).

11 "Born in the Wrong Body, Summer Camp, Full Documentary," https://youtu.be/N90m5B2jm80.

12 Safety and Tolerability Profile, https://www.supprelinla.com/hcp/safety-tolerability-profile/; https://www.lupronpedpro.com/content/lupronped-hcp/countries/north-america/us/en_us/pages.html, https://www.accessdata.fda.gov/drugsatfda_docs/label/2014/020517s 036_019732s041lbl.pdf.

13 "Package leaflet: Decapeptyl® SR 11.25 mg," Ipsen Ltd. 2017, retrieved from http://www.medicines.org.uk/emc/product/780/pil.

14 Cf. Biggs, "The Tavistock's Experiment with Puberty Blockers," 6.

15 The Tavistock and Portman NHS Foundation Trust, Board of Directors, June 23, 2015; Cf. Cohen, Deborah and Hannah Barnes, "Transgender treatment: Puberty blockers study under investigation," BBC Newsnight (July 22, 2019).

16 Cf. Biggs, "The Tavistock's Experiment with Puberty Blockers," 9.

17 P. Carmichael et al., "Short-term Outcomes of Pubertal Suppression in a Selected Cohort of 12 to 15 Year Old Young People with Persistent Gender Dysphoria in the UK," *PLoS One* 16:2 (February 2, 2021).

18 G. Fink et al., "Estrogen Control of Central Neurotransmission: Effect on Mood, Mental State, and Memory," *Cellular and Molecular Neurobiology*, 16:3 (1996), 325–344.

19 Blum, *Sex on the Brain*, 206.

20 Cf. Chandler Marrs, "Lupron Side Effects Survey Results Part One: Scope and Severity," Hormones Matter, October 4, 2017.

21 Cf. M. Schneider et al., "Brain Maturation, Cognition and Voice Pattern in a Gender Dysphoria Case under Pubertal Suppression," *Frontiers in Human Neuroscience* 11 (November 2017), 1, 4–6; "Gender Dysphoria in Children: Understanding the Science and Medicine," https://www.youtube.com/watch?v=GOniPhuyXeY.

22 Cf. Biggs, "The Tavistock's Experiment with Puberty Blockers," 5.

23 Cf. D. Klink et al., "Bone Mass in Young Adulthood Following Gonadotrophin-Releasing Hormone Analog Treatments and Cross-Sex Hormone Treatment in Adolescents with Gender Dysphoria," *Journal of Clinical Endocrinology & Metabolism* 100 (2015), E270–E275; M. Vlot et al., "Effect of Pubertal Suppression and Cross-Sex Hormone Therapy on Bone Turnover Markers and Bone Mineral Apparent Density (BMAD) in Transgender Adolescents," *Bone* 95 (February 2017), 11–19; Megan Twohey and Christina Jewett, "They Paused Puberty, but Is there a Cost?" *New York Times*, November 14, 2022.

24 Biggs, "The Tavistock's Experimentation with Puberty Blockers," 18.

25 Christina Jewett, "Drug Used to Halt Puberty in Children May Cause Lasting Health Problems," Kaiser Health News (February 2, 2017).

26 Jewett, "Drug Used to Halt Puberty in Children May Cause Lasting Health Problems."

27 Cf. Brie Jontry, "Does Prepubertal Medical Transition Impact Adult Sexual Function?," July 8, 2018, retrieved from http://4thwavenow.com/tag/puberty-blockers-and-sexual-function/.

28 P. Cohen-Kettenis et al., "Puberty Suppression in a Gender-Dysphoric Adolescent: A 22-Year Follow-Up," *Archives of Sexual Behavior*, 40:4 (2011), 845.

29 Cf. Gender Identity Research and Education Society, "Consensus Report on Symposium in May 2005," retrieved from http://www.gires.org.uk/consensus-report-on-symposium-in- may-2005/.

30 Cf. AbbVie 2021 Annual Report on Form 10-K.

31 "TAP Pharmaceutical Products Inc. and Seven Others Charged with Health Care Crimes; Company Agrees to Pay $875 Million to Settle Charges," United States Department of Justice, October 3, 2001.

32 Biggs, "The Tavistock's Experiment with Puberty Blockers," 10.

33 Cf. A. DeVries et al., "Puberty Suppression in Gender Identity Disorder: The Amsterdam Experience," *National Review of Endocrinology*, 17:7 (2011), 466–472; A. DeVries et al., "Puberty

Suppression in Adolescents with Gender Identity Disorder," Journal of Sexual 2276–2283.

34   P. Hruz, L. Mayer, and P. McHugh, "Growing Pains: The Problems with Puberty Suppression in Treating Gender Dysphoria," *New Atlantis* 52 (Spring 2017).

35   Cf. P. Carmichael et al., "Gender Dysphoria in Younger Children: Support and Care in an Evolving Context," WPATH 24th Scientific Symposium, June 19, 2016.

36   Cf. "The Hormone Health Crisis, with Endocrinologist William Malone, MD," https://www.youtube.com/watch?v=z4RYl75zdMY.

37   Cf. Lisa Nainggolan, "Hormone Tx of Youth with Gender Dysphoria Stops in Sweden," *Medscape* (May 12, 2021), https://www.medscape.com/viewarticle/950964; "One Year Since Finland Broke with WPATH 'Standards of Care': Finland Prioritizes Psychotherapy over Hormones, and Rejects Surgeries for Gender-Dysphoric Minors," *SEGM* (July 2, 2021).

38   Cf. Q&A for Dr. Kenneth Zucker: "Children and Adolescents with Gender Dysphoria," CMB Lecture at McGill University, January 23, 2020.

39   Cf. L. Nahata et al., "Low Fertility Preservation Utilization Among Transgender Youth," *Journal of Adolescent Health* 61:1 (July 2017), 40–44; D. Chen et al., "Fertility Preservation for Transgender Adolescents," *Journal of Adolescent Health* 61:1 (July 2017): 120–123.

40   Shrier, *Irreversible Damage*, 47.

41   "UK Bans Puberty Blockers for Trans Children," https://www.youtube.com/watch?v=EwgjGlrCdrw.

10.   Cross-sex hormones are beneficial for people who experience gender dysphoria.

1   World Professional Association for Transgender Health, "Standards of Care for the Health of Transgender and Gender Diverse People, Version 8," *International Journal of Transgender Health* (2022).

2   Cf. M. Colizzi et al., "Transsexual Patients' Psychiatric Comorbidity and Positive Effect of Cross-Hormonal Treatment on Mental Health: Results from a Longitudinal Study," *Psychoneuroendocrinology* 39 (2014), 65–73; G. Heylens et al., "Effects of Different Steps in Gender Reassignment Therapy on Psychopathology: A Prospective Study of Persons with a Gender Identity Disorder," *Journal of Sexual Medicine* 11 (2014), 119–126; A. Green et al., "Association of Gender-Affirming Hormone Therapy with Depression, Thoughts of Suicide, and Attempted Suicide Among Transgender and Nonbinary Youth," *Journal of Adolescent Health*, 70:4 (2021).

3   Cf. "Gender Dysphoria/Gender Incongruence Guideline Resources" Endocrine Society, September 01, 2017.

4   Cf. Johanna Olson-Kennedy, "The Impact of Early Medical Treatment in Transgender Youth," Progress report/change document, 2017.

5   Cf. Monica and Victor Wang, "For Trans Students, Health Care Only First Step," *Yale Daily News*, October 9, 2015.

6   Cf. World Professional Association for Transgender Health, "Standards of Care for the Health of Transgender and Gender Diverse People.".

7   "Response to Julia Serano: Detransition, Desistance, and Disinformation," https://www.youtube.com/watch?v=9L2jyEDwpEw.

8   Cf. Talal Alzahrani et al., "Cardiovascular Disease Risk Factors and Myocardial Infarction in the Transgender Population," *Circulation: Cardiovascular Quality and Outcomes* 12:4 (April 5, 2019).

9   Cf. Dario Getahun et al., "Cross-Sex Hormones And Acute Cardiovascular Events in Transgender Persons: A Cohort Study," *Annals of Internal Medicine* 169:4 (August 21, 2018), 205–213.

10   "Trans vs Conservative Men: Is Masculinity Disappearing in America?, Middle Ground," https://youtu.be/nDEyQB0Jjkw.

11   "Biological Woman's Hour—Keira Bell," https://www.youtube.com/watch?v=R6X5e3OmxSA

12   Keira Bell, "Keira Bell: My Story," Persuasion, April 7, 2021, https://www.persuasion.community/p/keira-bell- my-story.

13   "A Story of Detransitioning, Michael Knowles Interview," https://youtu.be/5HbPzJy9gkY.

14   "A Story of Detransitioning."

15   Serano, *Whipping Girl*, 69.

16   "Growing Up Trans (full documentary)."

17   As quoted in Shrier, *Irreversible Damage*, 190.

18   "DETRANSITION Q&A (#1)," https://youtu.be/kxVmSGTgNxI.

19   Cf. Carl Heneghan, "Gender-affirming hormone in children and adolescents," *BMJ EBM Spotlight* (25th February 2019).

20   Carl Heneghan, "Gender-affirming hormone in children and adolescents," *BMJ EBM Spotlight* (25th February 2019).

21   Wylie C. Hembree et al., "Endocrine Treatment of Transsexual Persons: An Endocrine Society Clinical Practice Guideline," *Journal of Clinical Endocrinology and Metabolism* 94 (September 2009): 3132.

22   "Growing Up Trans (full documentary)."

23   Bell, "Keira Bell: My Story."

24   As quoted in Joyce, *Trans*, 90.

25   Judiciary of England and Wales, *R (on the application of) Quincy Bell and A v. Tavistock and Portman NHS Trust and others*, EWHC 3274, December 1, 2020, Summary.

26   *Quincy Bell and Mrs. A v. The Tavistock and Portman NHS Foundation Trust*, EWHC 3274, High Court of Justice Administrative Court, December 21, 2020.

27   Libby Brooks, "Tavistock Gender Identity Clinic Is Closing: What Happens Next?," *Guardian*, July 28, 2022.

28   S. Levine et al., "Reconsidering Informed Consent for Trans-Identified Children, Adolescents, and Young Adults," *Journal of Sex & Marital Therapy* 48:7 (2022), 706–727; Jane Robbins, "Revisiting the Impossibility of Informed Consent for Transgender Interventions," PublicDiscourse.com, July 19, 2022.

29   "Dr. Johanna Olson-Kennedy Speaks About Cross-Sex Hormones and Surgery for Minors," https://www.youtube.com/watch?v=pO8v--tztSg.

30   As quoted in Finley, *Sexual Identity*, 231.

11. Gender-affirming surgery is a life-saving intervention.

1   Cf. M. Murad et al., "Hormonal Therapy and Sex Reassignment: A Systematic Review and Meta-Analysis of Quality of Life and Psychosocial Outcomes," *Clinical Endocrinology* 72 (2010), 214–231; A. DeVries et al., "Young Adult Psychological Outcome After Puberty Suppression and Gender Reassignment," *Pediatrics* 134 (2014), 696–704.

2   Cf. A. Lawrence, "Factors Associated with Satisfaction or Regret Following Male-to-Female Sex Reassignment Surgery," *Archives of Sexual Behavior* 32:4 (August 1, 2003), 299–315; K. Zucker and Nicola Brown, "Gender Dysphoria," in *Principles and Practice of Sex Therapy* (New York: Guilford, 2014), 238; C. Dhejne et al., "An Analysis of All Applications for Sex Reassignment Surgery in Sweden, 1960–2010: Prevalence, Incidence, and Regrets," *Archives of Sexual Behavior* 43:8 (2014), 1535–1545.

3   Gabriel Mac, "My Penis, Myself," *New York* magazine (December 20, 2021).

4   Serano, *Whipping Girl*, 11.

5   Cf. M. Hermann and A. Thorstenson, "A Rare Case of Male- to-Eunuch Gender Dysphoria," *Sexual Medicine* 3:4 (2015), 331–133; K. Hsu, "Erotic Target Identity Inversions in Male Furries, Adult Baby/Diaper Lovers, and Eunuchs" (PhD dissertation; Northwestern University, 2019).

6   Cf. Joanne Meyerowitz, *How Sex Changed: A History of Transsexuality in the United States* (Cambridge, MA: Harvard University Press, 2002), 142, 221–222.

7   Cf. J. Herman et al., "2015 U.S. Transgender Survey," National Center for Transgender Equality, 100.

8   Cf. "2020 Plastic Surgery Statistics Report," American Society of Plastic Surgeons.

9   "Watch This Before You Get Top Surgery w/Ash Hardell," https://www.youtube.com/watch?v=hcKZ2dxumgk.

10   Cf. Herman et al., "2015 U.S. Transgender Survey," 101, 102.

11   Cf. Gender Affirming Orchiectomy, Mark S. Litwin, MD, UCLAMDChat, https://www.youtube.com/watch?v=De3Iytw05TA.

12   Mac, "My Penis, Myself."

13   Mac, "My Penis, Myself."

14   Dr. Johanna Olson-Kennedy et al., "Chest Reconstruction and Chest Dysphoria in Transmasculine Minors and Young Adults," *JAMA Pediatrics* (May 2018), 431–436.

15   C. Dhejne et al., "Long-Term Follow-Up of Transsexual Persons Undergoing Sex Reassignment Surgery: Cohort Study in Sweden," *PLoS One* 6:2 (2011), e16885.

16   "DETRANSITION: My Story, And What I Wish I Knew," https://www.youtube.com/watch?v=rC7EtIeWrPs.

17   "Watch This Before You Get Top Surgery // w/ Ash Hardell."

18   "The Call Is Coming from Inside the House," https://www.youtube.com/watch?v=PBInNGgdF2M&t=654s.

19   "The Call Is Coming from Inside the House."

20   "Damaged by Gender, A Detrans Story, with Garrett," https://www.youtube.com/watch?v=6-ryJegz7no.

21   "Transgender Healthcare," *60 Minutes*, CBS, May 23, 2021.

22   T. Jensen et al., "Decision Memo for Gender Dysphoria and Gender Reassignment Surgery (CAG-00446N)," Centers for Medicare & Medicaid Services, June 2, 2016.

23   Centers for Medicare & Medicaid Services, "Decision Memo, Gender Dysphoria and Gender Reassignment Surgery," August 2016.

24   M. Murad et al., "Hormonal Therapy and Sex Reassignment: A Systematic Review and Meta-Analysis of Quality of Life and Psychosocial Outcomes," *Clinical Endocrinology* 72 (2010).

25   Cf. P. Hruz, "Deficiencies in Scientific Evidence for Medical Management of Gender Dysphoria," *Linacre Quarterly* 87:1 (September 20, 2019), 1–9; Dhejne et al., "Long-Term Follow-Up of Transsexual Persons Undergoing Sex Reassignment Surgery: Cohort Study in Sweden," 1–8; R. Costa, "Psychological Support, Puberty Suppression, and Psychosocial Functioning in Adolescents with Gender Dysphoria," *Journal of Sexual Medicine* 12:11 (2015), 2206–2214.

26   Cf. Dhejne et al., "Long-Term Follow-Up of Transsexual Persons Undergoing Sex Reassignment Surgery: Cohort Study in Sweden," Table 2.

27   Oregon Revised Statutes 431.925–431.955; Oregon Laws 2013, chapter 411.

28   Cf. "Tanning Restrictions for Minors," Oregon Health Authority, Oregon.gov.

29   Cf. Chapter 8.52 Tattoo Parlors, Portland.gov.

30   Cf. S. Blakemore and T. Robbins, "Decision-Making in the Adolescent Brain," *Nature Neuroscience* 15:9 (September 2012), 1184–1191; Sara B. Johnson et al., "Adolescent Maturity and the Brain: The Promise and Pitfalls of Neuroscience Research in Adolescent Health Policy," *Journal of Adolescent Health* 45:3 (September 2009), 216–221.

31   Cf. Minor Rights: Access and Consent to Health Care, Oregon Health Authority, Public Health Division (August 2016); Guideline for Gender Dysphoria: Frequently Asked Questions. Oregon.gov.

32   Cf. National Women's Health Network, "At What Age Can I Get a Hysterectomy?," Shaniqua Seth, October 13, 2016.

33   "Is This Appropriate Treatment? Dr. Johanna Olson-Kennedy Explains Why Mastectomies for Healthy Teen Girls Is No Big Deal," https://www.youtube.com/watch?v=5Y6espcXPJ.

34   Finley, *Sexual Identity*, 207.

35   "Dr. Johanna Olson-Kennedy Speaks About Cross-Sex Hormones and Surgery for Minors."

36   Cf. B. Schoumaker, "Across the World, Is Men's Fertility Different from That of Women?," *Population & Societies* 548:9 (2017): 1–4.

37   Cf. L. Nahata et al., "Low Fertility Preservation Utilization Among Transgender Youth," *Journal of Adolescent Health* 61:1 (July 2017), 40–44; K. Wierckx et al., "Reproductive Wish in Transsexual Men," *Human Reproduction* 27 (2012), 483–487.

38   "Dr. Mary Rice Hasson, Is the Fight Against Gender Ideology 'Reality's Last Stand?,'" https://www.youtube.com/watch?v=S96KBTBiYuA.

39   "'Transgender' Is an Identity Not a Diagnosis," https://www.youtube.com/watch?v=ZyGZnU_6tj4.

40   Paul R. McHugh, "Surgical Sex," *First Things*, November 2004.

41   Cf. Sumant Ugalmugle and Rupali Swain, "Sex Reassignment Surgery Market Size by

Gender Transition (Male to Female [Facial, Breast, Genitals], Female to Male [Facial, Chest, Genitals]), Industry Analysis Report, Regional Outlook, Application Potential, Price Trends, Competitive Market Share & Forecast, 2020–2026," Global Market Insights, Report ID: GMI2926 (March 2020), https://www.gminsights.com/industry-analysis/sex-reassignment- surgery-market; Grand View Research, "U.S. Sex Reassignment Surgery Market Size, Share & Trends Analysis Report by Gender Transition (Male to Female, Female to Male), and Segment Forecasts, 2020–2027."

42   Michael K. Laidlaw, "The Gender Identity Phantom," MercatorNet, November 11, 2018.

43   "Hey Doc, Some Boys Are Born Girls: Decker Moss at TEDxColumbus."

44   Andrea Long Chu, "My New Vagina Won't Make Me Happy: And It Shouldn't Have To," *New York Times*, November 24, 2018.

45   Cf. https://www.reddit.com/r/detrans/; https://www.detransvoices.org/resource-directory/websites-blogs-by- detransitioners-desisters/; Detransitioners Anonymous (DetransitionersAnonymous@protonmail.com); Pique Resilience Project (www. piqueresproject.com); Post Trans (https://post-trans.com/); Sex Change Regret (www .sexchangeregret.com).

46   L. Littman, "Individuals Treated for Gender Dysphoria with Medical and/or Surgical Transition Who Subsequently Detransitioned: A Survey of 100 Detransitioners," *Archives of Sexual Behavior* 50 (2021), 3359.

47   As quoted in Maria Keffler, *Desist, Detrans & Detox* (Arlington, VA: Advocates Protecting Children, 2021).

12. People who transition rarely express regret.

1   Cf. K. MacKinnon et al., "Preventing Transition 'Regret': An Institutional Ethnography of Gender-Affirming Care Assessment Practices in Canada," *Social Science and Medicine* 291 (2021); F. Pfäfflin, "Regrets After Sex Reassignment Surgery," *Journal of Psychology & Human Sexuality* 5:4 (1993), 69–85; Dhejne et al., "An Analysis of All Applications for Sex Reassignment Surgery in Sweden, 1960–2010: Prevalence, Incidence, and Regrets," *Archives of Sexual Behavior* 43:8 (2014), 1535–1545; WPATH, SOC-7, 8.

2   Cf. Kahlenberg et al., "Patient Satisfaction After Total Knee Replacement: A Systematic Review," *HSS Journal* 14:2 (2018), 192–201.

3   "Let's Talk About Detransitioning," https://www.youtube.com/watch?v=Fbhv1Znv4Lk.

4   "Let's Talk About Detransitioning."

5   Cf. Dhejne et al., "An Analysis of all Applications for Sex Reassignment Surgery in Sweden, 1960–2010: Prevalence, Incidence, and Regrets," 1535–1545.

6   Carey Callahan, "Gender Identity Is Hard but Jumping to Medical Solutions Is Worse," *Economist*, December 3, 2019.

7   "An Open Letter to Julia Serano from One of the Detransitioned People You Claim to 'Support,'" Crashchaoscats, August 8, 2016.

8   Cf. O. Bodlund and G. Kullgren, "Transsexualism—General Outcome and Prognostic Factors: A Five-Year Follow-up Study of Nineteen Transsexuals in the Process of Changing Sex," *Archives of Sexual Behavior* 25 (1996), 303–316; M. Stein et al., "Follow-Up Observations of Operated Male-to-Female Transsexuals," *Journal of Urology* 143 (1990): 1188–1192.

9   Paul Rhodes Eddy, "Rethinking Transition: On the History, Experience and Current Research Regarding Gender Transition, Transition Regret and Detransition," Center for Faith, Sexuality & Gender, September 2022, 204.

10   Cf. W. Tsoi, "Follow-Up Study of Transsexuals After Sex-Reassignment Surgery," *Singapore Medical Journal* 34:6 (1993), 515–17; J. Rehman et al., "The Reported Sex and Surgery Satisfactions of 28 Postoperative Male-to-Female Transsexual Patients," *Archives of Sexual Behavior* 28:1 (1999), 71–89; P. Cohen-Kettenis and S. van Goozen, "Sex Reassignment of Adolescent Transsexuals: A Follow-Up Study," *Journal of the American Academy of Child and Adolescent Psychiatry* 36 (1997), 263–271; James Barrett, "Psychological and Social Function Before and After Phalloplasty," *International Journal of Transgenderism* 2:1 (1998), 1–8; M. Stein et al., "Follow-up Observations of Operated Male-to-Female Transsexuals," *Journal of Urology* 143 (1990), 1188–1192.

11   Cf. G. Weinforth et al., "Quality of Life Following Male-To-Female Sex Reassignment

Surgery," *Deutsches Ärzteblatt International* 116:15 (2019), 253–260; N. Papadopulos et al., "Quality of Life and Patient Satisfaction Following Male-to-Female Sex Reassignment Surgery," *Journal of Sexual Medicine* 14/5 (2017), 721–730; T. van de Grift et al., "Surgical Satisfaction, Quality of Life, and Their Association After Gender-Affirming Surgery: A Follow-Up Study," *Journal of Sex & Marital Therapy* 44/2 (2018), 138–148; C. McNichols et al., "Patient-Reported Satisfaction and Quality of Life After Trans Male Gender Affirming Surgery," *International Journal of Transgender Health* 21/4 (2020), 410–417; L. Jellestad et al., "Quality of Life in Transitioned Trans Persons: A Retrospective Cross-Sectional Cohort Study," *Hindawi—BioMed Research International* (2018), 8684625, 10.

12   J. Dettori, "Loss to Follow-Up," *Evidence-Based Spine-Care Journal* 2/1 (2011), 7–10.

13   Richard Horton, "Offline: What Is Medicine's 5 Sigma?" *Lancet*, 385 (April 11, 2015).

14   Cf. Eddy, "Rethinking Transition: On the History, Experience and Current Research Regarding Gender Transition, Transition Regret and Detransition," 207.

15   Restingmyfeet, Instagram, https://www.instagram.com/p/CTmxyu6rrgb.

16   Cari Stella, "Female Detransition and Reidentification: Survey Results and Interpretation" [Post], Tumblr, September 3, 2016,, https://guideonragingstars.tumblr.com/post/149877706175/female-detransition-and- reidentification-survey; Cf. Elie Vandenbussche, "Detransition-Related Needs and Support: A Cross-Sectional Online Survey," *Journal of Homosexuality* 69/9 (2022), 1602–1620; Lisa Littman, "Individuals Treated for Gender Dysphoria with Medical and/or Surgical Transition Who Subsequently Detransitioned: A Survey of 100 Detransitioners," *Archives of Sexual Behavior* 50:8 (2021), 3353–3369.

17   Soh, *The End of Gender*, 184.

18   "Growing Up Trans (full documentary)."

19   "Reversing a Gender Transition," https://www.youtube.com/watch?v=V6V0p3_bd6w.

20   "Detransition TikToks compilation—June & July 2021," https://www.youtube.com/watch?v=xG5rOpNc8t0.

21   Cf. S. Lockwood, "Hundreds" of Young Trans People Seeking Help to Return to Original Sex," Sky News, October 5, 2019.

22   "Detransition TikToks compilation—June & July 2021.".

23   "Coercion & Abuse in the Gender ID Community with ⚥ GNC-Centric ⚥, https://www.youtube.com/watch?v=QAMar22S0ck.

24   "DETRANSITION: How My Voice Has Changed," https://www.youtube.com/watch?v=4UvqwOm3dD0.

25   Cf. Stella O'Malley, "The Arc of Detransition," March 10, 2022, https://genspect.org/the-arc-of-detransition/.

26   As quoted in Keffler, *Desist, Detrans & Detox*, 148.

27   As quoted in Joyce, *Trans*, 103.

28   "DETRANSITION: How My Voice Has Changed."

29   "Detransitioning: Reversing a Gender Transition—BBC Newsnight," https://www.youtube.com/watch?v=fDi-jFVBLA8.

30   "FtMtF Transition & Detransition Timeline," https://www.youtube.com/watch?v=Z2AIAX8-CqQ.

13. Refusing to affirm a person's gender identity leads to suicide.

1   World Professional Association for Transgender Health, "Standards of Care for the Health of Transgender and Gender Diverse People, Version 8," *International Journal of Transgender Health* (2022), S20.

2   M. Clarke et al., "Gender-Affirming Care Is Trauma-Informed Care," National Center for Child Traumatic Stress (2022), 1.

3   Serano, *Whipping Girl*, 117.

4   POTUS, tweet, March 31, 2022.

5   "How Radical Gender Ideology Is Taking Over Public Schools & Harming Kids," https://youtu.be/k33KeLh8aOk.

6   Littman, "Parent Reports of Adolescents and Young Adults Perceived to Show Signs of a Rapid Onset of Gender Dysphoria," 20.

7   Littman, "Parent Reports of Adolescents and Young Adults Perceived to Show Signs of a Rapid Onset of Gender Dysphoria," 21.

8   Helen Joyce, "Speaking Up for Female Eunuchs," *Standpoint*, February 2020.

9   Cf. Scott Mosser, "FTM/N Breast Binding Guide and Safety Before Surgery," Gender Confirmation Center.

10   E. Sievert et al., "Not Social Transition Status, but Peer Relations and Family Functioning Predict Psychological Functioning in a German Clinical Sample of Children with Gender Dysphoria," *Clinical Child Psychology and Psychiatry* 26:1 (2021): 79–95; W. Wong et al., "Childhood Social Gender Transition and Psychosocial Well-Being: A Comparison to Cisgender Gender-Variant Children," *Clinical Practice in Pediatric Psychology* 7:3 (2019), 241–253.

11   Cf. K. Zucker et al., "Puberty-Blocking Hormonal Therapy for Adolescents with Gender Identity Disorder: A Descriptive Clinical Study," *Journal of Gay & Lesbian Mental Health* 15 (2011), 58–82; T. Steensma et al., "Factors Associated with Desistence and Persistence of Childhood Gender Dysphoria: A Quantitative Follow-Up Study," *Journal of the American Academy of Child and Adolescent Psychiatry* 52:6 (June 2013), 582–590.

12   Cf. A. Haas et al., "Suicide Attempts Among Transgender and Gender Nonconforming Adults: Findings of the National Transgender Discrimination Survey," Williams Institute, 2014.

13   Cf. K. Zucker, "Adolescents with Gender Dysphoria: Reflections on Some Contemporary Clinical and Research Issues," *Archives of Sexual Behavior* (July 18, 2019); M. Biggs, "Suicide by Clinic-Referred Transgender Adolescents in the United Kingdom," *Archives of Sexual Behavior* 51 (2022), 685–690; N. Graaf et al., "Suicidality in clinic-referred transgender adolescents," *European Child & Adolescent Psychiatry* (Nov. 9, 2020); "The 41% Trans Suicide Attempt Rate: A Tale of Flawed Data and Lazy Journalists," 4thWaveNow, August 3, 2015; J. Michael Bailey and Ray Blanchard, "Suicide or Transition: The Only Options for Gender Dysphoric Kids?," 4thWaveNow, September 8, 2017.

14   Finley, *Sexual Identity*, 223.

15   C. Dhejne et al., "Long-Term Follow-Up of Transsexual Persons Undergoing Sex Reassignment Surgery: Cohort Study in Sweden," 7.

16   C. Dhejne et al., "Long-Term Follow-Up of Transsexual Persons Undergoing Sex Reassignment Surgery: Cohort Study in Sweden," 1.

17   Centers for Medicare & Medicaid Services, Decision Memo, Gender Dysphoria and Gender Reassignment Surgery, August 2016, https://www.cms.gov/medicare-coverage-database/view/ncacal-decision-memo.aspx?proposed=N&NCAId=282.

18   As quoted in *Transgender Issues in Catholic Healthcare* (Philadelphia: National Catholic Bioethics Center, 2021), 19.

19   Cf. D. Burgess et al., "Effects of Perceived Discrimination on Mental Health and Mental Health Services Utilization Among Gay, Lesbian, Bisexual and Transgender Persons," *Journal of LGBT Health Research* 3:4 (2008), 1–14.

20   Haas et al., "Suicide Attempts Among Transgender and Gender Nonconforming Adults: Findings of the National Transgender Discrimination Survey," 13.

21   McHugh and Mayer, "Sexuality and Gender," Part Two.

22   Cf. Dhejne et al., "Long-Term Follow-Up of Transsexual Persons Undergoing Sex Reassignment Surgery: Cohort Study in Sweden,", 1–8; H. Asscheman et al., "A Long-Term Follow-Up Study of Mortality in Transsexuals Receiving Treatment with Cross-Sex Hormones," *European Journal of Endocrinology* 164:4 (April 2011), 635–642; N. Adams et al., "Varied Reports of Adult Transgender Suicidality," *Transgender Health* 2:1 (2017), 60–75.

23   Jay Greene, "Puberty Blockers, Cross-Sex Hormones, and Youth Suicide," Heritage Foundation, June 13, 2022).

24   J. Bertolote and A. Fleischmann, "Suicide and Psychiatric Diagnosis: A Worldwide Perspective," *World Psychiatry* 1:3 (2002), 181–185; R. Hirschfeld and J. Russel, "Assessment and Treatment of Suicidal Patients," *New England Journal of Medicine* 337:13 (September 25, 1997), 910–915.

25   "Johanna Olson, MD, Talks About Research on Transgender Youth," https://www.youtube.com/watch?v=jjtRJsC16HE.

26   Cf. Aydin Olson-Kennedy, 2019 EPATH Conference slide presentation, in Keffler, *Desist, Detrans & Detox*, 17.

27 Lisa Littman, "Parent Reports of Adolescents and Young Adults Perceived to Show Signs of a Rapid Onset of Gender Dysphoria," PLoS One 13:8 (2018), 13.

28 T. Becerra-Culqui et al., "Mental Health of Transgender and Gender Nonconforming Youth Compared with Their Peers," Pediatrics 141:5 (May 1, 2018).

29 Cf. Hruz, "Deficiencies in Scientific Evidence for Medical Management of Gender Dysphoria," 1–9; C. Dhejne et al., "Long-Term Follow-Up of Transsexual Persons Undergoing Sex Reassignment Surgery: Cohort Study in Sweden," 1–8; R. Costa, "Psychological Support, Puberty Suppression, and Psychosocial Functioning in Adolescents with Gender Dysphoria," Journal of Sexual Medicine 12:11 (2015), 2206–2214.

30 Cf. "Board of Directors Part One: Agenda and Papers of a Meeting to Be Held in Public," Tavistock and Portman NHS Foundation Trust, 53.

31 Soh, The End of Gender, 185.

32 Cf. "Special Report: NHS 'Over-Diagnosing' Transgender Children," https://www.youtube.com/watch?v=qXvdrSkBFqw.

33 "The Truth About Trans Kids, from Trans Adults," https://youtu.be/f8GtmWxKbO8.

34 "The Hormone Health Crisis, with Endocrinologist William Malone, MD," https://www.youtube.com/watch?v=z4RYl75zdMY&t=2284s.

35 James M. Cantor, "Transgender and Gender Diverse Children and Adolescents: Fact-Checking of AAP Policy," Journal of Sex & Marital Therapy 14:4 (2020), 307–313; P. Eddy and P. Sprinkle, "The Problems with Correlating Sexual Orientation Change Efforts and Gender Identity Change Efforts," The Center for Faith, Sexuality & Gender 3 (2021).

36 Eddy, "Rethinking Transition: On the History, Experience and Current Research Regarding Gender Transition, Transition Regret and Detransition," The Center for Faith, Sexuality & Gender (September, 2022), 245; Cf. Geoffrey L. Ream, "Concepts of Sexual Orientation and Gender Identity," in Violence Against LGBTQ+ Persons: Research, Practice and Advocacy, eds. E. M. Lund, C. Burgess, and A. J. Johnson (New York: Springer, 2021), 8; L. Diamond and C. Rosky, "Scrutinizing Immutability: Research on Sexual Orientation and U.S. Legal Advocacy for Sexual Minorities," Journal of Sex Research 53 4–5 (2016): 363–391.

37 Eddy and Sprinkle, "The Problems with Correlating Sexual Orientation Change Efforts and Gender Identity Change Efforts," 8.

38 Eddy and Sprinkle, "The Problems with Correlating Sexual Orientation Change Efforts and Gender Identity Change Efforts," 66.

39 Kate Bornstein, Gender Outlaw: On Men, Women, and the Rest of Us (New York: Routledge, 1994), 52.

40 Serano, Whipping Girl, 226.

41 Soh, The End of Gender, 169.

42 Soh, The End of Gender, 152.

43 Cf. K. Zucker et al., "A Developmental, Biopsychosocial Model for the Treatment of Children with Gender Identity Disorder," Journal of Homosexuality 59 (2012), 369–397; L. Lothstein et al., "Expressive Psychotherapy with Gender Dysphoric Patients," Archives of General Psychiatry 38:8 (August 1981), 924–929; J. Kronberg et al., "Treatment of Transsexualism in Adolescence," Journal of Adolescence 4.2 (1981), 177–185.

44 Cf. Kelley D. Drummond et al., "A Follow-Up Study of Girls with Gender Identity Disorder," Developmental Psychology 44, no. 1 (2008): 34–45.

45 K. Zucker et al., "A Developmental, Biopsychosocial Model for the Treatment of Children with Gender Identity Disorder," 369–397.

46 Cantor, "Transgender and Gender Diverse Children and Adolescents: Fact-Checking of AAP Policy," 307–313.

47 Natacha Kennedy, "Protest Against Transphobic Psychologist Kenneth Zucker in London," Indymedia London, October 1, 2008, http://www.indymedia.org.uk/en/regions/london/2008/09/409405.html.

48 Cf. Affirming Sexual Orientation and Gender Identity Act, 2015, S.O. 2015, c. 18 - Bill 77.

49 Anderson, When Harry Became Sally, 142.

14. Gender identity is innate.

1 Serano, *Whipping Girl*, 188.
2 J. Campo et al., "Psychiatric Comorbidity of Gender Identity Disorders: A Survey Among Dutch Psychiatrists," *American Journal of Psychiatry* 160 (2003), 1332–1336.
3 M. Connolly et al., "The Mental Health of Transgender Youth: Advances in Understanding," *Journal of Adolescent Health* 59:5 (2016), 489–495; R. Rajkumar, "Gender Identity Disorder and Schizophrenia: Neurodevelopmental Disorders with Common Causal Mechanisms?" *Schizophrenia Research and Treatment* (2014); A. DeVries et al., "Autism Spectrum Disorders in Gender Dysphoric Children and Adolescents," *Journal of Autism and Developmental Disorders* 40:8 (2010), 930–936.
4 Cf. Jay Stringer, *Unwanted* (Colorado Springs, CO: NavPress, 2018).
5 Robert Leahy, "How Big a Problem Is Anxiety?," *Psychology Today*, April 30, 2008.
6 Shrier, *Irreversible Damage*, 6.
7 Pope Francis, *Amoris Laetitia,* 286.
8 Pope Francis, General Audience, April 15, 2015.
9 Soh, *The End of Gender*, 261.
10 Joyce, *Trans*, 37.
11 "Thousands of 'Trans' Teens Want to DETRANSITION (Women, Lesbians, Homophobia)," https://www.youtube.com/watch?v=bHOASkcG-zY&t=151s.
12 Littman, "Parent Reports of Adolescents and Young Adults Perceived to Show Signs of a Rapid Onset of Gender Dysphoria."
13 Cf. "To the Young Gender Questioners, I Was You," Third Way, September 21, 2014.
14 R. Blanchard, "Typology of Male-to-Female Transsexualism," *Archives of Sexual Behavior* 14:3 (1985), 247– 61; R. Blanchard, "The Concept of Autogynephilia and the Typology of Male Gender Dysphoria," *Journal of Nervous and Mental Disease* 177 (1989), 616–623.
15 Cf. D. Bem, "Exotic Becomes Erotic: A Developmental Theory of Sexual Orientation," *Psychological Review* 103:2 (1996), 320–335; D. Bem, "Exotic Becomes Erotic: Interpreting the Biological Correlates of Sexual Orientation," *Archives of Sexual Behavior* 29:6 (2000), 531–548.
16 Littman, "Individuals Treated for Gender Dysphoria with Medical and/or Surgical Transition Who Subsequently Detransitioned: A Survey of 100 Detransitioners," 3363.
17 "Damaged by Gender, A Detrans Story, with Garrett," https://www.youtube.com/watch?v=6-ryJegz7no
18 "Biology Isn't Bigotry: Why Sex Matters in the Age of Gender Identity," https://www.youtube.com/watch?v=Rt9DW4e1Cvw.
19 Littman, "Parent Reports of Adolescents and Young Adults Perceived to Show Signs of a Rapid Onset of Gender Dysphoria," 35.
20 "Reversing a Gender Transition," https://www.youtube.com/watch?v=V6V0p3_bd6w.
21 Littman, "Individuals Treated for Gender Dysphoria with Medical and/or Surgical Transition Who Subsequently Detransitioned: A Survey of 100 Detransitioners," 3369.
22 Soh, *The End of Gender*, 170.
23 "Transgender" Is an Identity Not a Diagnosis," https://www.youtube.com/watch?v=ZyGZnU_6tj4.
24 K. Zucker et al., "A Developmental, Biopsychosocial Model for the Treatment of Children with Gender Identity Disorder," *Journal of Homosexuality* 59 (2012), 369–397.
25 Littman, "Parent Reports of Adolescents and Young Adults Perceived to Show Signs of a Rapid Onset of Gender Dysphoria,"16.
26 "DETRANSITION: My Story, and What I Wish I Knew."
27 Cf. D. Wailing et al., "Dissociation in a Transsexual Population," *Journal of Sex Education and Therapy* 23 (1998), 121–23; Judith Trowell, "Child Sexual Abuse and Gender Identity Development: Some Understanding from Work with Girls Who Have Been Sexually Abused," in Di Ceglie and Freedman, *Stranger in My Own Body* (New York: Routledge, 1998), 154–172.
28 "Why I Detransitioned (made for USPATH presentation)," https://www.youtube.com/watch?v=1-UmPiinIFo.
29 "Growing Up Trans (full documentary)."
30 Cf. "Tranzformed—Finding Peace with Your God Given Gender."

31 K. Kozlowska et al., "Australian Children and Adolescents with Gender Dysphoria: Clinical Presentations and Challenges Experienced by a Multidisciplinary Team and Gender Service," *Human Systems* 1:1 (2021), 70–95.

32 Cf. M. Daspe et al., "When Pornography Use Feels Out of Control: The Moderation Effect of Relationship and Sexual Satisfaction," *Journal of Sex and Marital Therapy* (December 2017).

33 Cf. A. Bridges et al., "Aggression and Sexual Behavior in Best-Selling Pornography Videos: A Content Analysis Update," *Violence Against Women* 16 (2010), 1065–1085.

34 Littman, "Individuals Treated for Gender Dysphoria with Medical and/or Surgical Transition Who Subsequently Detransitioned: A Survey of 100 Detransitioners," 3359.

35 K. J. Zucker et al., "Psychopathology in the Parents of Boys with Gender Identity Disorder," *Journal of the American Academy of Child and Adolescent Psychiatry* 42 (2003), 2–4.

36 Cf. K. Kozlowska et al., "Attachment Patterns in Children and Adolescents with Gender Dysphoria," *Frontiers in Psychology* (January 12, 2021).

37 Cf. D. Perry et al., "Gender Identity in Childhood," *International Journal of Behavioral Development* 43:3 (April 2, 2019); David R. Shaffer, *Developmental Psychology: Childhood and Adolescence*, 6th ed. (Belmont, CA: Wadsworth/Thomson Learning, 2002), 464–465; K. Kozlowska et al., "Attachment Patterns in Children and Adolescents With Gender Dysphoria," *Frontiers in Psychology* (January 12, 2021); G. Giovanardi et al, "Attachment Patterns and Complex Trauma in a Sample of Adults Diagnosed with Gender Dysphoria," *Frontiers in Psychology* 9:60 (February 1, 2018).

38 Cf. K. Zucker, "Children with Gender Identity Disorder: Is There a Best Practice?," *Neuropsychiatrie de l'Enfance et de l-Adolescence* 56 (September 2008).

39 Cf. Kenneth J. Zucker and Susan J. Bradley, *Gender Identity Disorder and Psychosexual Problems in Children and Adolescents* (New York: Guilford Press, 1995); J. Veale et al., "Biological and Psychosocial Correlates of Adult Gender Variant Identities: A Review," *Personality and Individual Differences* 48 (2009), 357–366; H. Meyer-Bahlburg, "Gender Identity Disorder in Boys: A Parent- and Peer-Based Treatment Protocol," *Clinical Child Psychology and Psychiatry* 7:2 (2002), 360–376; P. Cohen-Kettenis and W. Arrindell, "Perceived Parental Rearing Style, Parental Divorce and Transsexualism: A Controlled Study," *Psychological Medicine* 20 (1990), 613–620; M. Hogan Findlay, *Development of the Cross Gender Lifestyle and Comparison of Cross Gendered Men with Heterosexual Controls* (PhD diss.; Carleton University, Ottawa, Canada, 1995); R. Schott, "The Childhood and Family Dynamics of Transvestites," *Archives of Sexual Behavior* 24 (1995), 309–327; D. Ghering and G. Knudson, "Prevalence of Childhood Trauma in a Clinical Population of Transsexual People," *International Journal of Transgenderism* 8 (2005), 22–30.

40 "Transgender and the Gospel: A Conversation with Heather Skriba," https://youtu.be/eKuftYuby5I.

41 "Gender Dysphoria in Children: Understanding the Science and Medicine," https://www.youtube.com/watch?v=GOniPhuyXeY.

42 "Tranzformed—Finding Peace with Your God Given Gender," 4.

43 Walt Heyer, "Transgender Characters May Win Emmys, But Transgender People Hurt Themselves," *Federalist*, February 22, 2015.

44 "Gender Identity Documentary. My Experiences of Changing Gender. Only Human," https://youtu.be/K_YDHAxbTmk.

45 "My Life Felt Ruined"—Talk w/ Detransitioned Woman," https://www.youtube.com/watch?v=xJNAD6dJanA.

46 "DETRANSITION: How My Voice Has Changed."

47 Cf. "Coercion & Abuse in the Gender ID Community, with ♀ GNC-Centric ♀."

48 "Adult Transgender Care: An Interdisciplinary Approach for Training Mental Health Professionals," ed. Michael Kauth and Jillian Shipherd (New York: Routledge, 2018).

49 Cf. DSM-5, 55; S. Stagg, "Autistic Traits in Individuals Self-Defining as Transgender or Nonbinary," *European Psychiatry* 61 (September 2019), 17–22.

50 Cf. Swaab, *We Are Our Brains*, 186.

51 James Shupe, "I Was America's First 'Nonbinary' Person. It Was All a Sham," Daily Signal (March 10, 2019), https://www.dailysignal.com/2019/03/10/i-was-americas-first-non-binary-person-it-was-all-a-sham/.

52   Ray Blanchard, "Gender Identity Disorders in Adult Men," in *Clinical Management of Gender Identity Disorders in Children and Adults,* ed. Ray Blanchard and B.V. Steiner (Washington, D.C.: American Psychiatric Publishing, 1990): 49–75.

53   Serano, *Whipping Girl,* 296–297.

54   Cf. Blanchard, "The Concept of Autogynephilia and the Typology of Male Gender Dysphoria," 616–617.

55   J. Bailey, "What Many Transgender Activists Don't Want You to Know: and Why You Should Know It Anyway," *Perspectives in Biology and Medicine* 50:4 (February 2007), 521–534.

56   Anne Lawrence, *Men Trapped in Men's Bodies* (New York: Springer, 2013).

57   As quoted in Joyce, *Trans,* 44.

58   R. Blanchard, "The Origins of the Concept of Autogynephilia," *Archives of Sexual Behavior* 34:4 (2005), 439–446.

59   "Rapid-Onset Gender Dysphoria: A Miffed Response," https://www.youtube.com/watch?v=9BZvAeOwAvU.

60   J. Kay, "An Interview with Lisa Littman, Who Coined the Term 'Rapid Onset Gender Dysphoria,'" quillette.com, March 19, 2019.

61   "Growing Up Trans (full documentary)."

62   Mary Eberstadt, *Primal Screams* (West Conshohocken, PA: Templeton Press, 2019), 78.

63   A Story of Detransitioning, Michael Knowles Interview," https://youtu.be/5HbPzJy9gkY

64   Littman, "Parent Reports of Adolescents and Young Adults Perceived to Show Signs of a Rapid Onset of Gender Dysphoria," 13; A. Meybodi et al., "Psychiatric Axis I Comorbidities among Patients with Gender Dysphoria," *Psychiatric Journal* (2014), 1–5.

65   Cf. Littman, "Parent Reports of Adolescents and Young Adults Perceived to Show Signs of a Rapid Onset of Gender Dysphoria,"22.

66   L. Littman, "Individuals Treated for Gender Dysphoria with Medical and/or Surgical Transition Who Subsequently Detransitioned: A Survey of 100 Detransitioners," 3365.

67   Littman, "Individuals Treated for Gender Dysphoria with Medical and/or Surgical Transition Who Subsequently Detransitioned: A Survey of 100 Detransitioners," 3365.

68   Littman, ""Parent Reports of Adolescents and Young Adults Perceived to Show Signs of a Rapid Onset of Gender Dysphoria," 25.

69   "Q&A for Dr. Kenneth Zucker: "Children and Adolescents with Gender Dysphoria," CMB Lecture at McGill," https://www.youtube.com/watch?v=RYKnz8NW9_w.

70   Littman, ""Parent Reports of Adolescents and Young Adults Perceived to Show Signs of a Rapid Onset of Gender Dysphoria," 36.

15. You should use whatever pronoun a person prefers.

1   Mann, *Not 'Him' or 'Her,'* 25.

2   Cf. NYC Commission on Human Rights "Legal Enforcement Guidance on Discrimination on the Basis of Gender Identity or Expression: Local Law No. 3" (2002); N.Y.C. Admin. Code § 8-102.

3   Cf. Michael Lee, "Wisconsin Middle Schoolers Accused of Sexual Harassment for Using Wrong Gender Pronouns," Fox News, May 15, 2022.

4   Pronouns—A How-To Guide, 2011, 2016 UW-Milwaukee LGBT Resource Center.

5   University of Washington, "IT Inclusive Language Guide," August 8, 2022.

6   "Lesbian Feminist Explains How the Equality Act Promotes Inequality," https://www.youtube.com/watch?v=_l1DoUXAdH0.

7   Mann, *Not 'Him' or 'Her,'* 33–35.

8   Mann, *Not 'Him' or 'Her,'* 38.

9   Keffler, *Desist, Detrans & Detox,* 79.

10   As quoted in Shrier, *Irreversible Damage,* 188.

11   Shrier, *Irreversible Damage,* 113.

12   Most Rev. Michael F. Burbidge, "A Catechesis on the Human Person and Gender Ideology," Diocese of Arlington, August 12, 2021.

13   Mann, *Not 'Him' or 'Her,'* 24, 31.

14   William Smith, "You Do the Truth in Love," interview with John Mallon, in *Sooner Catholic,* Archdiocese of Oklahoma City, June 4, 1995.

16. Trans people should be free to compete in sports, use restrooms, and enter public spaces that align with their gender identity.

1 B. Jones et al., "Sport and Transgender People: A Systematic Review of the Literature Relating to Sport Participation and Competitive Sport Policies," *Sports Medicine* 47:4 (2017), 701–716.

2 Katie Barnes, "Former University of Pennsylvania Swimmer Lia Thomas Responds to Critics: 'Trans Women Competing in Women's Sports Does Not Threaten Women's Sports,'" ESPN.com, May 31, 2022.

3 Valerie Richardson, "Penn's Lia Thomas Wins Two Races, Loses Third to Another Transgender Swimmer," *Washington Times*, January 9, 2022.

4 Fox News, January 18, 2022.

5 Cf. Joyce, *Trans*, 212.

6 Fallon Fox, tweet, June 2020.

7 Steve Warren, "Doctors Verify the 'Scientific Evidence' Proves Trans Swimmer Lia Thomas' Unfair Advantage Over Females," CBNNews.com, May 31, 2022.

8 Cf. I. Janssen et al., "Skeletal Muscle Mass and Distribution in 468 Men and Women Aged 18–88 Yr," *Journal of Applied Physiology* 89 (2000), 81–88.

9 Cf. A. Miller et al., "Gender Differences in Strength and Muscle Fiber Characteristics," *European Journal of Applied Physiology and Occupational Physiology* 66:3 (1993), 254–262; C. Harms, "Does Gender Affect Pulmonary Function and Exercise Capacity?," *Respiratory Physiology & Neurobiology* 151:2–3 (April 18, 2006): 124–131; Hanjabam Barun Sharma and Jyotsna Kailashiya, "Gender Difference in Aerobic Capacity and the Contribution by Body Composition and Haemoglobin Concentration: A Study in Young Indian National Hockey Players," *Journal of Clinical and Diagnostic Research* 10:11 (November 1, 2016), CC09–CC13.

10 Cf. V. Naganathan and P. Sambrook, "Gender differences in Volumetric Bone Density: A Study of Opposite-Sex Twins," *Osteoporosis International* 14:7 (July 2003), 564–569.

11 Cf. Michael Sokolove, "The Uneven Playing Field," *New York Times Magazine* (May 11, 2008); Michael Sokolove, *Warrior Girls: Protecting Our Daughters Against the Injury Epidemic in Women's Sports* (New York: Simon & Schuster, 2008); S. Magnusson et al., "The Adaptability of Tendon to Loading Differs in Men and Women," *International Journal of Experimental Pathology* 88:4 (2007), 237–240.

12 Cf. D. Leyk et al., "Hand-Grip Strength of Young Men, Women and Highly Trained Female Athletes," *European Journal of Applied Physiology* 99 (2007), 415–241.

13 Cf. Mayo Clinic, "Testosterone, Total, Bioavailable, and Free, Serum," Mayo Medical Laboratories, https://www.mayomedicallaboratories.com/test-catalog/Clinical+and+Interpretive/83686.

14 Cf. E. Hilton and T. Lundberg, "Transgender Women in the Female Category of Sport: Perspectives on Testosterone Suppression and Performance Advantage," *Sports Medicine* 51:2 (February 2021), 199–214; D. Handelsman et al., "Circulating Testosterone as the Hormonal Basis of Sex Differences in Athletic Performance," *Endocrine Reviews* 39:5 (2018), 803–829.

15 Cf. K. Kivlighan et al., "Gender Differences in Testosterone and Cortisol Response to Competition," *Psychoneuroendocrinology* 30:1 (2005), 58–71; J. Carré et al., "Changes in Testosterone Mediate the Effect of Winning on Subsequent Aggressive Behaviour," *Psychoneuroendocrinology* 38:10 (2013), 2034–2041; S. White et al., "Putting the Flight in 'Fight-or-Flight': Testosterone Reactivity to Skydiving Is Modulated by Autonomic Activation," *Biological Psychology* 143 (April 2019), 93–102.

16 Cf. Associated Press, "Transgender Boy Wins Texas Girls' Wrestling Title," *New York Times*, February 25, 2017.

17 Doriane Lambelet Coleman and Wickliffe Shreve, "Comparing Athletic Performances: The Best Elite Women to Boys and Men," Duke Law: Center for Sports Law and Policy; Emma Hilton, "Harder, Better, Faster, Stronger: Why We Must Protect Female Sports," https://fondofbeetles.wordpress.com/2018/10/01/harder-better-faster-stronger-why-we-must-protect-female-sports/.

18 "Karsten Braasch: The Smoker Who Ridiculed the Williams Sisters," So Press, April 9, 2013.

19 Cf. "'Bathroom Bill' to Cost North Carolina $3.76 Billion," CNBC.com, March 27, 2017.

20   Littman, "Individuals Treated for Gender Dysphoria with Medical and/or Surgical Transition Who Subsequently Detransitioned: A Survey of 100 Detransitioners," 3369.
21   "Toilets, Bowties, Gender and Me, Audrey Mason-Hyde, TEDxAdelaide," https://youtu.be/NCLoNwVJA-0.
22   Chase Strangio, "What Is a 'Male Body'?," Slate.com, July 19, 2016.
23   Cf. Ryan T. Anderson and Melody Wood, "Gender Identity Policies in Schools: What Congress, the Courts, and the Trump Administration Should Do," Heritage Foundation Backgrounder 3201 (March 23, 2017).
24   Cf. "Forced to Share a Room with Transgender Woman in Toronto Shelter, Sex Abuse Victim Files Human Rights Complaint," *National Post*, August 2, 2018.
25   Cf. "Shelter Forced Women to Shower with Person Who Identified as a Transgender Woman and Sexually Harassed Them, Lawsuit Says," ABC30 Action News, May 24, 2018.
26   Cf. U.S. Department of Housing and Urban Development, "HUD Issues Final Rule to Ensure Equal Access to Housing and Services Regardless of Gender Identity," press release, September 20, 2016.
27   Cf. Dhejne et al., "Long-Term Follow-up of Transsexual Persons Undergoing Sex Reassignment Surgery: Cohort Study from Sweden."
28   Cf. "How Many Transgender Inmates Are There?," BBC News, August 13, 2018, https://www.bbc.com/news/uk-42221629
29   Cf. "Karen White: How 'Manipulative' Transgender Inmate Attacked Again," *Guardian*, February 11, 2018.
30   Joyce, *Trans*, 166.
31   Cf. "First UK Transgender Prison to Open," BBC News, March 3, 2019.
32   As quoted in Kara Dansky, *The Abolition of Sex* (New York: Post Hill Press, 2021).
33   Cf. IPSO, "Guidance on Researching and Reporting Stories Involving Transgender Individuals," September 2016, https://www.ipso.co.uk/media/1275/guidance_transgender-reporting.pdf.
34   Kathleen Stock, *Material Girls* (London: Fleet/Little, Brown: 2021), 161.
35   Jill Harmacinski, "Woman Gets 30 Years for Child Sex Abuse," *Eagle-Tribune*, June 10, 2021.
36   "Male, Transgender Youth Arrested for Raping 4-Year-Old Girl, Distributing Videos, Photos of the Act," WomenAreHuman.com.
37   Joyce, *Trans*, 168.
38   Joyce, *Trans*, 299–300.

17. Parents and educators ought to affirm any child who identifies as trans.

1   Cf. J. Herman et al., "2015 U.S. Transgender Survey," National Center for Transgender Equality, 65.
2   Julian Vigo, "Capitulating to Bullies: Brown University and the Transgender Lobby vs. Science," *Public Discourse* (October 7, 2018).
3   Cf. Ryan Anderson, "Parents Denied Custody of Child for Refusing Support of Transgenderism: Here's What You Need to Know," Lifesitenews.com, February 19, 2018.
4   "DETRANSITION Q&A (#1)," https://youtu.be/kxVmSGTgNxI.
5   Mark Yarhouse and Julia Sadusky, *Emerging Gender Identities* (Ada, MI: Brazos Press, 2020), 67.
6   "DETRANSITION Q&A (#1)."
7   Cf. Yarhouse and Sadusky, *Emerging Gender Identities*, 66.
8   Keffler, *Desist, Detrans & Detox*, 26.
9   As quoted in Keffler, *Desist, Detrans & Detox*, 141.
10   Father Jean C. J. d'Elbé, *I Believe in Love* (Manchester, NH: Sophia Institute Press, 2001), 195, 203–204.
11   Preston Sprinkle, *Embodied* (Colorado Springs, CO: David C. Cook, 2021), 62.
12   Sprinkle, *Embodied*, 62.
13   "What Is Gender Dysphoria," https://youtu.be/CMqiD_4KslA.
14   "Gender Dysphoria, Dr. Mark Yarhouse," https://youtu.be/0-I2eMpHfo8.
15   Yarhouse, *Understanding Gender Dysphoria*, 41.

18. If you struggle with gender dysphoria, you should accept that God made you trans.

1   M. Barringer and D. Gay, "Happily Religious: The Surprising Sources of Happiness Among Lesbian, Gay, Bisexual, and Transgender Adults," *Sociological Inquiry* 87:1 (2017), 75–96.
2   "An Open Letter to Julia Serano from One of the Detransitioned People You Claim to 'Support.'"
3   "DETRANSITION Q&A (#1)."
4   "I Regret Transitioning"—Talk w/ Teen De-transitioner," https://www.youtube.com/watch?v=tPBLyb8H_iE
5   Jacques Philippe, *The Way of Trust and Love* (New York: Scepter Books, 2012), 129.
6   "Tranzformed—Finding Peace With Your God Given Gender."
7   Saint Augustine, *Letter to Proba*, 14.
8   Cf. Psalms 6, 22, 42, 88.
9   As quoted in Mark Yarhouse, *Understanding Gender Dysphoria*, 141.